450

RETURN TO OASIS
War Poems and Recollections
from the Middle East
1940–1946

War Poet

by Sidney Keyes

I am the man who looked for peace and found
My own eyes barbed.
I am the man who groped for words and found
An arrow in my hand.
I am the builder whose firm walls surround
A slipping land.
When I grow sick or mad
Mock me not nor chain me;
When I reach for the wind
Cast me not down
Though my face is a burnt book
And a wasted town.

March 1942

"We'll soon be digging in at Shepheard's"

'Two Types', 1942.

'Two Types', 1942.

"My brother says he's on a lonely gunsite in Yorkshire—
two miles from the nearest pub!"

Two contemporary cartoons by JON

RETURN TO OASIS

War Poems and Recollections
from the Middle East
1940–1946

Editors
Victor Selwyn: Erik de Mauny, Ian Fletcher,
G. S. Fraser, John Waller

Consultants
Tambimuttu, John Cromer

with Introduction by
LAWRENCE DURRELL

Shepheard-Walwyn
in association with

Editions Poetry London for
The Salamander Oasis Trust

This edition first published 1980 by
Shepheard-Walwyn (Publishers) Ltd
51 Vineyard Hill Road,
London SW19

ISBN 0 85683 047 X (cased)
ISBN 0 85683 051 8 (limp)

Of this edition the first one hundred
copies have been numbered

Printed in Great Britain by
Mather Bros (Printers) Ltd, Preston

Dedication

Let us reflect. The wealth of a people and the heritage they pass on lives in their knowledge, their skills and culture . . . the written word, music, painting, sculpture and shadows on a screen.

Of all literary forms, poetry expresses man's deepest thoughts and feelings. For the poet perceives; he feels; he creates; he hands on to posterity and so becomes our history. His poetry belongs to us all. It is not the privilege of a group. We sing poetry in our songs. We recite poetry when we pray—psalms written by inspired men in the Judean hills nearly three millenia ago.

There are objects of the moment. There is that which endures—the spirit of man, the flame of the poet. The tragedy is that it takes a war—kill or be killed—to move man to the heights, to write the finest verse, the most moving lines.

To those who shared the sand with the flies, who wrote in exercise books on the tail-board of a truck or hammered an Army Oliver on a trestle-table, we who came back say your task is now done. We hand on treasure from man's most wasteful occupation.

V.S.

Acknowledgements

We say thank you to John Checkley (ex-*Daily Mirror* and *National Enquirer*) for generous help with subbing; Brian Sutherland (*Daily Mirror*) for advice and Dermot Purgavie (*Now!*); to Jane Crosthwaite (and Maggie and Laura) who gave the Trust a home at 24 Beauchamp Place; to Edward Lucie-Smith (*Evening Standard*) for telling us Tambi was back in business. We thank Chris Rees (*Daily Mail*), Colin Welch (*Daily Telegraph*), Peter Reed (*Daily Mirror*), Richard Findlater (*Observer*) for letters published; John Parry (B.B.C.) for the 'World at One' spot; Moyna Rimington for secretarial help, Christine Fretten (House of Commons Library), and Creative Design Workshop, Lewes (Trixie Selwyn, Jeremy Shearing), for front cover design produced overnight.

But truly, we are overwhelmed by the response to our appeals for poetry from those who served in the Middle East. Nearly a thousand poems came in, poems that had been kept for nearly forty years. The poems and the letters that accompanied them moved us deeply. Yet, as in Cairo, we still have not the space. But the exercise has not been in vain, for historians of the future will be able to read all the poems, published and unpublished, that we are placing (with permission) in the Imperial War Museum, with copies to Reading University.

We gratefully acknowledge permission to reproduce poems from the following: *Orisons, Picaresque and Metaphysical* (Ian Fletcher), Editions Poetry London; *Poems of the War Years*, Macmillan; *More Poems from the Forces*, George Routledge & Sons; *Alamein to Zem-Zem* (Keith Douglas), Editions Poetry London; *Poems from the Desert*, Harrap; *Libya* (Louis Challoner), Romford Poetry Centre; *Libyan Winter* (P. M. Clothier), Central News Agency, South Africa; *Songs of Soldiers* (C. P. S. Denholm-Young), published privately; *Home Town Elegy* (G. S. Fraser), Editions Poetry London; *Collected Poems of John Gawsworth*, Sidgwick & Jackson; *Elegies for the Dead in Cyrenaica* (Hamish Henderson), EUSPB, Edinburgh; *Atlantic Anthology*, Fortune Press; *Firework Music* (Peter Hellings), Fortune Press; *Poems* (John Jarmain), Collins; *Poetry Now*, Faber & Faber; *Poetry in War-Time*, Faber & Faber; *Middle East Anthology*, Lindsay Drummond; *The Horses of Falaise* (Victor West), Salamander; *Libya 1942, Sicily 1943 Poems* (N. T. Morris), published privately; *Sun and Sand* (John Warry), Fortune Press; *Desert Wind* (Thomas Eastwood), Fortune Press; *Inferior Verse* (Harold Ian Bransom), published privately for 124th Field Regiment R.A. We also acknowledge gratefully permission to reproduce 'L.R.D.G.' (J. G. Meddemmen), 'Air Raid' (Charles Robinson) and the wartime 'Two Types' cartoons (JON), *Daily Mail*.

We apologize for any omissions or if we have failed to trace the publisher.

We thank, too, the following for contributing poems by other writers from the Forces: F. Frost; Mrs Pat Hefferon; K. Warburton; Chas V. Rigby; K. Pickersgill.

Contents

II. Previously Published Middle East Verse

Preface

The Setting

Before the jet shrank the world, before television and transistors gave us instant entertainment—and noise—and before yesterday had become a dirty word, Britain shipped an army to an alien desert. They travelled by slow boat to Suez, three months round the Cape, sleeping three tiers to an airless deck, zig-zagging in slow convoys of converted cattle boats—a lucky few travelling in the luxury of ocean liners fast enough to go it alone.

They went to fight and share the desert with the flies, stinging flies and the wandering Bedouins who appeared from nowhere to trade in marble-sized hard-boiled eggs. They went to experience the loneliness of four long years exile from home, to live in wooden huts with the characteristic smell of bed bugs and in tents dug-in against the *khamseen*, the hot desert wind, an existence governed by the shifting front—and sands—of a Desert War which ranged from the Nile Valley, the comfort of Cairo and Alexandria, to Tripoli and beyond.

This was the world for most until World War Two was over, first with the Desert Army, then the Eighth Army, fighting the last large scale campaign Britain, aided by the Commonwealth, directed alone as a first-league power.

For many, too many, their world also ended in the desert sand.

They were defending freedom which has now, like democracy, become an overworked word. But in Middle East Command in those days freedom was very much alive and well and, within the military constraints, the men of these armies enjoyed a freedom for which we can find no parallel. In retrospect many events occurring then seem hard to believe. But they did occur. As evidence we have the *Oasis* anthology on which *Return to Oasis* is based.

It was launched in Cairo in war-time (1942/43) by three volunteer editors whose highest rank was corporal—true, war substantive, but still corporal—with no official status. The completed anthology had its Foreword signed by no less than the Commander-in-Chief, Middle East Force, General 'Jumbo' Wilson. We tell more of the *Oasis* story later in this book. It happened in a war against an authoritarian threat. There, freedom began in men's minds. It became a way of life in a desert that stretched endlessly with no 'idiot box' to occupy lonely hours, no non-stop radio to aneasthetize the mind. Newspapers often never arrived. Men read serious books, argued and discussed. The books were often Penguins, cheap reprints of sixpenny and ninepenny classics (two-and-a-half pence and four pence or in U.S. money five and eight cents) which had just broken into the publishing world. The discussions and arguments went on while brewing up on the 'Benghazi Cooker'—an inverted can filled with petrol-soaked sand and ignited.

The official handbook for officers and N.C.O.s sent out to inform the troops on current affairs—following the Cromwell dictum that an army should know why it fights and love what it knows—carried the instruction: 'Never force your opinions on the group. An intelligent instructor will avoid ramming his own views down men's throats. It is one of the cardinal sins . . .'

No one COULD force opinions down the throats of these men, particularly if those opinions bore the official stamp. It was 'us' versus 'them' and 'them' were not the enemy but a distant higher authority at home—with unbrowned knees—who could be counted on to screw things up—and often succeeded! Not that it made the troops less loyal. Not at all! They would win THEIR war in THEIR way, just to show 'them' how to do it, an attitude shared by British, New Zealand and Australian forces alike. To survive, they adapted and innovated[1]. They invented a 'uniform' if that be the right word. (See the 'Two Types' cartoons by JON in the frontispiece.)

The Command became a paradise for eccentrics and mavericks. A character called Popski ran a private army. The Long Range Desert Group (L.R.D.G.) operated independently for weeks behind enemy lines. This inspired David Sterling to found the S.A.S. Whilst the best known maverick of all, Montgomery, won the last vital battles. The soldiers saw him as one of their own—not one of 'them'. He shared their desert, threw staff officers out of Cairo comfort, festooned his Aussie felt hat with cap badges collected from units at the front. He boosted morale. Morale wins wars, even against a better armed enemy. The Eighth Army conquered—and moved on to Tunis and Sicily and Italy, a legend in our time.

They left behind a 'flower' that had blossomed in the desert and in the Cairo base—a collection of the finest poetry written during the Second World War. Unwittingly, the War Office back in London helped. For a vital element of Middle East creativity stemmed from higher authority posting so many writers and poets to that Command. They did so to staff the myriad of Intelligence units in Cairo[2]. As a result this bustling city of many languages and people became the cultural centre of the war outside Britain.

The Poetry

A myth has evolved, repeated so often that people believe it, that in contrast

---

[1] Few could adapt better or innovate more freely than the British and Commonwealth Forces. In the end it enabled them to beat a usually better equipped opposition—a more organized opposition, too organized!

[2] Intelligence units were earmarked for places improbable and impossible, including Eastern Europe and the Balkans. In the end they watched each other.

to World War One, the Second World War produced only three poets of note. This belief formed the conclusion of a B.B.C. Radio 4 probe into 'Where are the war poets?' in March 1978, repeated weeks later by a Sunday newspaper critic who prefaced his remarks about there being only three poets, with the words: 'as we all know.' That settled that!

'*As we all know*'! This three poet summary of World War Two has just one slight drawback. The facts don't fit, the story just does not stand up. A visit to any library, or the Imperial War Museum would kill the myth even before publication of *Return to Oasis*. There is a tendency now to denigrate much of what Britain and its soldiers achieved between 1939–45, and maybe that extends to the poetry they wrote.

Certainly, after the War, our late colleague G. S. Fraser felt that a gap appeared in our poetry, for many who came back did not continue writing and were lost to view. And when we mention Second World War poetry, especially that of the Middle East where it mostly happened, we receive blank stares even from academics who teach tomorrow's generation. The names of Owen, Brooke, Sassoon, Edwards, Graves, and Grenfell from the First World War remain bright. Yet, a silence shrouds their Second World War successors except for a few reprints—so much so, that we are in danger of losing part of our cultural heritage.

In a memorandum for this book Fraser wrote: 'The Middle East in World War Two produced far more—and at times even finer—poetry than all the years of attrition on the Western Front in World War One. The poetry came from a more literate and aware generation. They had read more, and employed a wider range of styles and techniques.' Our late colleague had an advantage. He had written, and served in the Middle East as the most unlikely sergeant-major ever—see Lawrence Durrell's description in the Introduction to this book.

Return to Oasis reproduces the neglected Middle East poetry from the widest possible spectrum; from the professional poet, to the sailor, soldier or airman, whose inspiration flared for a dramatic moment then died. In such dramatic moments of inspiration men added a few personal brush strokes to the picture of a war.

The Selection

The criteria for inclusion in *Return to Oasis* remain the same as for the original *Oasis* in Cairo. The poet must have served in the Forces in the Middle East theatre of war in the 1940s and have written his or her poems at the time[1]. This military qualification sadly excludes poems from such as Bernard

---

[1] B. Cole's poem, 'Anniversary' forms one exception in that he wrote it years after the War, but the theme is so relevant that it has been included as the last poem.

Spencer or Terrence Tiller, who were in Cairo, but as civilians, as was Lawrence Durrell who has so kindly written the Introduction. But a boundary line had to be drawn. *What did the poets in uniform write*[1].

The reader will note a contrast between *Oasis* and the poems chosen for Part III (previously unpublished) and, to a lesser extent, with those in Part II (previously published). At the time of compiling *Oasis* we felt less need to describe a war. We were in it. Poems could be more reflective; an *Oasis* in fact! However, a generation later, when choosing poems to supplement *Oasis*, we realised that we were presenting a picture of yesterday to today. So we have chosen more poems that tell of the war, more poems of action. Many have a rougher edge, as they should, for war is not a neat affair. We have incidentally rejected poems we suspected from a professional source far away, having learnt from one Desert anthology (produced in Britain) that included a poem purporting to come from a soldier in a slit trench.

Some of the poems in Part III G. S. Fraser termed 'Soldiers' Verse and Ballads', which correctly describes them. Many were written or typed on a heavy Army typewriter (Oliver) and passed hand-to-hand. Some sent to us just fell apart. Maybe critics will describe a few as doggerel. That is their privilege. What is or is not poetry must be somewhat subjective. However, it is significant that all who took part in selecting—they had gone their separate ways after the War for over thirty years—hardly differed on what to include. As Ian Fletcher observes in his contribution to this book 'the poems selected themselves'.

Inevitably many poems on the same theme were received. Occasionally the poet had let himself down by the odd word or phrase that he would have corrected if he had had time. A few alterations (G. S. Fraser chiefly) and deletions have improved some poems, at least in our view[2] but in the main the blue pencil and scissors have been resisted, so as not to lose the flavour of the moment, the feel, the emotion, when the poet is moved to write. (As many a

---

[1] If we included civilian M. E. poetry we would need twice the space. As Lawrence Durrell has written to Tambi, there was a verse war between Cairo and Alexandria '. . . not since Troy was there such a bash-up. On the one side Robert Liddell Gwyn, D. Bryn Davis [and himself] and on the other, Robin Fedden, Bernard Spencer, Terrence Tiller, Ruth Speirs, Charles Hepburn, George Seferis, Elie Papadimitrious.' His letter adds . . . 'Diana Gould walked up and down the lines encouraging the troops and firing off nasty epigrams about us all. When she left Alexandria the Army went into mourning like Achilles (Robin, Bernard, Gwyn and me). Her arrival in Naples to dance for ENSA coincided with an eruption of Etna, so Gwyn wrote:

The proof that you're in Naples, not with us,
is the misbehaviour of Vesuvius'.

[2] This differs, though, from the unjustifiable alterations made to Keith Douglas's poems, revealed by Tambimuttu in his 'Last Lunch with Keith Douglas'. Keith Douglas had revised and polished his own work, so that the final manuscripts needed no improvement.

reporter will testify his first on-the-spot story reads better than his revised copy when he has had too much time to think).

Finally, as Tambi so rightly says, poetry becomes history. In these poems the thoughts, beliefs and experiences, expressed in verse, of the servicemen and women in the Middle East in World War Two are presented. The world they saw, in the way they saw it, is in this book. The rough with the smooth. That was forty years ago. Regimes have changed, relationships have changed, standards of living have been raised. So much of the world has changed. But man is still man.

Our credentials for this task are simple. *We were there*. We—the editors[1]—all served in the Middle East Forces in World War Two and all took part in the unique collection, *Oasis, The Middle East Anthology of Poetry from the Forces*, compiled and produced in Cairo in 1942/43—its poets and editors were all members of the services. The Salamander Society, Cairo, who published it, comprised both military and civilian writers and poets.

So, a generation later we pick up the threads again. We have found each other, formed a literary trust, The Salamander Oasis Trust, appointed an editorial board from amongst us, and linked with a colleague of those days, Tambimuttu of Editions Poetry London. The Middle East poetry we present divides into three parts:

The original *Oasis* anthology in full. This slim volume has become a collectors' item to trade at under the counter prices.

A selection of poems already published from well known names, and from those deserving better recognition.

Finally, poems, written at the time and place, that have not been published before. Some of these are by our *Oasis* poets, but mostly they came in response to our appeals carried in the letters pages of two newspapers, the *Daily Telegraph* and the *Daily Mirror*. The appeal ran to only three paragraphs, yet nearly a thousand poems arrived. They include army ballads that were written or typed to be passed hand-to-hand. When they reached us, some fell apart. Widows and children often sent us poems a man had treasured, along with his medals and war records, as part of his life.

We have added a fourth part to the book to enable some of the *Oasis* poets and editors to express in their own words what it was like. There are maps, a chronology of the war, explanatory notes on the poems and biographies of the poets to give the modern reader some of the background and context.

We knew from *Oasis* in Cairo that there were many unpublished poems from the Middle East. Yet again, space prevents us publishing all. However,

---

[1] and The Salamander Oasis Trustees.

we have sought permission from the writers and their families to pass on manuscripts to the Imperial War Museum with copies to the University of Reading, so that future historians and poets can read them. They will not be lost.

The original *Oasis* in war-time took us four months to produce. *Return to Oasis* has taken us four years. At times we even considered printing it ourselves on a hand press. In the end *Return to Oasis* has happened. We say thank you to those who made it possible.

Profits from the original *Oasis* went to the Red Cross. Our share of royalties from its successor will go to new projects. For there is so much to be done.

V.S. and J.Ch.

Sketch by Keith Douglas.

Introduction

The dire events of 1939–40 had been so long awaited, so long dreaded, that when at last things came to a head and the Nazi storm broke, it created a curious sense of anticlimax; almost of relief, for now at least we would know the worst that had to be faced. The card-houses of European politics tumbled down almost at once; the politicians and their policies were swept away by the impetus of the German armies. Within weeks, within months, Europe was ringed about with battlefields, nations were knocked about like ninepins. Nothing, it then seemed, could withstand the German might, and we in the Mediterranean realized that we were castaways on the waterlogged rafts of countries like Egypt, Greece, Turkey and Syria. It seems incredible now that we managed to go on believing that things might come right, yet believe we did; it was hope against hope, hope against all reason.

In Egypt the sense of alienation and distance was made even more marked by the apparent normality of everyday life. The country basked in its fictitious neutrality, the shops were crammed, the cinemas packed; the Allied armies marooned here sharpened their claws in preparation for the desert battles to come, but in fact it seemed extraordinary to live in such oriental splendour with a battlefield which was only an hour's drive away. The cities had been declared 'open'. Cairo was one blaze of light all night long. The phrase 'flesh-pots of Egypt' took on new meaning when one saw such fortunes being made and spent by army contractors. Later, in a year or two, would come the crisis of 'shipping space' which would cause a number of serious shortages, but they were always sporadic and intermittent. People flown out from bombed and rationed England stared aghast at the bulging shops, the crowded nightclubs, the blazing lighted thoroughfares of Cairo—made all the more grotesque by the glaring poverty of the *fellaheen*, by the beggars which flocked everywhere. Hardship and profligacy lived side by side. Walking home late one night from a party an English civilian was accosted by a beggar who offered to 'show him a dead Egyptian' for two piastres. The sores, the leprosy, the smallpox, syphilis and bilharzia completed the throbbing panorama of the night life with its swirling *souks*[1] and tinsel brothels. It is true that Alexandria harbour was bombed once or twice, but Cairo was never, as far as I can remember, even reconnoitred; the skies were open day and night. An occasional snarl of tanks wound their way through the town after midnight, but in such slow calm

---

[1] Markets

order that they seemed to chime with the occasional padding strings of camels that passed, fetching clover to the markets in the *bercim*[1].

There was no sense of dramatic urgency about things; the General Staff went about its business in a quiet and reserved way. Of course, this apparent nonchalance masked fearful anxieties, but it deluded the Egyptians into believing that we had something up our sleeves, and this was useful in a country seething with spies and spycraft. However, the really striking thing about the psychological atmosphere was the sudden realization that everyone was hungry for reading matter. As books became in short supply the libraries were besieged by the Welfare Services cadging reading matter for the Eighth Army. My publishers reported with some astonishment from London that several editions of poems by young poets had been bought up almost overnight by the general public. Perhaps the sharpened sense of death in the air gave a new resonance to life. People felt that they might die without having really tangled with any of the great religious and philosophical problems of their time. One suddenly realized that, after all, the British were at bottom poets and poetry lovers, and not just football philistines. It took moments of dearth like this to bring it out in them. Among people cadging books for the desert I met one weary Education Officer who told me of the boredom and misery of being stuck out there in the sand with only the *Egyptian Gazette* to read. In despair he had erected a three-ply notice board and pinned up a few rapidly fabricated poems and satires on it, asking for further contributions. Within the same day the whole board was covered with every kind of poetry and prose production, down to brilliant limericks. He had been obliged to increase the size of the board!

It was only too appropriate in this context that the Commander-in-Chief was himself a poetry-lover and spent his time (in between wrapping up the Italian Forces in the most brilliant battle of the desert war) in compiling an anthology of his favourite verse and Lord Wavell was not the only soldier on the beach, there were many other soldiers who were writers. This world crisis caused an upsurge of creative effort which is admirably illustrated by the contents of this anthology, expressing as it does the nostalgia and enchantment of that far away epoch spent between the two deserts, divided by the placid and beautiful Nile, with danger in the air, plus the sense of participation in major historical events which would shape the world to come in unpredictable ways.

There were many different aspects of the book shortage, some of them diverting, as when the largest bookshop in Cairo announced to customers that it had been swindled by some wholesaler in London to whom it had sent a blank cheque asking for several crates of unspecified 'stock'; I must say it *was*

---

[1] Panniers

rather a swiz, for the wily London bookseller had off-loaded a mountain of unreadable seventeenth-century theology, memoirs and sermons on his Cairo colleague who had so blithely trusted him for his advice. I saw with misgiving this whole wall of dreadful indigestible fare exposed to human view in the Cairo bookshop. Its owner wrung his hands the while and cursed his rascally London contact. Who on earth would wade through all this stuff? I could hold out no hope to the moaning bookseller. But two days later the New Zealand Division arrived. I cannot say if they were all divinity students or curates in the bud, but all I can attest to is the disappearance of all these fat unreadable tomes in a matter of twenty-four hours. I had a wild vision of the desert being littered with *Bishop Dodderidge's Sermons* in twenty volumes, *Tuke's Theological Axioms, Holy Living and Dying* by Jeremy Taylor . . . *The Collected Pamphlets and Exhortations of Mottram and Mink*, plus astringent pamphlets with titles like 'A Swift bunk-up from behind for a hard-arsed Christian' . . . What on earth would the Germans make of all this?

Individual memory became precious; an actor like Colin Keith-Johnstone, who had the whole of Shakespeare by heart, found his recitals packed out by the poetry-hungry in uniform. He did an anthology of great Shakespearean heroes and great scenes which brought us the best of what we had left behind at the Old Vic. Sybil Thorndyke, en route for some Far Eastern tournée for ENSA dropped in on our modest Brain's Trusts with poetry that seemed freshly minted; she had the Oxford Book by heart it would seem. We began to see some point in the old-fashioned type of school education where much store was set upon memory, upon recitation; prizes were given for it. Shan Sedgewick, the Correspondent said: 'I am not a religious man, but thank goodness I have the whole Prelude of Wordsworth by heart. I recite the whole thing every morning as I shave.' One thinks of other phenomenal memories— Paddy Leigh-Fermor who knew all Palgrave right through, and much else besides. It was as if the notion of poetry had found its true fulcrum in the thought of the freedoms which were so much at stake.

And of course the poetic upsurge brought us many eccentrics. I recall George Fraser visiting me in the press department of the Embassy to deliver some poems of his for *Personal Landscape*. I was horrified to see that, though in uniform, he was wearing tennis shoes and a dirty scarf while his trousers were fastened with string. I asked with concern whether he wasn't reprimanded for such wear and he said that he never had been, probably because his boss was a writer too. When the war sharpened its focus and the armies expanded Cairo became a brilliant intellectual centre. It seemed at times that every poet and painter from London was in our midst. And, of course, inevitably the King of Redonda, the Bard, John Gawsworth, arrived and set up shop in a sort of underground Arab café near GHQ. Here he caused considerable alarm by his flamboyant conversation. He was only an aircraftman, and thus denied access to the hotels and cafés reserved for officers. But he carried his lowly rank off with an air, protesting that he had only accepted it to honour the memory of T. E. Lawrence. He had given my name as a reference and in next to no time I had a heavily breathing Security Officer sitting in front of me in the office showing the whites of his eyes and expatiating upon my friend.

'He says,' he remarked grimly 'that he is descended from the Dark Lady of The Sonnets—whoever *she* may be—one can't know everything—and that the rightful heir to the Throne of England is Prince Rupprecht of Bavaria. Well, that may be all right, but he is encouraging his fellow aircraftmen to drink toasts to him in warm beer. Now this could easily come under "suborning", compromising their allegiance to the Crown. He could get beheaded for this. And he says he is a friend of yours.'

It was difficult to know what to say.

'He is a colleague of the quill, and a writer to be prized. Perhaps a mild reprimand might finish with the affair.'

The Security Officer said: 'I should prefer him to be beheaded, but if you think he is all right and are prepared to vouch . . .'

I said I was prepared to vouch—though with misgiving. And in a month Gawsworth was posted and we breathed again.

The Chancery of the Embassy had several secretaries of a literary persuasion and one fine poet, Charles Hepburn, who afterwards helped us with contributions to our little paper. It may have been he who asked me to go round to the Greek Embassy and teach English to the new President of the Greek Government in exile, Panagiotis Cannellopolous. He was a fine poet in Greek as well as a statesman, and I had met him in Athens. He knew no English and was anxious to learn. When I presented myself he told me that he wished to learn the language, but he had no time to bother with trifles. He wanted to start with Yeats. It seemed hopeless, as he knew no grammar whatsoever. I told him that this could not turn out well and a long discussion ensued, during which I explained our problems over *Personal Landscape*, which was a kind of little chapbook of verse printed among private friends. Robin Fedden had found an old press and some paper and we thought it would be a pleasant act of friendship—it fitted into the general atmosphere of the time—but as for the money . . . it was quite an expensive production, and while we were all in jobs the cost of the first two numbers was quite a wrench. The Greek ardour of Cannellopolous blazed up, and as I took my leave of him he said: 'All the funds of the Greek Government in exile are at the disposition of your paper!'

It was a marvellously Greek thought and we treasured it. But as all the funds of the Greek Government in exile came from London we somehow felt that the offer would prove unrealizable. Nevertheless the gesture proves the temper of those times when poetry counted so very much.

All hungers march together, says the proverb. Books played an enormous role in the life of those who had been used to more spacious times and whom the war had surprised. It was not a question of morale, it was literally a question of spiritual survival. In this context even the war had its uses; I recall a commando friend telling me 'Thank God for the war; I should never have found the time to read the whole of Proust had I not been holed up in an icy Cretan cave for three whole months while the Germans combed the valley below me.'

One day the officer in charge of Special Operations dropped into my office and said: 'I wonder if one of you writer people can help me with a little problem. We have only got a couple of agents in Albania and we have persuaded the RAF to do a Christmas moondrop with presents for them. We asked them what they would like for the Yuletide season and they replied forthwith. But old X said that he only wants a box of Havanas and a copy of Spengler in English. Now where the devil should I look for a copy of the *Decline of The West?*'

Spengler! Vague memories of having seen the stout volume somewhere stirred me. I closed me eyes and thought. Yes, I had seen it at Schindler's Bookshop. 'If the Anzacs haven't wolfed it I think I know where to find a copy' I said and lifted the telephone. By luck the book was still there and off it was packed to this solitary secret agent sitting in a cave in the desolate Albanian mountains.

All these diverse incidents should, I hope, go towards making up an impressionistic picture of the role that words played during these difficult and tragic years; by the same token these poems by many hands will make up a composite sketch of deeper concerns which stirred the hearts and minds of these poets in their Egyptian exile.

LAWRENCE DURRELL

By coincidence the first person to meet Lawrence Durrell on his arrival at Alexandria from Greece in 1941 was John Cromer Braun who describes the incident on the following page.

Lawrence Durrell's Arrival
at Alexandria

When Greece was being evacuated in 1941, I was tweaked from the Field Security Office in Cairo and transported along with two other sergeants to Alexandria to help with the security reception of refugees. One particular boatload was expected, but days passed and we were kept in idleness, broken by eating ice-cream, drinking coffee and regaling ourselves in the evening with some fine meals. Suddenly, at 4 a.m. we were awakened in our barracks and told to bustle down to the docks. The boat had arrived, dodging the Stukas which had sought to destroy it. I was assigned to a gangway and told to let nobody pass until the word was given. No sooner did I appear at the head of the gangway than I was assailed by a clamouring group of journalists, each trying to get away first to file copy. The rudest and most insistent was Tom Driberg but even he could not get ashore until clearance was given. (Thirty-five years later, on the anniversary of Pearl Harbour Day a Requiem Mass was celebrated for Lord Bradwell—alas poor Tom.)

As the passengers filed off, for the most part a pathetic line of retired schoolteachers, professors, widows and other expatriates from Athens and the Peloponnese, a stocky, round-faced figure with wife and child in tow came to the gangway. I took his passport and read 'Lawrence Durrell'.

'Writer?'

'Yes.'

'Once of the Villa Seurat?'

'Yes.'

'Friend of Henry Miller?'

'Yes, anything wrong with that?'

'Not at all, would you step aside please.'

I was not thinking then of security risks but of the chance to talk about a world which was far removed from Alex docks. As the parties were made up and sent off to Cairo, Durrell and I conversed in a slit trench in a sandy transit camp through the night, while the Alexandria barrage sent up its innumerable tracers to chase the German raiders from the sky. Finally Durrell rejoined his wife and daughter and the three of them went off by lorry to be installed at the Luna Park Hotel in Cairo. I went back to work in the office.

JOHN BRAUN
Chairman, Salamander Oasis Trust

War Anthologies

Anthologies require no defence. In the first place, anthologists were responsible for preserving much of Greek tragic and lyric poetry. Secondly, they are succinct, portable: good for dangerous days. Thirdly, they are a window into the past or the present: they have both aesthetic and documentary value. And finally, they condition expectation and taste. They should not be read at a sitting, but rather dipped into here and there.

The war of 1939–45 though so different was fought under the shadow of the first. A far higher proportion of troops were actually involved in the earlier fighting: casualties and first-hand experience of battle were more intense. In the Middle East theatre it took, I believe, nine men at the rear echelons to keep one man in action at the front, as war became ever more mechanized, more specialized; then there were the usual flurries when the cooks and the clerks (as in April 1918) were hurriedly thrown into the melée. It seems that the Duke of Wellington's comment 'I don't know what effect you'll have on the enemy but by God you frighten me' would be misapplied in this case for at that point the enemy were rolled back. If there was boredom on the Western Front, it was punctuated for the most part by danger.

Boredom, sand and flies made up much of my own personal experience in the Middle East. But for the front line troops, the realities of war were less tenuous. And by all accounts the campaigns, the tank battles, recalled a little of the ideal war of the old cavalry, the white arm. The weather of Flanders and the general feel of the landscape, though, might at least present some faint resemblance to the English scene; but the desert, none. So that this anthology, these 'flowers' of the desert, often it may be thought as brilliant in bloom and as quick in withering as the flora of North Africa, are different in kind from those culled from Northern France.

The poetry of the Middle East theatre may seem to divide itself into those with battle experience and those rotting gently on the lines of communication. More importantly, perhaps, than the variousness of the experience is the variousness of the sensibilities, talents and education of the contributors. There were the 'art' poets for whom the war and the army were merely a phase in a larger career; then the educated voices of those who were moved under the pressures of exile and acute, unfamiliar experience, to a poetry of occasion, and finally, the record of the almost inarticulate, the artless, the oral; those blunt, often poignant songs of complaint or of an innocent patriotism.

This anthology not only presents that microcosm of a nation and a society at war, in exile; but is of further documentary value in gathering such fugitives; records of immediate and authentic experience, where the words have no time to go dishonest, emerging after forty years in tattered typescript, in painful capitals. And, as Victor Selwyn has recorded, enclosed in letters from elderly veterans, recalling comrades either dead in battle or more recently lost, these perhaps the most moving documents, more moving than the art poetry, even when written by such richly talented poets as Keith Douglas, or than the occasional poetry of the educated.

It is to be hoped that this anthology then is both a document and a memorial. What it is not, unlike some anthologies, is the expression of a temperament; or very much of a personal choice. *These poems seem to have chosen themselves.*

IAN FLETCHER
Professor of English,
University of Reading

On War Poetry and *Oasis*

A war is one of the few periods in English history, in this century, when a large number of people who might not otherwise think of themselves as poets feel a need to write poems. The main themes of the poems of the two world wars were very different. In 1914, there had been the Crimean War, the Mutiny, and the Boer War, but these were all wars of professional soldiers and might touch the feelings but not the experience of poets—give or take a few exceptions like Tennyson on the 'Charge of the Light Brigade' or Kipling's Boer War poems which are not up in quality, on the whole, to his poems on peace-time soldiering in India.

The two world wars were the first wars in our history to use the bulk of the fit young manhood of the nation, outside reserved jobs. The pattern in each, however, was different. The 1914–18 war was a long static war of attrition in which neither side really achieved a breakthrough of a stalemate position. It was far more costly in British lives (though not in German or Russian lives) than the Second World War. The pattern of war poetry is from the early romantic enthusiasm of Rupert Brooke or Julian Grenfell to the compassion and sense of the pointlessness of the whole operation of Owen, Rosenberg, and Sassoon (with Sassoon's satire an additional personal quality). Graves bears the horrors, as Sassoon says, by almost exaggerating them; Blunden finds glimpses of the natural beauty which is his real subject even in France and

I suspect, humane man though he was, what moved him most was the desecration of good forest and farmland, the war against nature, even more than the deaths of men.

The poets of the Second World War, particularly those in the Near East, faced a different situation. The war in the desert with first-rate commanders like Rommel and Montgomery on either side was mobile, exciting, horrifying in some ways but much less costly in life than trench warfare. A feeling of grimly almost enjoying the war, like some rough game, marks for instance Keith Douglas's poems. The special feelings that *Oasis* poets express are often a reaction to new, strange, and picturesque surroundings (the mixture of opulence and squalor in Cairo, for instance), homesickness, loneliness (typical feelings of the civilian soldier), but not the pessimism of the First World War poems.

It is difficult, in retrospect, to feel that the First World War was necessary; longer-sighted diplomats might have avoided it. None of the combatant countries in the long run gained anything from it. The post-First World War policy of reparations led to the rise of Hitler. No serving man in the Second World War felt, as Sassoon had done about the First, that the war was pointless; Hitlerism was something which threatened the very humanity of man and had to be destroyed. The *universal* theme of the poems in *Oasis* seems, therefore, to be less protest against war as such than feelings of a personal kind shared by many soldiers and to some degree hopes for a better world after the war. Both the sense of loneliness and the sense of comradeship are important. Most of these poets are able to express feelings that were widely shared by their comrades in a direct and natural way. Some (not, I think, the majority) went on to pursue careers, if not as poets, at least as writers of some sort after the war but for many the war had been a special stimulus, and they fell silent. One may add that the public fairly rapidly lost a wide interest in war poetry after the war, and that as far as any clear new trends in British poetry were concerned the years between 1945 and 1953, say—early work of poets like Philip Larkin and Thom Gunn—were rather a blank.

G. S. FRASER

The Salamander Oasis Trust[1]

On 17th July, 1976 the *Daily Mail*, London, carried a brief appeal, signed by Erik de Mauny (B.B.C.) and G. S. Fraser (Leicester University), for two of the editors and the poets who had contributed to *Oasis, The Middle East Anthology of Poetry from the Forces* (Cairo 1943), to contact Victor Selwyn, an *Oasis* editor in London.

A generation after it had been published, *Oasis*—a unique collection having been compiled and published in its theatre of war by those who were there—began to appear on university curricula and traded at under the counter prices. A decision was taken to reprint this collectors' item which had acquired an historical interest over the years.

A B.B.C. 'World At One' slot followed the *Daily Mail* appeal. John Rimington's poem 'Danse Grotesque' was read. John's wife, Moyna, heard the broadcast and John Rimington was put in touch. John Cromer Braun picked up a copy of the *Daily Mail* on a plane going back to Brussels, where he worked at the Commission. Thus the link with the Salamander Society of Cairo which had published *Oasis* in 1943 was re-established.

Detective work by two *Oasis* poets, librarian Edward Dudley and retired headmaster Louis Challoner, led to the first reunion of *Oasis* poets and editors on 1st November, 1976 at the Sols Arms in Hampstead Road, London, two blocks away from Thames T.V. and Capitol Radio. From that reunion of thirteen poets came an editorial board and a board of trustees to form The Salamander Oasis Trust.

By the end of the year thirty-one of the fifty-one *Oasis* poets had been located. So had the two editors outside the U.K., Denis Saunders (Almendro) in Johannesburg, where he toiled seven days a week as a homoeopathic doctor and David Burk, the European Roving Editor of an American weekly, based in Switzerland. Today David has moved to Hamburg and works for a German magazine.

Whilst the Trust went through the formalities of becoming a registered charity, the Editorial Board had decided to enlarge the original *Oasis* into a new collection of Middle East poetry, adding vignettes and background to explain yesterday to today. *Oasis* would become *Return to Oasis*. It would even include Middle East verse no one had seen before—apart from the

---

[1] Registered Charity 274654

poets and their families—which were gathered in following letters in the *Daily Telegraph* and *Daily Mirror*. Details were requested from contributors to ensure that they had served in the Middle East Forces and that only those poems were accepted which had been written there at the time.

Oasis had certainly grown. It needed a publisher. Those who had poetry on their lists were approached —in vain! It is a disturbing thought, that had the Trust not been founded, the present and future generations would be unaware of the men and women, who went to war in the Middle East in the 1940's and wrote superb poetry. Part of our cultural heritage would have been lost. We are glad, too, to have found Tambimuttu again. He knew many of us all those years ago, published poetry in the War and was the man to whom Keith Douglas entrusted his manuscripts before his death in Normandy in 1944.

En route two of the trustees, John Rimington and G. S. Fraser have been lost. John died in Plymouth. As a Director of Brunnings Advertising, he had gone there to pitch for a new account. He raised the funds to pay our legal fees when we set up as a Trust from the Litton Trust (Hovis). George Sutherland Fraser died in the first week of this year. He contributed greatly to the editorial decisions of *Return to Oasis*. The Editors leaned on his judgment. Ian Fletcher, Professor at Reading, and a Middle East poet, stepped in for him.

The Trustees today are:
John Cromer Braun, O.B.E. (Chairman)
Victor Selwyn (Managing)
Louis Challoner
Erik de Mauny
Alan Freedman
George Norman
Sir John Waller, Bt
Dr Darrell Wilkinson

July 1980, London

Sketch by Keith Douglas.

THE MIDDLE EAST ===
ANTHOLOGY OF POETRY
=== FROM THE FORCES

OASIS

*"A fertile spot in a sandy desert.
Any place of rest or pleasure in
the midst of toil..."*

Chambers's Dictionary.

SALAMANDER PRODUCTIONS
121, Sh. Malika Nazli
CAIRO

FOREWORD

This Second World War has not as yet been so prolific in the production of Poetry as was the War of 1914-18, perhaps because the tempo is faster and the lands more foreign and barren than those experienced by the majority of fighting men in the last War. I consider OASIS very aptly named, because of the pleasure that it will give to many who have found War an aesthetic desert; and because most of us in the Middle East will always remember the feeling of excitement and anticipation on approaching those patches of greenness and water in the Western Desert; not knowing whether they would turn out to be real or mirage — I feel in the case of OASIS it will prove to be the former. I therefore wish it the greatest success and hope that it may be the source of pleasure to many.

GENERAL,
COMMANDER-IN-CHIEF,
MIDDLE EAST FORCE.

September, 1943.

In The Beginning

by THE EDITORS

The idea for compiling OASIS *was inspired by the atmosphere afforded by the coffee room at Music For All. Three of us were present: Denis Saunders (who is perhaps better known as Almendro), Victor Selwyn and David Burk. Denis is a poet, Victor a lecturer and David a journalist*[1].

We were discussing and criticizing Denis's latest poem and the book of verse he intended publishing in the near future, and one of us suddenly said: 'There must be a lot of poets in the Middle East. Men who have been encouraged by some inward feeling, induced by the war and by battle, to express in verse the many ideas flowing through their minds. It seems a pity for the gems which undoubtedly will have been produced to remain locked secretly in the poets' bosoms. Why not collect their works together and publish a Middle East anthology of servicemen's poetry?'

The suggestion went through a two-week period of eager discussion. All three were keen but many factors required consideration before any action could be taken. It was not a task into which one could plunge blindly and hope for the best. Soon, however, the plan was made and the anthology begun.

The scheme was advertised as widely as possible, for which thanks are due to the many newspapers and periodicals in the Middle East who carried a 'blurb' for us; and to the Egyptian State Broadcasting for their kindness in reading an announcement each day for a week.

The response from the services was magnificent and over a period of approximately three months, the editors read more than three thousand poems.

Working at distances, for no sooner had they started on the anthology than the editors found themselves separated by 'exigencies of the service', it has taken some time to select the poems required and thanks are due for the patience and consideration shown by the contributors in waiting for results.

But it is not intended in this foreword which the editors wish to keep as brief as possible to deal at any length with the poets whose works are included in OASIS. *The editors' main object here is to thank the many people who assisted readily in its compilation.*

Sincere thanks are due to Dr Worth Howard, of Music For All, for kind assistance; to Lt-Col. F. N. Stevenson, Command Education Officer, B.T.M., for untiring help and encouragement: Colonel Hurford Tatlow, O.B.E., M.C., Con-

---

[1] Denis Saunders had arrived from the South African Air Force in the Desert.

Victor Selwyn ran a tented map-reading and navigation unit.

David Burk was in transit between the Intelligence Corps and Army Newspapers.

troller of NAAFI, Middle East, and also to those who assisted in many smaller ways and whose names are far too numerous to be mentioned individually.

Lastly, but certainly not least, the editors have to thank the Salamander Society for assistance, encouragement and for seeing the edition through the press. Had not those enthusiasts Keith Bullen, John Cromer and Raoul Parme so generously for Poetry's sake, accepted the huge task of proof-reading and presentation, it would have gone hard with the editorial trio who eventually, for military reasons, became separated by continent-wide distances which made satisfactory administration an impossibility.

As they write this, the editors tremble, thinking they may have overlooked somebody, If they have, they ask only that their lapse may be taken as momentary and not as a sign of forgetfulness.

And thus, if everyone is satisfied, so are the editors, who would like to mention that, if OASIS *was hard work—it was nevertheless a pleasure.*

ALMENDRO
VICTOR SELWYN
DAVID BURK.

Preface

Most fittingly, following the victory of the Allied Forces in North Africa, there comes from the press an anthology of verses written by men who have served in the Middle East during the past three years or more. For all who have been in the services and whom we would honour, these poets say, 'Here we are—there are our dreams, our cries, our songs. Learn what has been the anguish and the grief, the joy and the faith of us in uniform.' We may think that we have known these soldiers and airman, seeing them by the thousand on the streets of the city, riding with them on packed trains or tram cars, sitting with them in the cinemas, chatting with them in service clubs, entertaining them in our homes. Yet by these poems, we may come to know the soldier of the Middle East in a fashion impossible hitherto. In addition, this volume marks, in a peculiar sense, the conclusion of an important period of the gigantic struggle; Africa is no longer a battlefield.

Details of the campaign and accounts of individual exploits of men of the army and the navy and the airforce have already been given to the world. Newsreels and daily broadcasts have kept the public far better informed of the progress of the forces than has been possible in any previous war. An untold number of photographs have been taken, showing men in action and recording the aftermath of battle. Cartoonists and artists have employed their skill to portray scenes on the battlefield and life away from the front.

The public will continue to receive other reports. Stories of escape which can now be only mentioned will be narrated in detail. Stories of the amazing adventures of the desert patrols and of combined operations will sometime be revealed. Carefully prepared histories of army divisions and air squadrons will be published in weighty tomes to find their places in libraries beside the musty records of past wars. In time, generals and other high-ranking officers will write their memoirs, quoting from secret documents to solve puzzles of the past.

But perhaps no record relating to the war in the Middle East will be closer to the spirit of the men who have served than this volume of poems. This is true because poetry has the quality of engaging our emotions so directly and so powerfully. By a word rightly chosen or by a phrase richly coined, a poet opens vistas or captures the heart as no other artificer may.

Doubtless we shall always think of the Battle of Egypt and of North Africa principally in terms of the desert. Airfields have been established and maintained on the sand; men have lived on the desert, enduring its intense heat in summer when a tent might suddenly burst into flames or its bitter cold in winter when rains might come to add discomfort and pain. In the swarms of flies and other insects the plagues of ancient Egypt may have seemed revived to require another Moses who never appeared. Men have been lonely; they have been weary; they have been harassed in body and spirit; yet they have been tempered and toughened; they have regained a happy simplicity of living; some have learned the vast resources of the human spirit.

And back they have come from the desert—sometimes bitter, sometimes desperate to catch life in some more colourful aspect—but so often they have returned eager simply for a bath, clean sheets, a good meal. To some it may have appeared that these men back on leave to the city, in their need for change, cared only for the sordid and the ugly. On the contrary, thousands of men have searched for beauty in a variety of forms. With what evident joy have they flocked to concert halls to hear a Beethoven sonata, a Brahms concerto, a Schubert symphony. Men have crowded the cathedral courtyard to listen to a Handel oratorio. They have sought hungrily for the privilege of good books. Men and officers have gathered to share their love of poetry—others have read and acted plays together. Discussion groups have sprung up, and good speakers on a wide range of topics have been in demand. Let no man say that all those in uniform have become simply cogs in a machine—that military discipline has made of them mere automatons. Their eager search for the good and the beautiful has been splendid proof of the cultural vitality of our democratic processes.

True, far too many men have been thwarted, many embittered; for, after all, war brings its casualties of the spirit as well as of the body. Yet for those who are the unhappiest about the conditions in which they find themselves or are the sourest in their outlook on life, we venture to predict that they will come to view the experiences of these months and years through a mist of fond memory. The minarets of Cairo and the hills of Palestine, desert dawns and shadowy streets, the teasing boot-black and the shouting *arbagi*, exotic flowering trees and choking desert storms, signs of extreme poverty and displays of oriental luxury—memories of matters such as these will be relics of an experience which some have already tried to put into letters, others into journals, and still others into sketches or paintings.

To the greater portion who have found no creative release for their adventures, this anthology should come as a welcome aid. That someone has captured a present experience in a mesh of words, that another has given shape to dreams of lovely desert nights, or that some other has unleashed questionings of society's conventions and restraints should be cause of gratitude. Here is a record for men of the services to refresh memories, give meaning to experiences, reveal values previously unsuspected or only glimpsed.

From another viewpoint, the collection is a memorial to those who have fought, died, or endured in battles of this Near Orient. Likewise, it is a message and an interpretation for those others in homes all over the world who have hoped for these men, loved them, and yearned for their return.

We are told not to expect great art in the midst of great conflict. No matter what the verdict of time is upon the rank of these poems, there is certainly assurance that the creative springs have not been choked by this awful sport of Mars.

WORTH HOWARD,
Acting Dean
Faculty of Arts and Sciences,
American University at Cairo.
Director of Literary Activities,
Music For All.

Poetry Today (1943)

It is the fashion and folly of critics and apologists of poetry to treat it as something inevitably bound up with the conventions and conditions of the day. If these conventions and conditions become disrupted and destroyed then the same fate should befall poetry. But this is not the case. Through wars, revolutions, social and economic upheavals the spirit of poetry lives on, not altogether unimpaired but sufficiently unbroken to survive.

It is easy to be revolutionary in word and action by destroying the insignia and literary canons of an existing regime. But mere destruction results in impasse unless a constructive pattern is built upon the ruins. And the bases of reconstruction will always be found among the debris, for no system which has lasted for centuries can be altogether bad, and no culture which has developed alongside social progress can be snuffed out like a candle. So it is with poetry.

In his preface to *Lyra* (expressed to be 'an anthology of new lyric' published in 1942) Herbert Read, the champion of Surrealism and new movements, stated, 'A new political world, a new economic world, a new practical world is being forced on us; we cannot drag after us into this new world the literary conventions of the old.' This statement fails entirely to take into account the nature of poetry, its basis upon and interrelation with the imagination. Furthermore it is dangerous. Dangerous because it aims at severing the future from the past and such an action can only result in sterility. For literature in general, and poetry in particular, to be whole and of permanent value it must include not only all experience but also all time, and the exclusion of poetical precedent is as fatal as dogmatic adherence. Art can never stand still, and new forms and new ideas are constantly being thought out and developed. But such development is evolutionary—the adaptation of the written word to changes in colloquial speech; streamlining of phrases; clothing of permanent ideas in the transient dress of the day. But the essence and the principle remain and it is upon these bases that the world of poetry is constructed.

There have been so many definitions of poetry throughout its history that it would be invidious to attempt any fresh interpretation. William Hazlitt, in the first of a series of lectures on English poets in 1818 has made as clear an exposition as could be found anywhere and the following extracts show how his remarks apply today and at all time; 'Poetry is the language of the imagination and the passions. It relates to whatever gives immediate pleasure or pain to the human mind. It comes home to the bosom and business of men, for nothing but what so comes home to them in the most general and intelligible shape can be a subject for poetry. Poetry is the universal language which the heart holds with nature itself. He who has a contempt for poetry cannot have much respect for himself, or for anything else. It is not a mere frivolous accomplishment, the trifling amusement of a few idle readers or leisure hours; it has been the study and delight of mankind in all ages. Many people suppose that poetry is something to be found only in books, contained in lines of ten syllables with like endings: but wherever there is a sense of beauty, or power, or harmony, as in the motion of a wave of the sea, in the growth of a flower that "spreads its sweet leaves to the air, and dedicates its heart to the sun"—*there* is poetry, in its birth . . . Fear is poetry, hope is poetry, love is poetry, hatred is poetry; contempt, jealousy, remorse, admiration, wonder, pity, despair, or madness, all are poetry. Poetry is that fine particle within us that expands, rarefies, refines, raises our whole being: without it man's life is poor as beast's.'

The trend of poetry has been to overlook the intuitive reaction and to bastardize the language of the imagination; passion and emotion have been subordinated to the intellect; the clinic has been substituted for the fairy glade. The fault lies partly with the poets, partly with the conniving critics and partly with the apathetic public. That there has been a movement away from lyrical impulse cannot be denied. A return to lyricism must be achieved, but this cannot be done by ignoring tradition and beauty in the written word, for the one is inherent in the other.

After the last war there was too great insistence upon experimentalism for experiment's sake, new art forms and esoteric production. As Cyril Connolly has written, 'Turning from the Georgians to the moderns we abandon the lyrical for the intellectual, for the poetry with a frown.' This frown became so menacing that the poetry-reading public took fright and the new voices spoke only to a limited audience who had passed through the initiation stages of psycho-analysis, political economy and brain-fag. Poetry wandered into the field of prose, retaining the name of poetry more by idiosyncrasy of presentation than by true imaginative content. Just as intelligence and intuition have different functions, so do prose and poetry have different appeals. It was the confusion of intelligence and intuition that resulted in a certain confusion in the poetry produced in the last quarter century. That period must now be looked upon as a period closed, and the lessons drawn from it should be well learned by the poets of this generation. For they are the poets of the future and will mould the shape of poetry for the next quarter century.

Although it is presumptuous to lay down rules, some of Hazlitt's dicta may well be remembered, for they go to the root of the nature and effect of poetry and give indications for the essential atmosphere without which future poetry will be barren. 'The universal language which the heart holds with nature and itself—that fine particle within us that expands, rarefies, refines, raises our whole being.' That is poetry and for all the camouflage of words which has hidden it from the modern public, that is what it remains. Nor does its expression depend upon strict rhyme, classical metrical form or fustian phrase. It calls for beauty of emotion and thought expressed with clarity and poise.

The tricks and sensationalism of certain bright young men have not been representative of the genuine searching for poetic expression and basic truth. Too much of the poetry of recent years has been hasty and improvised, and too many of the poets have failed to achieve the wealth of emotional experience vital for rich expression. The result has been a certain flimsiness and slickness which has caught the public eye more through its flash advertisement than through its real value. But there have been real poets among the scribblers who have sought to fashion good verse, and their work will achieve a lasting place in the realm of letters. The period of perplexity and scepticism became changed in character by the impact of war, the effect of which has been to re-awaken the poetic impulse and add zest to the writing of verse.

It may be argued that the ideal conditions for poetry writing are impossible to achieve during wartime and that when the age is one of ugliness and terror, the poet is an escapist who does not reflect these things. That is a short-sighted and erroneous supposition. It is because of the ugliness that the poet is urged to bring forth beauty to counteract the adverse emotional play. The facts of war may not be in themselves subjects for poetry, but rather left to novelists and journalists. The emotions produced by war are subjects for poetry and in all wars poets have been quick to appreciate this and capture the stress in their works. It is not all stress, and the human and at times comic relief all find reflection in verse, even down to the humble limerick.

It is only right to reflect awhile on the position of the poet. In wartime he fulfils an arduous and difficult role, for he plays the dual part of fighting and writing, and the same hand wields both pen and sword—though today it is no doubt manipulating typewriter and Tommy gun. The soldier-poet has a double allegiance—to the military machine of which he forms a part, and to his art to which he is bound. It is a fallacy to regard the poet merely as a dreamer of idle dreams, an escapist from reality; he may be an able soldier, quick to appriase situations and swift to act. His reactions are rapid in proportion to the volatility of his nature. He can adapt himself to conditions of war with rapidity, however much he may revolt within himself against those conditions. If one has any doubts about the success of a poet as a soldier, rove through history and recall the gallantry of Sir Philip Sidney, the military exploits of Byron, the poets of 1914–18—Rupert Brooke, Wilfred Owen, Siegfried Sassoon, the volunteers of the Spanish war—John Cornford and Christopher Caudwell. And so today, while the spirit of poetry still lives within the hearts of men, there are soldier-poets on every front.

From time to time in English literary circles the cry arises, 'Where are our war poets?' That cry has been answered by the appearance of a number of anthologies and a continuous stream of books of poetry. It may not all be good poetry, but it is symbolic of the men of our time and the poetry of all time, that despite the crises and difficulties which surround them, they continue to sing their songs and give out the benefit of their lyrical impulse and philosophic reflection. These men are not detached dreamers, but practical men fighting for principles which are embodied in their verse. Beauty, truth, liberty, happiness—all abstracts, but ideals which have stood before us through the ages as abstracts which are worth fighting and dying for, abstracts which men have constantly struggled and still are struggling to clothe in positive form in a world of peace and contentment.

That is the value of the poet—to preserve for the people the thought and feeling, the ideal and the substance of the spirit of mankind. Man in his humility of selflessness, in his understanding and compassion for his fellows; man in his search for truth and appreciation of beauty; man in the bliss of his love for woman and in the sublimity of his thanksgiving to his Creator. While military strategists plan the final victory for the free peoples of the world; while diplomats hover over the chessboard of international settlement; while politicians ring changes on war aims and post-war reconstruction; the poet holds the standard of liberty and culture high in the air for all to see and follow.

The hard-headed businessman and the sceptical soldier is not swayed by rhetoric, and asks at once, 'Has poetry any practical value now?' Let that be answered by Mary Rowlatt, who stated in her preface to *The Watcher on the Cliff*—'Poetry can lead men and women through a process of mind, spirit and will to constructive decision.' And such a result is at once admirable and vital. For both businessman and soldier need above all else the aptitude for constructive decision and it is the lack of this factor that leads to disaster. By its very exaltation, the pure spirit of poetry can induce in men and women a feeling of detachment from harassing circumstances and an access of power by which they can fortify themselves and fit themselves for some constructive action. By constructive action is meant action of the mind, spirit and will. This may be further interpreted as a steeling or steadying of the nerves, a physio-spiritual act by which the whole bodily system is attuned to greater effort, both physically and mentally. It is the possession of this knowledge which has enabled the poets now in uniform to continue their writing while carrying out their military duties.

This anthology has been compiled from poems written by men and women serving in the Forces throughout the Middle East. Some of them may not have survived to see their poems in this collection, but all were inspired by the same ideal. All felt within them the leaping flame which fired their imagination and created their poetry. Some are known, some are unknown, but all are part of the same brotherhood. All have been on foreign soil and a prey to the nostalgia and agony of separation from their homes and families. Conditions have been easy for none of them to write their poems. They have been denied, for the most part, the beauty of natural surroundings, the leisure for contemplation, the quietude for writing. But they have overcome their difficulties as this volume testifies.

It should be a matter of some pride for the peoples of the United Nations that the men and women of those forces who have achieved victories by armed assault on foreign soil should at the same time be maintaining the victory of culture and beauty over the horror and ugliness of the time.

JOHN CROMER

Almendro

Night Preceding Battle

Spoamy,
Slashing at the shore,
Salt skimmering in the moonlight,
And always that roar
Like a family quarrel. Tonight
I look across the disarranged sea,
Undulating unaltered, only I,
Different and detached, divining Me
Formulated as a breathing question-mark
Crivelling in lust-pregnated casing,
Like bee seducing pollened virgin,
Questions 'Why?'

Why dust-born society advancing dust's decay,
Cradled in metal-moulded rhetoric, insane
Distortion of armed arbitration?
With this 'Why?' pounding, thumping in my brain
I demand God end His holiday
And influence the situation.

Yesterday I embraced my plough with Masochistic pleasure,
Worrying if my economic seeds would be enough
To feed the hungry. Soil and work were the measure
Of my education.

Today I killed a man. God forgive me!
Tomorrow I shall sow another political corpse,
Or be dead myself. And strangely
I am satisfied to be applauded killer.
Holy Mary plead my dutied sin's legality.
Is there no end, reason, answer? Damn the sea!

Spoamy,
Slashing at the shore,
Salt skimmering in the moonlight,
And always that roar
Like a family quarrel. Tonight
They are rolling up the guns for tomorrow's battle.
I must not be late to hear Death rattle
In my enemy's throat.

The flame of Hell pythoning
Around my trigger finger insinuates coercion,
And feeling body's blooded-reeds contracting,
Dispose of humanity's humiliated feelings
And know that I am ready.

Christ, it's cold tonight!

Trepidation

There are moonbeams weeping on the desert sand,
And the dew is softly dripping
Where the opal waves are lapping 'gainst the land
And the wind is lithely tripping . . .

Shall we dance—
In the shadows, or in the latticed light,
Criss-crossing as the careless moon caresses cloud
In the blackened bowl, with the stars' eternity—
To the mellifluous voices of the Night,
Which, with the passage of the Time, become more loud,
Until lo! we swoon with the sound: end our ditty?

Then are we Yogi . . . all the Secrets know . . .
We are inspired . . . our souls, unloosed away have fled
To the lost Spirits of the Air, crying 'panic!'
For oh, who shall bear the lantern, to show
Us into the aisle of the long quiescent dead,
Or the railed throne of the Kingdom Satanic?

Sweet zephyrs of the dawn, O bring us balm!
Let the end be what it will.
Now are we automatons in a charm,
Sportive in the chase and kill . . .

Let us die
And let our graves be by the littoral,
That we might be soothed by the sea's soft, silky chant.
So, in the evening's close, perhaps we shall
Ethereally return, and lying on the slant
Of a wadi, in trepidation await
For the zero-hour's mishandling of our fate,
With the moonbeams weeping on the desert sand,
And the dew so softly dripping
Where the opal waves are lapping 'gainst the land
And the wind is lithely tripping.

Egyptian Dancer

It seemed the very sunlight shamed,
Half-holding from the exhibition room,
Yet on her shapely legs it flamed
To leave her face and upraised hands in gloom.
And as she swiftly spun, it tightly spiralled round
Her naked body, like a snake, then fell to ground
And was lifeless.

With the silence broken by the beat
Of music pounded on the door,
And the softened shuffling of her feet
Scraping on the hard, bare floor,
While like castanets, the clacking of her finger . . .
For her no joy in this endeavour
Bought by men whose lustful, bulging gaze will linger
Until it scar her soul forever.

So must the poor besmirch the Spirit
To ensure continuance of it.

J. G. Barker

Vision

I saw young men in youth and pride
Grow god-like, laughing in the sun.
I saw them strangely deified.
I saw them clearly, one by one,
Quicken and change, and pass along
Reborn because their thoughts were strong
In images of subtle right.
Yet some were shattered in a day,
And all the glory passed away,
I saw two nations smitten poor,
Two nations, neither wholly wrong,
Grow weak and bitter, evil, old,
Oppressed by politics to war,
By priests, advisers, greed of gold.
I saw their men in mystery,
    Mystical their pride;
I saw them on Gethsemane;
    I saw them crucified.

J. A. K. Boninger

Elegy

Feel me like music beautiful with pain
Be hers in passion and then quietly hear
your heart redeeming all the purple fear
of living. Bending in all cooling rain
the echoes sound like south-wind in the plain
and violins must call like floating wings
of nightingales and vanished moonlight sings
in us, and turns all wisdom back to care

So I remember you as part in me
A part undying with a soundless past
and seeing you as I would always see
infinite moments and my music tells
of poverty and warmth that would not last
A broken trumpet, which at last rebels.

Max Bowden

Myriad Destiny in Neat Black Shoes . . .

With minimum bow-wave
The convoy glides persistently
Determined sheep guarded by brawny shepherd
Swallowing opposed distance

Sweating ghosts from reeking troop-decks
Man bleak unsmiling guns
Like devils' fingers jeering at God
And all balanced on a restless eiderdown
That gives no rest

Eyes like women's fingers
Attempted to smooth ruffled surfaces
Lay a constant stare by day and night
Focusing the impossible
Optic nerves ache and minds dull
At constant illusion of small waves

This monstrous iron womb
Teeming with obscure life
Holds torturous course
Steered by epaulettes flanking a teak face
Grey pulp throbbing in bony cup
Under bald head and peak cap
Myriad destiny in neat black shoes.

Desert Memories

How grey and greenly graceful
The beeches on the hillside
Cathedral cool shade in the woods
Every blade of grass
Every wild flower
Tangled in the ditches
Rain-drenched and sun-drenched
Like your eyes and hair
How many aeons since was that?

Come back memory!
Back to your fossil, desert state
Your fingers reaching out
Clutch at the heart.

Through the bitter-sweet miasma
I see the fresh and fertile beauty of peace
Personified
In your own vivid loveliness.
Halt! Who goes there?
Sharp challenge of a sentry
Ripping the desert night
Jerks the puppet strings
And my mind shrivels
Becoming a hard pebble in the desert.

Desert

The sand, the spewed up, shattered rock,
    The chaos of hours, the tired confusion
And days which heap upon each other's backs—
    The mating beasts that breed delusion.

A familiar echo in the brain
    Of thought once stridently expressed
Memory, music, colour fades
    With senses callously repressed.

We stumble through the hours of night
  That jut like clumsy lumps of stone
With penetrating shafts of fear
  The light that searches nerve and bone.

Sand whipped by all the varying winds of hate,
  Blast, howling through exasperated mind,
But in the fog small kindnesses persist—
  The border line of hell is ill-defined.

Space choked by time and time oppressed by space,
  The simple things corroded by sterility
The formed hate beneath affection's mask
  Sees reason searching death with strange futility.

John Bristow

Circles

I watched the slow footing of the ox
Tracing circumference over circumference,
Bound to the radius of a crooked beam;
With his bandaged eyes, and his sides sunken, ah sunken!
I looked and saw how they trace their circles,
Each traces his circle through space and time:
The world, the roundabout and the ox.
Each follows the self-same path;
The first two giddy with spinning.
But the ox does not hasten his step;
He knows that he will outlive Eternity,
Dragging his beam to no oxenish end,
Neither peering through his bandage like a curious schoolboy.
I find, ox, that I like you, though I expect
That you are as tiresome as the Marx brothers to live with.

Douglas Burnie

Seven Pints of Ale

Seven men in Cairo,
Seven men in gaol
Mad as hell and drunk as well—
Waiting for their bail.
Seven men in khaki
Looking rather pale . . .
All because they couldn't hold
Seven pints of ale.

One had been in Syria
Wiping up the French,
One in Crete, had faced defeat
With a monkey-wrench.
They had been in luck then
Now they were in gaol . . .
All because they couldn't hold
Seven pints of ale.

One escaped from Norway,
One had fled from Greece;
In Palestine they drank their wine
And wove their Golden Fleece.
They had had to run then,
Couldn't run from gaol . . .
Held the Nazis, couldn't hold
Seven pints of ale.

One was bombed in Mersa,
One at Singapore;
One knew the way from Mandalay
And took it . . . to the shore.
Seven men in Cairo,
Seven men in gaol . . .
Because they smashed the tout who hashed
Seven pints of ale.

19

Louis Challoner

Sonnet

Weave me a web of mem'ry fine and close,
A tapestry of rich and vivid themes,
Rare with the fitful imag'ry of dreams
And textured as the petals of a rose;

Bearing the dew of morning's tenderness
Regretless tear of voluntary love.
And to the form the fleeting shadows prove
Fashion a garment like the dawn's caress

That garbs the filtering landscape of the Fylde—
Or like the glittering veil the twilight draws
Over wild moorlands' lonely cliffs and shores,
Lulling in half-tones her wind-worn child.

So weave, so fashion, so engarb my heart
That none may know it from your own apart.

Sonnet

I find no place in strife, no hope in war;
For all that battle, all that courage gains
The hero's but a momentary star
That gleams at midnight and with morning wanes.
My pleasure has been found in simpler things—
A woman's smile, the laughter of a child,
The comfort that a silent friendship brings,
And hills of home, by man yet undefiled.

Remember me as one who brought you light
To see the joys writ small in Nature's book.
But bright their beauty seen in friendship's sight,
The lovers' fairer flowers, the greener grass
As one who loved the sunset at Tobruk,
And found a violet on Halfaya Pass.

Outward Bound

Grey gulls gleaming on the grey river—
White wings weaving in the wan sky—
Thrust the flanks and the bows quiver
    As the dark waves roll by;

Green heads heaving in the blue distance—
White wake surging from the grey land—
Strong the salt and the spray's fragrance—
    The grip of the clenched hand.

Stern strength striving in the ship's motion—
Dull thoughts drumming in the dark brain—
Hopes that drown in the deep ocean
    Will not start tears again.

White wings words from my pale lips sweeping—
Grey gulls gleaning from my damp eyes—
Eager waves to my hand leaping
    Carry home my goodbyes.

Dudley Charles

Twilight on Carmel

The fading light of evening and the first star
Stealing its sorrow through me and I know
How they hung their harps upon the trees and wept
    For thee, Jerusalem

The faint clatter of venetian blinds, the dim Path
Winding a narrow way where witches dwell
I hear through the far forest the boughs
    Whispering wickedly

Wailing of village dogs; unhappy echoes
Cry to the tender moon a spectral woe
Vague indefinable longing, melancholic
    Moves within me

Murmur of muted power, the distant sea
Whispers old secrets to the passive shore
Old was I when great Solomon
　　Tasted his glory

Harvest golden the earth; a glad Shalom
Rings through the land—'Come ye, my people'
Ache of the ages stilled . . .
　　　　　　　　　　　Oh, but the wind
　　　　Is mournful tonight.

John Charnock

Down on the Sands Flinging

Down on the sands flinging!
　　A heart restless,
　　With pain swollen:
　　Conscious only of a tautness
　　And a wild singing—
　　The wild singing of the whispering waves
　　And the rolling ocean,
　　Lapping the sands with a rhythmic motion.

Down on the sands flinging!
　　A heart for ever aching:
　　Listening to the ceaseless sounding
　　Of the sea on the sand—
　　The wild rhythm of restless passion,
　　The rolling motion of love.

Down on the sands flinging!
　　A body hurt with longing
　　And the endless swinging of the waves,
　　And the endless lapping of the waves
　　On the warm sand—
　　Like the kissing
　　And the rolling rhythm of the love
　　The body seeks,
　　Far from the loved one.

Down on the sands flinging!
  A body seeking the calm sleeping,
  Lapp'd in love, which passion lent—
  Like the swelling of the ocean
  When the wild waves have roared restless
  And pass'd over,
  Leaving the ocean,
  Happy but spent.

God made the rolling ocean.
God! Why am I far from my loved one?

J. M. Collard

Death of a Man of Kent

Now he could see the fields that lay below,
The tiny chequered towns, the London train
Just steaming into Canterbury with slow
And sinuous movement. Then the steel rain
Of bullet after bullet seemed to tear
His Hurricane in pieces. As he fell
He thought he heard come to his dying ear
Church bells from Wingham tolling out his knell.

The land he loved stretched out her arms to meet him,
The land he'd fought to save now called him home;
The smiling fields of Kent were there to greet him,
And to his graveside all his neighbours come;
Men with bowed heads, and girls dissolved in tears,
As if he'd died in bed and full of years.

To a Daughter Never Seen

If I should never see you in this world,
If war's inconsequence should claim me too,
God grant me this, that I may come to you
When you're asleep, with tiny fingers curled.
Around your pillow, with the moon's white rays
Making a halo round your golden hair.
Give me an hour to let me watch you there
Midway between this life and death's dark ways.

And then perhaps when many years have passed,
You will recall a long forgotten dream,
Of how a stranger came when you were fast
Asleep, and stooped and kissed your curly head.
And as you think of me there'll be a gleam
Of light upon the valley of the dead.

Molly Corbally

. . . Ad Astra

I took my leave of the earth and men,
And soared aloft to the lonely sky,
Thro' the gathering dark, to the silent stars,
And the whisper of Angels passing by.

I heard the beat of the Angels' wings,
In the silent watch of the starlit night.
I felt His touch, and I heard His Voice.
I, Man, communed with the Infinite.

Far below lies a burnt-out wreck,
Soft, the strains of the bugles sound.
The Ensign flutters a last salute
As another pilot is laid to ground.

Men are sighing, and women weep.
Ah! foolish friends, do not grieve for me,
For I heard God call in the silent night,
And flew on, into Eternity.

John Cromer

Asleep in War

I called you once, but you were sleeping,
Gold in your hair the moonlight gleamed.
I stood quite still, but my heart was leaping
Though I knew not what were the dreams you dreamed.

I called you again, you still were sleeping,
Pale was your face, no smile was there.
Your eyes were tired with too much weeping,
The splendid lustre had left your hair.

I called once more, you were not sleeping,
A trickle of blood lay by your head.
The sky was clear, no searchlights sweeping;
Raiders had passed—but you were dead.

Reverie

I walk in the tranquil shadow hours of twilight,
Before the golden zenith of the moon,
Alone, and grateful for my solitude
To drift and dream away the lagging hours.
It is good to forget the death that is in the air,
To breathe again the fresh pure breath of living;
It is good to remember Nature and her joys,
To hear again the song of nightingales.
There is always peace behind the blaze of gunfire;
There is always quiet beyond the wire-tipped hills;
There is grief in thoughts of death and separation,
From these I turn and look another way
To see afar the broad fields of the future.
There lie the fallen seeds of destiny,
Waiting for warmth and peace to bud and flower.
That time will come and I will be there with them,
Content and happy at that shining hour.

Egyptian Evening

This is the country of long sleeping dust,
Land of forgotten twilight
Where memory dies with the sun;
Where only the moon is cold
And the stars reflect its chill.
Dusk blends into the pastel afterglow,
Slipping beneath the shadow of night
In the hasty retinue of time.
The silhouette of palms against the sand,
The warm wind of the desert
And the lost cries across the moon
Embalm in peace this Egyptian evening.

J. A. R. Dakin

Bonds

O, I would tie you inextricably
Into a knot symbolic in design;
A lover's sigh
Merging in mine
The name that gives you separate identity

O, I would bind you inescapably
Twixt you and me the bonds would intertwine
Line over line
Till we combine
To live and die in Love's great unity.

A. C. J. Davies

We Are Dust . . .

We are dust, and must
As dying leaves which fall
Sodden in the autumn rain,
Golden and brown, quivering down
Be dust to dust again.

Why then this fight, if light
Be only for a day,
Oh God, why all this pain?
We fighting die, wondering why
Our dust by dust is slain.

Stella Day

Bataan

Have I a pen of flame
To write of deeds
That fabled gods and heroes never dreamed?
Or are my spoken words
Trumpets of gold, to wring from mortal sound
The thrilling paean of each soaring name?

Never shall history speak or books make known
That assured truth of horror these men found.
No words conceived within the speech of men
Could truly prison deeds so conquering fear,
That Bravery's self paid homage to his own.

What need have they of old, stale words of praise,
Void of the understanding that they know?
Each man, by his own separate soul and heart,
Has built a temple on Olympian heights,
Eternal shrine for all the Future's days.

Erik de Mauny

Steeplejack

I

Uncover the lenses, hush the crying,
Let the wind stop in the restless trees,
Dam the stream, stay the fountain.
Slow the winter, slow the dying,
So hush the crying.
Here come the quick,
Here come the living.

Forget the conventions, abandon the articles,
Arrest the eternally moving picture.
With your hand on your heart or your heart in your mouth,
Examine the particles.

Or by a quieter insistence
To reaffirm the imperative:

Now a crystal morning in the sunlight,
With bells chiming, swallows on the grass,
The wrought iron of the cafe table
Throwing a baroque shadow, the air
Clean even of flowers, the motor horns,
The screaming children, all smothered
Or lulled by the hour, the strident headlines
Gone, the newsboys vanished,
The war a thousand leagues behind a green hill;
The heart quiet awaiting the questions
With the hot answer, like the lover's kiss;
Is a good time for a benediction,
Or a vision.

Nothing is fixed. Let us postpone judgements.
The sea, drifting and edging up the sand
Is repulsed with a disconcerting rattle of pebbles.
Fevers and loves ride the mind like combers,
But the waves suck back, out, out to the deep.
In the morning everything is the same,
Except for a little sea-weed and sea wrack.

Postpone your judgement on blanket assertions.
Children are frightened without the lamplight,
Men have their own big dark fear: saying

   'How at the mercy of these tides
   Could we live at ease or live at all.
   Learn to say white is white, God is good,
   Seize happiness in this rigid rut.
   Take care of the pressure of hands,
   Chiaroscuros, innuendos,
   Between the lines, diminuendos
   And nuances by violins.
   Cultivate the bright brass band.'

II

In the end the struggle for remoteness
Is unequal. Just as sure as the blue ocean
In summer makes its siren call,
So the voices of action clamour like riveters' hammers
On the brain: the unjustly dead
Cry for intervention. Perhaps because
The shattered bodies of children whose quicksilver
Has run away, or the women whose mature joy
Ended with a bayonet in a dark back room,
Cannot be related tangibly on marble slabs
Before your eyes as jurymen
Their demand impinges with a deeper insistence,
Claiming denouncement of their anonymity,
The squalid burials.

   'All, all over into the ditch.'

   'Even the stars are afraid to come out tonight.'

   'Quiet, my friend, we have created a power
   That blackens the sky. Heave, into the ditch,
   And let the dogs kick over a cover,
   Or the birds make the service unnecessary.'

We have a morality which baffles
The computations of spring and autumn,

Contradicts the calendars of living, eating,
Mating and dying.
We, who are from the celestial stud-book,
Must inherit the earth; which
Involves a certain responsibility.

III

Yet there is a high tor and an icy wind blowing,
And loneliness, a cold wind before and behind,
The head wind and slip-stream round a skier.
Can you stand the cold? That, and having
Your heart frozen always to silence?
Then you will find a strange renaissance,
A spring within the ice,
Feel yourself tugged out of gravity,
Beyond even the vertigo of the steeplejack.

Boats going out, seagulls going out, dreams
Going out in the cold douche of the grey morning.
Hitler speaking over the radio, son saying to father
'Oh, turn that rot off, we want some jazz.'
Snails in a hundred gardens slowly trailing
Their silver calligraphy across the opening leaf.

A bird leaving the bare branch, chasing the sun
Into the darkness. Trams disgorging pouch-eyed workers.
The old, brown-faced peasant woman suddenly
Kneeling in the empty field, pleading
'Oh God, let Albert come home safe: if not today
Tomorrow . . .'

Leaves and the wafer skeletons of leaves
Swirling down the swollen rivers. The mind
Watching, a thousand feet up, watching and counting
These things dispassionately, like a man trying to sleep
Counting sheep. One, two, three,

And slowly feeling the urgency of the task
Come out of hiding within, unfold,
Like the green leaf uncurling,
The unconscious spring unfolding.

Maizefield Near Cairo

The green sea whose smooth swathe
laps from rivershore to rock
peopled by spasmodic trees
lightens to the summer wraith.
Luminous and calm this stock
stands in seried phalanges
leaning spears into the last
tremors of the evening breeze.
Horizon west the city lies
grey wound, at dusk, too old to bleed
while all the tired men turn and mumble
under the rose miracle of the skies.
By the city of abstract sound
and men whose eyes look back through time
searching the hurt, the green tide sways
and flowers and sings about the wound.

Season

In summer dusks the fierce sky
Burned behind sombre mountains like
Rose essence distilled in the crucible of twilight.

Licking the city steps the waters rose
Wine-dark jungle of moon-snakes softly weaving
Interminable creations into a childhood's dream.

Scent was the evening world, smoke and fume,
Tired breath of streets, hot sigh as the lights pricked up
Yellow ears and eyes in the melting darkness.

Warm bloom of haste on cheeks, we softly climbed
Then, in those late days (can they come again?)
With hands, eyes, of love, into the cloaking hills

Above the muted city, the snake-quiet water,
The parks, the breathing woods, were furred with lovers
Dark symmetries half resolved in the merging night.

Was it far, that climb out of the world? That far
Glister of stars that veiled our faces then
Hides in cloudburst, now all's war

And the slow sad rustle of fading, falling men.

E. P. Dudley

Stalingrad

Once before
You counted this city
Symbol of young freedom.
Now your hands your nerves
your blood
Repeat
Thousandfold projection of battle
Your desires

time was more
than clocks ticking
away our lives
time was more
than lives touching
the cells of death

Till now our dreams are false
Pointers to nowhere.
With passionate life
You walled your city with death—
Triumphant
Swept away together
Dead thought
Dying fears
Our barriers of expression
Built our springing hope
With the tissues of your pain.

David Dunhill

Summer Afternoon

You, mingled in the sense of summer grasses
tingling the white flesh speckles
with the tasselled field's eyelashes,
blinked a touch upon the quickness
of my skin, and sent the thin
pores dancing with a passion's wind.

So the cool, firm dust
(as orthodox, religious men believe)
sank in the white quicksand of your skin.
And the coldness of your arm
was swallowed, as dust might be
in swirling particles I called desire.

The grasses dance,
too-heavy in their dusty, pollened heads,
and touch; by chance, maybe,
transmute their careless choreography.

And we on the river-flanked, uncut hay
were sifted, had ourselves drawn together,
jerked apart in the rootless sway.

Nobody Waves

'This is what war is . . . two ships pass
each other and nobody waves his hand.'
CHRISTOPHER ISHERWOOD.

They wave to us from the triangular villas
With lathered hand stuck on a washday brow.
And children, high to the hip, remember how
They, too, have waved, have had response
Or else the cold-blood, fearful adult stare.

The troop train passes and they wave again,
Return the insistent, hopeful, phallus thumb,
The upturned, tousled smile of boys who come
Unknown, unknowing, from back single rooms,
From bicycles in passages, and ride to war.

For motion wins, unfreezes relationships,
Forbids communication and precludes the stare:
The carriage window of a person, where
The loneliness, the privacy are stalked
By hurried, platform pacing up and down

Looks on a world of which he is afraid,
On faces where the upturned smile is dead.
Only retreating, rushing can he rear the head
Retracting at each tunnel, each
Heraldic, engine's petrifying shriek.

And now, in war, the motion is not arrested.
Fears have only been replaced by fears.
The speed is faster and the accident
Must be—must wait the pause between
The child's grazed knee, the welling, fist-eyed tears.

After the buffers are broken, the wills have telescoped,
After the travellers are denied the hopes they hardly hoped,
The quick response is broken, and the children are aware
Uniquely of the cold-blood, fearful, so-called adult stare.

G. S. Fraser

Lament

In a dismal air; a light of breaking summer
Under the conspicuous dolour of a leaden sky,
We walk by the river, beneath the deciduous branches;
Cold in the water the webs of the cold light lie.

Always the sky bleeds with sorrow that no light stanches
In the evenings of autumn, when rust coloured crisp leaves fly,
Always the heart is uneasy and full of foreboding:
Always the heart is uneasy and cannot tell why.

Always the rust of the leaves and the light is corroding
The steel of the evening, gun-metal blue of the sky.
Always the river is lisping and lapping of sorrow.
Like the leaves and the light, the incontinent impulses die.

No more appointments to meet and continue tomorrow.
No more postponements of parting, with hesitant sigh.
Here's the great year in its circle, announcing departure.
Here are your hard lips on mine and goodbye and goodbye.

Summer resumes the occasion but not the adventure.
Always the heart is uneasy and cannot tell why.
In a dismal air; a light of breaking summer,
Cold in the water the webs of the cold light lie.

The Two Dreams

You who have forgotten me now completely, remain
A durable image, standing like a column
Whose marble in the storm winds takes no stain:
Tall like Athene, straight, and white, and solemn,
You vanish last in the dismembering night
That flays and opens all the good and fair:
You are the morning, very cold and white:
You are the room for which I climb the stair.
You are the lucid and forgiving page

That lends a shiftless history point and order:
You are the challenge and the noble rage:
You are the happy land across the border.
You are these dreams, but of your dreams not one
Is this hurt creature you took pity on.

Egypt

Who knows the lights at last, who knows the cities
And the unloving hands upon the thighs
Would yet return to his home-town pretties
For the shy finger-tips and sidelong eyes,

Who knows the world, the flesh, the compromises
Would go back to the theory in the book:
Who knows the place the poster advertises
Back to the poster for another look.

But nets the fellah spreads beside the river
Where the green waters criss-cross in the sun
End certain migratory hopes for ever;
In that white light, all shadows are undone.

The desert slays. But safe from Allah's Justice
Where the broad river of His Mercy lies,
Where ground for labour, or where scope for lust is,
The crooked and tall and cunning cities rise.

The green Nile irrigates a barren region,
All the coarse palms are ankle-deep in sand:
No love roots deep, though easy loves are legion:
The heart's as hot and hungry as the hand.

In airless evenings, at the cafe table,
The soldier sips his thick sweet coffee up:
The dry grounds, like the moral to my fable,
Are bitter at the bottom of the cup.

Alan Freedman

African Port

Heat!
And the headland blurred amid the steaming rain.
Plague!
And all the breeze a rotting warmth about the mouth.
Flies!
And the swamp breath, the sun a burning pain.
That's the blazing haven of a harbour in the South.

God! How we longed for smoke trails, the English ships,
A cool familiar face and a friendly eye
But for us there were black minds and heavy lips
And always the fury leaping avid from the sky.

Night!
And mosquitos with their needle-note of doom.
Dawn!
And the climate like a weight
Day!
And the colour, yet disease within the loom,
That's the evil beauty of a tropic-beaten port.

Harold M. Fridjohn

If I Could Stay

If I could stay the flood of time,
impound the fickle moment ere
it sweeps on into the past;
hold time's drop—like crystal rime
is firm by winter held—clear
of seconds scudding fast,
I'd pluck the time-beat when you pealed,
'I'm nineteen now.'
                                    Within that phrase
your unsaying said
'On, youth. On into life. Wield

the power of your Spring. Gaze
beyond the red
Of shattered human wrecks, beyond
the crimson slough of our inheritance.
On, youth. You are
today held in tomorrow's bond
to make life's living void of chance
and want.'

'I'm nineteen now,' you said.

W. G. Graham

Song of the Young Men

We will go down and fasten back the gate;
For the hills are cool, and the dews on the grass are cool,
And the rivers are slow, and the fields are grey and still;
Under the streaming mists the furrows wait
For the hand of the sower, and the morning skill
Of the casting of seed, and the rake, and the gentle rain:
We will go down that the reapers may not wait,
That the sickles be not ground by the reapers in vain—.

Last night we deeply drank with the idle old men,
And feasted, and in our folly spilled the wine,
And drunkenly rose, and stupidly watched it drain
On to the dusty floor, and lifted again
The empty cup, and with a drunkard pain
Crushed it into the palm of a bleeding hand:
Ah, fools were we to waste with the idle old men
That crimson wine of the first-fruit of our land—.

Aye, ye will go; yet still ere ye open the gate,
What will ye sow? lest at the harvesting
Silence may be, or weeping, for a song—.
We have the seed, and we will not be late;
The grass and the poppies shall grow again:
We cannot fail; for those who passed through the gate,
The reapers—what would they say of the sowers then?

Peter Hellings

Orientation

Sailing a sea of flame
That gilds our hull
With the false fire of reflection
And a world of dream,
We plough with austerity northward into Egypt,
Make small attempt to paralyse reaction,
But to arrest a sunset.

Black spars in the sky
At night, invest
Our cause with grandeur, for few question
The moon's brilliancy;
And we released from boredom by starred sleep
Relax lethargic limbs and breed conviction
In five seas of hope.

The high actinic quality
Of the sun
Has made us malleable, and inaction
Marred our reality:
The blue waste of the sea's perpetual flux
Mirrors our character with a mild refraction
And wastes our sex.

Now we like Caesar's troops,
War–ridden,
Seek to oppose contraction
Of our cooling hopes,
For in the navigation of historic seas
There can be no return or changed direction
Like that of Ulysses.

Sailing no sea of fame
Or myth, like heroes,
We are not free in action
But in name:
Like Rome, ironically race the seas again
To arrest no Roman Empire's disintegration
But that of the Island of Britain.

Hamish Henderson

Hospital Afternoon

In the hand projecting from the blue pyjamas
The nerves dart like a pond of minnows,
Betraying a brief agitation in the brain,
Timid deer start in the parkland spinneys:
Through our shutters the fine sand blows like rain.
The waves of heat loll lazy aggression
Against our feverish island of illness,
The bumble buzz of an electric fan
Makes a weakly wind in a covey of coolness.
Whispering starts behind the crimson screen.
We lie out of sheets in defeatist languour.
The wardrobe mirror takes up my attention.
After lunch feelings grow fat in the head.
My nihilist brain nods its own suspension,
On a tide of treacle drifts off towards sleep.

Norman Hudis

. . . And There Was Light

'To live it again
is past all endeavour.'

*Extract from popular pessimistic
hymn of the mid–twentieth century.*

Gaslight
pale eggish tremor of a London eve
an age gone: it was my boyhood. Grieve
for the death of it.
Naphtha
fierce bruiting above shining sweetsquares
and white elephants for sixpence,
stuffed pink-haired monkeys and teddy bears,
second–hand bowler hats. Sense
this street market as my bright Cathay:
double-headed monsters in each alley
it's true, but in the main
an artless wondrous joy, and the gurgle of the rain.

Hurricane
lamp, weathered, glassed, roundly against the night,
suffering smoky black from a malformed wick,
plopping exasperation, ugly winking sound and sight.
This now's the latest lighting trick;
tented Libyan interlude,
graceless, grassless étude.

Return
soon, the junk and toy rows, floodlit barrows,
the illumination of medium marrows
brazenly outshining Corporation incandescence;
and the awesome man with his long pole
floating the streets, an immortal carbon soul
engaged on light transference.
And, with a British Legion step
I'll through the market pass
noting on every pitch, a deathly farce,
a fatal link with other bazaars,
Derna, Cairo, Alep.
I will have walked the foreign strand,
a disciplined and humble Polo:
the smiling trees of Sarafand,
chill glories of the Sinai night,
sparse chanting of a Beirut band,
bleak birth of Daba light
all this I'll know . . . adult, solo.

And not a few grey alleys, with a formless glint
of evil, there, deeply swirling back . . .
this I'll vividly recall, more than gentle hint
of warlife . . . mocking, endless and a cul-de-sac.
Then will past happiness be sought
in the home stretch;
but years will walk with me, hard-bought
and more to fetch. And adventure will elude:
a bricked London street-scene
a Stepney étude.
The hissing beauty of the squalid had been
a breathless voyage to my half-forgotten child,
(why do we then grow aimless and defiled?)
But I'll see a 'bus, recall a desert jeep,
(why, for our infant projects do we weep?).

Dorvil Jones

For My Wife

I, too, remember daffodils,
With every golden head a-shake,
When laughter lazed among the hills,
And swans lay placid on the lake.

I, too, can see the water lie
With scarce a line upon its face,
As full of silence as the sky
And lovely with immobile grace.

We talked in murmurs, hushed and slow,
Our secret thoughts, our dearest dreams,
Of what we'd do and when, and how,
And pondered strange domestic themes.

Then, in those moments, did we frame
And from our love a world create,
And fondly dwelt upon a name
What time our love was consummate.

There will be times again, sweet wife,
When faith will gain its recompense,
And dreams will live beyond this strife,
Fulfilled in dear magnificence.

So let us heartful courage take,
Outbrave the present woes and ills;
Again we'll see the quiet lake
And glory in the daffodils.

Hugh Laming

Zito Hellas

Greek Memories 1941–1943

My son, the world forgets and turns its tired face
    From old regrets to new disgrace:
That is the way of the world, son,
    Dominus Dei, Thy Will be Done.

Spring came in all her loveliness to Greece,
    Green leaf on winter's trace.
And life and love took on new lease
    In Thessaly and Thrace.

South rode fair Spring—
    I saw her kiss
The noble pillars
    Of Acropolis.

South sped the Spring, but on her heels
    Came war: sullen rumbling of the wheels
Of Hate's grey chariot; and the beat of wings
    Black crossed Death's anthem sings.

Greece stood embattled where the eagles fly:
    Hellas who showed us how to live
Now taught us how to die.

Northing to block invaders' road
    A strange song-singing legion strode;
Men from beneath the Southern Cross
    And rain-swept Western Isles
Taking no count of bloody loss
    And marking the miles
With dead in their retreat
    Singing in their defeat.
And on St George's Day they held Thermopylae.

Two years, two weary years have fled,
　　Years to suffer and avenge the dead;
And now, praise God, a new Spring comes
　　With brave new banners and new beat of drums.
This Year of Grace shall Greece be free

　　Strike now for Greece and liberty.

L. K. Lawler

Poem

I have remained in the café
Long since the sour red wine
Sank to black dregs in my glass
And think if the chair next to mine
Will again be tenanted, who will come in
Before the café's beetle dark begins.

You, coming first with crinkled eyes
Into the yellow shout of light
And the stale smell, suddenly
From the unreceptive night's
Old fingers which our own new war unties
To blind in blackout streets the cars' weak eyes;

Sitting at my table, pretending
That no one watches you,
Hesitant, beginning politely to speak
How empty the time, having nothing to do;
Why were you quick-eyed frightened,
So that at each newcomer your throat muscles tightened.

Later the woman with a sloppy mouth,
Humped in the chair next to mine,
Not very hopeful amateur tart
Whose cheap hot smell spoilt the taste of wine;
Why were your meaty hands not still,
Not for a moment still.

I do not want your body
Or your soul, or your creed,
You have no glance, nor grace
Nor love that I need;
Though from the eyes the soul is fever ill
And the hands are never still.

Being nothing to me these are brethren,
Sloppy mouth, moth hands and loose eyes
These are the friends I have and will hold
In our hate and sentimental lies;
We are the ancient easy game, we are yet cheap
For power and slaughter; these are the friends I will keep.

Because I hate and want no reason,
No more of words or scientific logic,
No more the regretful, relentless
Equation of the economic;
These are my friends, whose eyes were put out
By those they do not know to hate.

R. B. Lester

Higgledypiggledy

I sometimes sit and dream about a world that's upside down
With houses standing on their heads in every dizzy town,
Where skylarks burrow underground and worms nest in the trees
And whales go whistling through the air and donkeys swim the seas,
Where daffodils grow in the sky and stars float past the door
And men walk on the ceiling for there isn't any floor.
And then again I'd like to see a world turned inside out
Where people sleep in flowerbeds while their Queen Anne tables sprout;
With kingcups in the kitchen, on a polished lawn we'd dine,
We'd have goldfish in the cellar and a fountain full of wine,
We could build a lofty coalmine, dig a lighthouse in the ground,
And deep inside the earth we'd watch the moon go waltzing round.
And what a merry place would be a world all back to front
Where little foxes chase the hounds each night at Boogle Hunt,
Where humming tops spin little boys and people pay to work
And microbes gaze through microscopes where men of science lurk;
We'd wake at midnight bleary-eyed and stagger off to sup,
We'd eat to get an appetite and drink to sober up!

Norman Longhurst

Sonnet—Strictly Personal

You will not change; for nought of Time's endeavour
   Can dim the dancing light within your eyes,
Nor passing years' prosaic passage measure
   In weeks and months the life that in them lies.
You will not change; for how shall moments capture
   The eager heart that greets each hour anew
And flings its beating warmth with careless rapture
   In challenge to the world, so brave and true?
You will not change; for Youth shall be your token
   Against the solemn rolling of the years—
And laughter, and the joy of life unbroken,
   And steady shining eyes that know no fears.
And I shall come, when wandering days are done,
   To warm my heart in Love's eternal sun.

The Trust

Keep these for me: the far high blue of Summer
   Wide-stretched across the sloping valley fields,
And Monk Wood lying sombre in the evening,
   And all the shadow'd mystery it shields:
The pillared green of tall trees in the sunlight—
   Long golden hours of laughter, careless, free—
Arms linked along the homeward stroll from tennis
   —Keep them for me.
And keep these too: dew-feathered lawns of Autumn,
   And morning mists soft-rolling from the sun;
October's winds a-prey on Summer's sweetness,
   And brown leaves fluttering earthwards one by one.
Stern Winter days, and lamplit dusks,—snow falling—
   Long cosy teas, and toast, and fire's bright hue;
   —Yes, keep them too.
Oh! Keep them all, for now my heart's sad longing
   Must hold them in its mirror, ever-clear,
Nor fading with the weary months of waiting
   —But most of all, oh, keep your smile, my dear!

T. W. Louch

The Exile

It is not that I pine for freedom
To sow the offsprings of my mind,
Or that this land—this ancient kingdom
Has fetters which it seeks to bind
Around my strong and youthful wrists.
It is not that my heart is frozen
In the chaste lake of absent love,
Or that this hand that war has chosen
Lies crushed within the iron glove
And memory stagnant in old mists.
   It is that I am starved for laughter;
   And exiled from the smooth caress
   And scarlet lips of Eve's own daughter—
   And golden sunlight in each tress.

Edward McHale

The Dreamers

Through the sand, and the dust, and the heat,
  Through the pain of our burning feet,
Through the sweat, and the flies, and the thirst,
  We dreamed as we wearily cursed.

  Is the meadow-green grass as green
    As it was when it last was seen
      From the quiet of a Turton lane?

Are the whinberries ripe on the moors?
  Does the heather sweep down to the shores
Of the road that goes up to Belmont?

  Do the oak and the elm and the beech
    Still crowd to the water's reach
      In that wood where the bluebells grow?

Through the sand, and the dust, and the heat,
  Through the pain of our burning feet,
Through the sweat, and the flies, and the thirst,
  We dreamed as we wearily cursed.

George Malcolm

Lament

As I walked under the African moon,
I heard the piper play;
And the last place ever I heard that tune
Was a thousand miles away.

Far to the west, in a deep-cut bay
By the ceaseless sound of the sea,
We lived and laughed in a happier day,
Archie and Johnnie and me.

For they'd be piping half of the night
At every ceilidh by,
And I'd be dancing with all my might
As long as they played, would I.

Many a time we were at the Games,
And many a prize had we;
And never a one but called our names,
Archie and Johnnie and me.

But Archie's dead on the Libyan sand.
And Johnnie was left in Crete,
And I'm alone in a distant land
With the music gone from my feet.

I heard him under the African moon,
That piper I could not see;
Yet certain I am he played that tune
For Archie and Johnnie and me.

A. W. Marsden

Infantry Training Blues

The rain blows west and the room grows colder,
Ruts are fuller and the rats grow bolder
This winter forty men will moulder,
And they'll bury 'em shallow, shoulder to shoulder.

The rain blows west and the moon is hazy,
The food is lousy and the cooks are lazy,
Maybe the forty weren't so crazy
When they changed their diet to salad-a-daisy.

The rain blows west and them forty's walking,
There many already has heard them talking,
And many to swear they've seen them stalking
With queerer things than a bat for hawking.

The rain blows west and my new girl's haughty,
Says the things I'd rathest do are naughty;
There's nothing to do but join them forty,
Thirty-nine steps, and I'm with the forty.

J. G. Meddemmen

War's Dullard

It is easy to talk of
    Intellect and Reason,
Spirit and Mind,
    Soul and Hate and
Even Love.

It is easy to suffer
    Now or for a season
War and the blind
    Unsatisfied passion;
Times can be rougher.

It is not easy to waken
    A full comprehension
Of what it now means
    To be legally killer;
Man is dulled, not shaken.

It is not easy to sever
    Word from declension;
For apathy gleans
    Now little discomfort
And maybe for ever.

G. C. Norman

Halt for Lunch

A light wind whips the flame to furnace heat.
'It's on the boil, throw out the milk and tea,'
Says Atkins, 'what we going to have to eat?'
Somebody stirs the petrol-sodden sand;
The dixie-lid spurts steam.
                      'There's M and V'
I say, 'as good as anything. And canned
Pineapple.'
            They agree. The cans are stood
In water on the fire-tin. Mercifully
The dust storm has died down.
                    'There is some wood
Somewhere inside the truck' says Cpl Dean.
The air is very still. A smell of bully,
And chips and onions fried in margarine,
Comes from a truck a hundred yards from ours.
The sky would match a Suffolk sky at home,
Pale blue and cloudless. Small sweet-scented flowers
Make sweet pretence of Spring. The burnt-out husk
Of a wild idea conceived in distant Rome
Stands near at hand, where desert scrub and musk
Have given place to strange, hewn wooden plants,
Whose harvest has been plucked, and whose rough branches
Are done with Spring forever.
                  Two spidery ants
With triply bulbous bodies come and go
In aimless haste.
          Some men are digging trenches
Unhurriedly. McCartney tries to sew
A button on his trousers at the back,
And turns round like a corkscrew.
               'Take 'em off'
Says Atkins.
       'What, in front of you?' says Mac,
And tries to blush. He does not find that easy,
Being older than us all in years and love,
Three times in jail, and twelve years in the Army.

I lean against the wheel and close my eyes,
The water in the tin is bubbling softly.
Two amorous and persistent desert flies
Whine in my ears. Small sounds can sometimes quell
The roaring of great silences.
                    Then faintly
A new sound strikes the air, a surge and swell
Like angry breakers on grim distant shores—
A sullen hateful sound, evil, portentous,
That grows in wrath and volume, till it roars
Its hatred and defiance overhead.
From half a score fierce throats.
                'Look out, they're Stukas!'
'Where's my tin hat?'
        Ghent has already fled.
We jump into a trench. The mighty throbbing
Is changing key. Two of us have a Bren
And one a rifle. Ghent is almost sobbing,
From breathlessness and panic. It is the first.
The planes turn round into the sun, and then:
A sudden pause.
        These moments are the worst.
Five dreadful seconds, five eternities,
Five bars of trembling silence.
                Nothing stirs.
Breathless and tense we listen. Here it is:
A throb, a hum, a deep full-throated roar,
The whistling of rushing air, and now our ears
Are helpless in the turmoil and furore
Of impact and explosion. As they land,
Bursting and crashing to a wild crescendo,
The bombs send up great founts of smoke and sand.
Wandering shrapnel whistles through the air,
Uttering a long-drawn sigh, as if in sorrow
At finding no soft mark or target there.
The planes are past us now. The last bombs fall,
The roaring dies away; and it is over.
We clamber up and dust ourselves. 'That's all,'
Says Atkins, 'that's our lot. Cups up for tea.'
And when the smoke has lifted we discover
One truck ablaze; one torch for Liberty.

G. O. Physick

November Evening

Trains clank up and down on iron tracks.
   In dank, clamorous hours,
      Nightfall lowers;
Dead men have burdens to their backs
   And on their graves, flowers.

The half-alive creep back into their cells,
   Dark curtains draw within
      To keep out sin;
For it would shout, as dead men's knells
   That to the dead make din.

And there are children, conceived in lust,
   That come, through shrieking birth,
      To filth of earth.
Theirs is the heritage till they are dust
   Of sorrow, with no dearth.

The earth I do believe is purgatory.
   How wind, whip-driven bleeds
      For God's dire needs;
And there is no peace, not even sanctuary
   In the whole night, where it bleeds.

Death in Libya

   Bury him by the pale sea
   Whose waves the whole night long
   Pour quietly, resignfully
   Down.

   Leave him by the cool sea
   And say for him no prayers:
   The waves are crying for him
   And wind blows back the tears.

John Rimington

Danse Grotesque

The Devil played the drums when Peter died
An overture of bombs and crashing sound
   A whirling slip of splinter caught his side
   And deftly set his body spinning round

Alas! He missed his final curtain calls
A khaki Harlequin in 'Danse Grotesque'
   With just a single vulture in the stalls
   To witness so superb an arabesque.

Jasper Sayer

Flight

High on the singing slopes
The voluntary conscription of the birds is taking place
And the moorland is abandoned to the lizards,
And unshielded sun, with flashing grace.

Upwards in a momentary sweep
They chatteringly propel a painted arc across the sky;
In this formation each is leader and the clouds
Can hold no terror while he need not die.

There is the everyday, fantastic flight,
Undetected down below the pin-point shrieking of the air,
For in the valley men are glancing over the gun sights
And their shoulders with disciplinary care.

Racing, turning swiftly south,
They shut off the power and coast down, effortlessly mute;
Encountering in flight a different breed,
They dip in civilized salute.

Christopher Scaife

Soldier to Artist

I am no traitor, do not think me so;
I burn your books and bring your towers low,
But you, the unconformer on the verge,
Destroy the order that I cause to grow.

This is our opposition, every man
Can see; but we in truth are other than
We seem, not foes, but allied against Chance,
Both ordering, trying to shape and plan.

I have, indeed, done much I blush to see,
Riots, and rapes, and drunken cruelty;
But you, have you not much that brings you shame?
Volumes and miles of mind's debauchery?

At worst, we both have fled, time and again;
Best—you to Nothing give, by brush and pen,
Significance, my bugle stirs, through shape
To strength, the formless energy of men.

Look at me now, brother, do you not see
Our struggle's one, though we act differently,
To draw an order from the ancient world,
Warmth out of coldness, joy from misery?

Write If You Can

Write, if you can, exquisite phrases
Balanced like flowers, and, if you can,
Arrange rare images upon your pages
Remote from this harsh present-day of Man.

Fill, if you can, well-lighted chambers
With past imaginings, hands, work where still,
Familiar once, a spirit called beauty slumbers;
Familiar, before Man made a tyrant of his will.

Who would not follow you, and leave this present—
Day without sunshine, and a starless night—
Who would not free himself from the persistent
Will, the tyrant conjuror with wrong and right?

All its achievement who would not change, and all
The spoil of conquest and the gain of human strife,
For things, the fruit of Man's whole nature, full
Of that spirit called beauty—filled with life?

Bhag Singh

Thirst Epigraph

I am thirsty . . .
For the sweet water of life that flows so rare on this parched earth—
Some cups are bitter, others are tasteless.

But sweetness comes from thee . . .
When in thrills I drank a few deep draughts.
Ever it increased my unsatiated desire . . .

I refused all drinks, I sacrificed all fountains
For the Font of thy sweetness.

How can I forget those blissful sips.

Throw out if thou so desireth
A thirsty life lies writhing on the burning sand:
So parched am I with thirst . . .

Forbid be the full cup with all thy heart,
Why refuse a few draughts—from thy perennial fountain
Oh thou cruel charmer . . .

Yet in all sincerity of love I *sing*.

Alan Smithies

The Dejected Singer

Miranda, it is past time for songs and singing,
　I have sung so long, and I have found no peace;
No peace . . . and all the Christmas bells are ringing—
　I think that it is time the songs should cease . . .

I kept for you a proud heart, and a lonely
　Spirit, I stood defiant, and alone
And no peace came, Miranda—it is only
　Within your life that I may find my own.

Our love sounds like a wistful Chopin piece,
　In its divine, overshadowing poetry
Of passion—but the splendid songs must cease;
There is no music written which can sound
　The silent depths of bitterness in me,
The restlessness of spirit, the profound,
　　The desperate misery.

Arnold Smithies

Morning After

I

Now I plunge into mud,
After child fancies of the same
I well remember:
Crude graspings finding beauty,
Through an implacable energy
Digesting filth.

(Who thus purveyed my life
To vent a madder groping without tears
In these red years?
In this dark compromise, pursuing Truth,
I see with alcoholic eyes derelict Youth
Fighting, in dissipation, the birth-pangs of stagnation.)

Judge me—
I beg you, judge me!
And watch a faltering hand
Gratingly-intimate with sand,
Turn to the fine-tinged corridors of heart
It has traversed.

II

Only that rain be on my face
On a wild day,
Walking with vaguely-searching pace
In the old, child way.
Only that consciousness embrace
Valley, turf and trees,
And the cloak of dull clouds; the clamouring peace,
My sensitivities . . .
In a bowl of silence, with thoughts turned upwards,
Dropping and falling in slow fertility.

To a Woman in England

It is that through the port-hole of my pain
You seep with larger rhythms. I maintain
A jutted consciousness, weakened in hardness . . .
The freeze of the moonlight hardened my love.

It is that in the longings of the child,
Sick for affection, fiercely made and mild—
There of frustrated cinder-dust you made
A wholesome fuel, fearful of a flame

A lurid thought escaped and dwelt,
Aloof and wan. Conspiracy of pain.
Dear, let us stand and see a wall appearing,
And turn our backs to live another creed
In all its unbelief and grime and flowers.

Catherine Smithies

Sonnet

Ah, yes, I have remembered, as I said,
And Beauty, constant, has remembered, too;
She sent her messengers with silent tread
To scatter silver tokens fit for you.
Her robins came, and pleased the waiting hour
With liquid notes that summoned old delights,
Awakening hidden dreams to conscious power
That sent them surging upwards to the heights.
Invisible and soundless craftsmen wove,
At Beauty's bidding, veils of finest lace,
To hang on every tree in dale and grove,
While well-loved hills were dowered with new grace

Yes, Beauty has remembered, faithful yet;
I, too, keep faith,—for how could I forget?

Christopher Stanley

Poor Mist

Soft padded, shyly fumbling with numb fingers
          across the street,
The mist but lightly pauses, crouches, lingers
          on stealthy feet.

And then, with murky shrug forlorn,
Treads vanquished on before the dawn
          Dead beat.

Windswept

The wind romped laughing up the hill
And pirouetted round the mill—
                    But I stood still.

The trees splashed wild, as fingers tear
At fabric, with their manes: saw ne'er
                    That you were there.

And wild geese calling, roughly hurled,
Thrust, crumpled as the wind unfurled
                    And round me whirled.

The leaves in gaudy handfulls played,
Dim-mirrored pools of light and shade—
                    So there you stayed.

The pale, the grimmer sombre sky
Envelop'd earth and hugged close by
                    The trees and I.

You saw me—ran—soft-panting rose,
And there we lay so breathless close—
                    In deathless pose.

T. Stephanides

The Marsh of Death

Of rusty wire are the brambles
That writhe o'er the sodden plain,
Of shell-burst the lowering cloud-banks
And of iron the pelting rain.
The shadows are lurking perils,
The breezes a poison breath,
And the Very-lights are the will-o'-the-wisps
    That dance o'er the Marsh of Death.

R. N. Walker

Living and Dead

These crimson bandages speak and move feebly,
But quickly establish their identity and enquire for others from their home
    town,
Becoming tender acquaintances instantly:
They wring the heart.
But the dead—
Makeshift mortuaries full, uncounted,
Uncountable—
The mind claps down its shutter, excludes the realization
That they ever lived, and ascribes the scene
To frenzied work left unfinished
In a waxworks factory.

John Waller

The Brave to whom Frontiers

The brave to whom frontiers
Seem calm before attacking
Who in dark corners
Fear no danger lurking
Are happy in story
Where success in loving
Is hero's reward
And the prize for doing.

So these make love
A second encounter
Ending as quickly
And even with laughter;
Heroic though they take
In this register
Life is too swift
And they miss the dearer.

But love is the death
That my heart dies from,
Passionate lips
And bright rebellion . . .
While even losing
And being alone
Is joyful sorrow
Of what was done.

So leave to others
The impersonal glories;
Being alive
Makes the finest stories.
Let pride remain
In a few memories
Growing more lovely,
No hour disparages.

Convoy

Like lazy ducks upon a placid pond
Only deep blue, and the sun drenching
Against shadows a hard dry light, the ships rule
Whose purpose is so firm and feminine,
Now power but heart lazy, the cool limbs
Safe on a certain journey, an end sure.

Now for a moment distance intensifies
Each personal tragedy, lends wings to wish,
New favour to frail. Certain moments
Make pictures for always, continual summer
On a separate island, over each heart
An enchanted figure, someone to adore.

Nina and Konstantin

From Tchehov's 'Seagull'

It is a story very like our own,
The seagull, seduced Nina, lured away
With her bird's beauty; a loveliness
False for success, drear harmer
To whom children are made as spoil!
So life at last despoiling you perhaps
Has even now enveloped and hurt
That shy youthfulness; and I, if only
I knew, would grieve as true
As Konstantin, hapless admirer
Of waywardness; because he loathes
Treegorin's kind, losing life itself
With memory of the time
Nina has coloured; he yields to death
All his advantages. Unlucky victims
Of the famous bogies, Irene and
Treegorin, these two children
Leave only a tale others may understand.

E. A. Walmsley

1914

They said, 'It shall not happen twice. We'll fight
To make the world a better place.' They died
And I was born. Foolish, I thought them right.
They lied.

Darrell Wilkinson

Apprehending the Morning

Tomorrow will there come again
an evening's apple-scented breath,
and will the warm-touched English night
around the closing petals wreathe?

Shall you and I again be quiet,
again my whispers in the air,
I cradling tresses in my arm,
you muffling kisses with your hair?

Will there be skies mauve-pink at dusk
and rustled leaves to shake the dawn—
or were these only broken dreams
that, restlessly, I waking mourn?

I have a fear that so much love,
and so much faith, these previous scents,
may turn insipid, and become
the strangling memory of events.

Tomorrow will there come again
an evening's apple-scented breath,
(or will my hours be spun tonight,
and hushed the day, and damp with death?—)

'Two Sailors Lost Their Lives'

It was only in the lessening rhythm of energy
that brought them together,
and in the terrible moment of companionship
their eyes stood proxy for their heart,
lips murmuring words they could not say:
faces bound horribly together
in the slimy thought of death,
but beautiful in a friend's unity.

Held on the churn'd piercing of the trident
they were twisted apart.

We are torn away;
but in the afterplay of emotion,
the subsident swell,
half-dead the body lies.
the while it drifts between the storms,
drip-salt in hair and cold beneath the stars,
we will remember each others' eyes.

Faith in Landing

Eyes cool
unhurried the gestures
beautiful the glances.

nights against the wind
heels ground into the pebbles,
and the waves
softly lapping;
watching
the lights of a ship
calmly figurative
the proceeding.

but there are so
many thoughts desires
lighting the boat,
do they know
they are bounden
by faith
and the changeable countenance?

they are lit by
so many desires
and move so slowly
your glances . . .

we are at present on the lee . . .

I have been thinking
of a ship
wishing to appreciate
all aspects
of the sea.

C. B. Wilson

Mood

The spindle of the world
is still tonight,
The gusty winds
all folded into bales;
A shroud of vapour
hangs across the moon,
A winding-sheet of mist
about the sails
of all the little ships.
The cold grey sea
is sewn with sleep,
And there is none can bring
Trinkets and toys
and gingerbreads for me,
A sad child
with a bobbin on a string.

II

Previously Published
Middle East Verse

Harold Ian Bransom

Tempus Fugit

(Hackneyed, but very true. Feared by those who are
unable to face the dignity and honour of retirement or
who probably deserve neither.)

When wars were fought as bard doth tell,
　　Leaders fell in their prime.
But now they're fought with shot and shell,
　　'They' hang on in decline.

11th March, 1942.

The Twenty-five Pounder

(Order received when on patrol,
16th March, 1942, 'Engage all Tanks!')

The tank we shoot at a thousand yards,
　　And he shoots us at double,
So don't take pains to lose your life,
　　For he'll save you the trouble.

Never let him have two thousand yards,
　　Restrict the Hun to one,
And wake me, mother darling,
　　When the wicked tank has gone.

The Game Old Gentleman

(To Battery Sergeant-Major Alfred Beattie)

Old Beattie has the '14 Star,
　　Deep wrinkles and grey hair;
And if there's trouble in this world,
　　'Clickerty' he'll be there.

Five years are one to this old man,
　　Or else he never mounted
The earlier years which clearly ran
　　Before he ever counted.

He gives his age as 'over-forty,'
    Perhaps some think it rather naughty,
For 'Click' is nearly fifty-four,
    But good for ten or twenty more.

One son fell serving at Hong Kong,
    Another stood at Calais,
And the Grand Old Man waits happily
    For the last Great Reveille.

                                    30th March, 1942.

I. Celner

Battle Interlude

The ground shuddered, the canvas shook,
In the darkness flash on flash
Swept from left to right
And right to left;
One here, another one there,
One this side, then that side,
Ever faster. Now
A dim horizon is a line of fire
And punctuated banging
Has become a palpitating roar;
Trains rushing near and not arriving,
Noise swelling up and not receding,
Glutting ear and brain.
In vain, a human word from human mouth,
Impossible tinkle of a bell,
Imagined crunch of boot on sand;
Like crazed, hypnotic tyrant
This savagery of sound
Weighs on its brutal yoke,
Commands obedience,
But find the freedom of the boy—
Cup your hand and hold it to your ear
And play at sea-shells.

(How often, as a child,
I broke the brittle case
And sought the living cause,
The absent mystery bewailed.)
But there it goes!
Disintegrating, dying;
And now, pleasantly,
Lone guns stubbornly
Beating a rhythmic drum.
Above me, yellow light.
A blinking flare,
Remindful of the bright
New lustre of the modern thoroughfare;
And yet a sickly, waxen light,
Moving, floating there,
I lie, close-walled,
The grateful touch of earth
Around, above me; chiselled
By my spade to frame my girth.

I think of mummies.
So feels a corpse, if corpse can feel.
I think of testimonies
Picturing the victim made to kneel
In grave. I see again my father's face;
So did those eyes take in this place;
The undertaker's nail, the gluey stain.
Above me, yellow light;
And bird-of-prey intentfully
Circling, searching in the night—
A purring plane resentfully.
The engine-echo of the pilot's mind
Tells me has yet to find
Our place; but listen! that harder tone!
His finger on the button; threatening moan;
The rush of air, the whining sound . . .
My body stiffens on the ground . . .
The screech, the all-obliterating blow,
The palsied earth, the panicked flow
Of startled air—and then the gentle, eerie patter
Of sarcastic shrapnel asking what's the matter?

The yellow light
Like midnight candle
Fast is dipping
Weary of the flight,
Now no anxious rattle
From the guns is tapping.
Murmur of a distant motor.
All the sweeter,
Like a drug, begins to seep
Delicious silence, bringing with it,—sleep.

Louis Challoner

Tripoli in Spring

Over her wounds Winter was weeping yet
When first we saw the city of the Trees,
The tumbled roofs gaped to the weeping skies
And shattered walls with rain and blood were wet;
Blinded the windows stared on sullen seas
Grim as the fear in little children's eyes.
Scenes too intense for sorrow or regret
Cling to the passing soldier's memories—

The bells that rang at Zavia for the dead,
The Stukas and the shelling at Kournine,
Bambinos by the wayside begging bread—
The hundred nameless horrors we have seen
Would darken victory, except for these
Gay wreaths of welcome in the flowering trees.

Alternative

The question rises almost daily
In the gunpit, grimly, gaily—
Is it the shelling you prefer
Or the bombing?—All the air
Crouching in silence, tensely waiting—
The distant thud—the daily hating—
The whining scream—the crashing roar,
Forever nearer,—ever more
Intimately:

Then are the strong weak and the brave
Lie flattened low in their sandy grave,
Counting the leaden seconds dropping
Heavy as heart-beats, slowly—stopping—
Knowing each moment, dearer, clearer,—
Death creeps methodically nearer—

Or shall we stand, hands to our eyes
And watch the foeman in the skies,
Knowing the peril but unheeding
For the sheer beauty of the speeding
Planes that dive and, turning, mount again—
Light of their silver load—count again
The known numbers, note foreseen effect,
The chaos, sand and limestone wrecked
Into a halo round the sun
A cloud about our friendly gun?

I'd rather look death in the face
Born by a bomber's speed and grace—
Swinging down its rainbow arc
Like a falcon to its mark—
Than grovel like a nerveless slave
With nothing but his skin to save,
Crouching beneath the ugly Hell
Made by the calculated shell.

P. M. Clothier

Libyan Winter

There is so little earth, and so much cold
Grey sky clamped down upon us that we seem
Cut off from any kinship with the world,
That safe sane world we knew once in a dream.
We have been set apart like fallen souls
Without a past or future to fulfil
Blindly a driving destiny that hurls
Us on towards a goal beyond our will.
We only know that nights are long, and sleep
Comes slow to shivering men who lie
On cold hard ground, and dawn brings no respite,
Only the pallid sun and sullen sky.
Always on every side our trucks intrude
Their stark forbidding shapes above the plain
Of stones and yellow earth and grey dwarf scrub,
Bleak under wind and clouds that bring no rain.
The idle anxious days draw out their length
Into uncharted seas of time, and all
The urgent incidents that stirred us once
Are blurred and fading, lost beyond recall.
We know capricious death drones overhead,
And, more insistent as our column runs
Into the unknown battles we must fight,
Lurks in the thudding menace of the guns.
And we are trapped, for there is no escape
From this colossal tumbril as it reels
On its relentless way towards the fate
That waits us in the west before our wheels.
But still we trick ourselves with poignant dreams
Of half-forgotten days, and long in vain
For the old easy life we knew at home
In peace—that we shall never know again.
Those things are not for us; ours is the way
That lies over the desert under sombre skies
Past rusting blackened wrecks of trucks and tanks
And graves of men who blazed it in this guise.

Western Desert, 1942.

73

Front Line

Here above Gazala, where the barren hills,
Pockmarked with shin-high scrub,
Look down over the brown plain to the blue sea,
Our days draw out in trivialities.
Now there is a parody of spring
And grey clouds send fleeting showers of rain.
Wild flowers bloom beside the bomb craters
And the wadis are threads of sober green.
The moon rides high in the cold night
And we think of girls we knew in another life.
It is the same over there at Tmimi,
But there they are Germans.
We are Manning the Front Line of Democracy, no doubt,
But soon it will be summer,
And there will be flies, fleas and mosquitoes.
When my last socks are too dirty to wear
How shall I wash them?

Libya, March 1942.

Death Valley, Gazala

The Buffs are lazy fellows:
So many of them lie
Upon their backs in Death Valley
Whenever we pass by.

Guards, fatigues and fighting done,
For them the bugles blow no more.
They were called upon to pay,
And paid, the last demand of war.

Among the shattered trucks and tanks,
And flowers, and glinting grass that waves,
Marked by tin hat or wooden cross,
They lie in lonely graves.

Though sea-ways wide divide them now
From their own English earth,
The desert stones that guard their bones
Know well their worth.

And threadbare Libyan springs will bring
Each year with scanty rain
Flowers and grass to Death Valley
About their graves again.

We who daily come this way
On routine patrols
See with careless callous eyes
This valley of forgotten souls,

Knowing as we leave them there
That if the fates had willed it so
They would ride and carry on
And we would lie below.

And if I join the Buffs tonight
Or on some distant desperate crest,
I know that I shall find with them
Good fellowship and rest.

John Cromer

Transition

I breathed and moved
In the long yesterday,
Clad only in my threadbare dreams,
Deeming them filigree and finery.
I spun my fancies in the dying air,
Caught thoughts upon the wing
And drifted in a gossamer of make-believe.
To me, that world was durable, strong.
Long in history, tradition bound,
A place for men to live and women to love—
But living was fraudulent and love a ghost,
Wan in the shadow of Freud.
Gaiety spun from a high trapeze,
A harlequin behind a sable mask,
Lost, lost with the rest of youth.

The lyrics I loved are anthems now,
The rumba a requiem,
The skip and jump a slow march for the dead.
Those smiling faces lie buried beneath the sand,
Those slim hands, nerveless now, will never touch again,
That sunburned body rots on the deep sea bed.

(All gone, the youth we knew, the lads we loved.)

I breathe and move
In the minute of today,
Thoughts scattered, hopes awry, faith holding yet;
My head is empty but my heart knows and is full—
There will be life for men and love for women
And love for men and life for all.
There will be singing again on the mountainside
And eager choirs in the valley.

Old myths have gone but new magic will appear;
The dead bane clutches but the fresh seed falls
And the anxious soil is ready.
We are all ready for the silent dawn
And the daylong clamour of life and love.

We are waiting and the world is waiting
For the sudden call and the quick response.

Erik de Mauny

News from Home

Here under the neutral, distempered wall
Of the shuttered hut in a transit camp
Or waiting in tent at pebbly dusk
Impatient as a traveller at an empty station
I have lived, hardly aware of you at all.
Stray thoughts of home make leaguer and decamp
Between the exile's smile and gesture.
For here I have learned another intonation:
The shadow of the year passes like a bird's,
Dark, treacherous and smooth across the banquet,

Life's bright plateaux and shining mountains.
(I'm sorry I sent you just a picture postcard:
The legions foundered in the snow.)
These are my trophies: beads and dead leaves,
An island mask and the programme of a show,
Pension receipts from the foreigners' foreshore—

Can I tell the girl who gave, the waves' thunder
As the moon sank? These you cannot know.
These, like the dreams of ruin or delight,
Happened to the jar and thrill of the fife,
Are pent for the bullet's or the fever's spending.
This last of ecstacy, life and no life
I will bring to bury in peace among you.
You will say: 'There is another day gone by.'
And I will smile and shrug: say yes
To a dear stranger's happiness.

C. P. S. Denholm-Young

Dead German Youth

He lay there, mutilated and forlorn,
Save that his face was woundless, and his hair
Drooped forward and caressed his boyish brow.
He looked so tired, as if his life had been
Too full of pain and anguish to endure,
And like a weary child who tires of play
He lay there, waiting for decay.
I feel no anger towards you, German boy,
Whom war has driven down the path of pain.
Would God we could have met in peace
And laughed and talked with tankards full of beer,
For I would rather hear your youthful mirth
At stories which I often loved to tell
Than stand here looking down at you
So terrible, so quiet and so still.

Rommel

You hurried us out of Benghazi,
You followed us back to Matruh,
You Stuka'd us daily with bombers,
You tried every trick that you knew.
You even persuaded your soldiers
They'd drive into Cairo in state,
And you booked your own room there in Shepheard's,
You even broadcasted the date.
But you reckoned without one small factor,
When you counted up all you would gain,
You bumped up against our position
Prepared for you round El Alamein.
This factor is always recurring,
Even out here in the tropical heat,
Yes, Erwin Von Rommel, Field Marshal,
We English don't know when we're beat.

Desert Phantasy

1942

You came to me, out there in the darkness
Of the sweltering desert night.
I was standing at the entrance to my bivouac,
And the sounds of distant gunfire
Had receded to a mere rumbling.
I had been thinking about you.
All that evening I had longed for the sweetness
Which I always felt when you were near.
I longed to hear your voice,
To feast my eyes upon the gentle roundness of your cheeks.
I longed to press your lips against my own
And scent the elusive perfume of your breath,
To clasp you in my arms and try to speak
In futile words the utter longing
Deep down in my heart.
The vastness of the desert almost hurt,
And then, I felt your presence very near.

I called to you, dear heart,
With all the pent up passion of my soul.
I stood there, listening, in the fetid air
Which cast a blanket o'er the tropic night.
When, suddenly, I sensed you by my side.
Across those cruel miles which did divide
You came to me, my darling and my heart.

Brew-up

Brew-up! Brew-up!
Stop and dig some sand.
Fill up half a petrol tin
And sprinkle in some spirit
From your can.
Take another petrol tin,
Tip some water in it,
Strike a match and light your fire
And in another minute
You can make a cup of tea
For all your crew to drink.

Thus did half-a-million men
Make their daily brew,
From Daba back to Alamein,
From Fuka to Matruh,
In the good old days,
In the good old ways
All we Desert Rats knew.

Keith Douglas

Devils

My mind's silence is not that of a wood
warm and full of the sun's patience,
who peers through the leaves waiting
perhaps the arrival of a god,
silence I welcomed when I could:
but this deceptive quiet is
the fastening of a soundproof trap
whose idiot crew must not escape.
Only within they make their noise;
all night, against my sleep, their cries.
Outside the usual crowd of devils
are flying in the clouds, are running
on the earth, imperceptibly spinning
through the black air alive with evils
and turning, diving in the wind's channels:
Inside the unsubstantial wall
these idiots of the mind can't hear
the demons talking in the air
who think my mind void. That's all;
there'll be an alliance of devils if it fall.

Egypt, 1942.

The Offensive

I

Tonight's a moonlit cup
and holds the liquid time
that will run out in flame
in poison we shall sup.

the moon's at home in a passion
of foreboding. Her lord
the martial sun, abroad
this month will see Time fashion

the action we begin
and Time will cage again
the devils we let run
whether we lose or win:

in the month's dregs will
a month hence some descry
the too late prophecy
of what the month lets fall.

This overture of quiet
is a minute to think on
the quiet like a curtain
when the piece is complete.

So in conjecture stands
my starlit body; the mind
mobile as a fox sneaks round
the sleepers waiting for their wounds.

This overture of quiet
is a minute to think on
the quiet like a curtain
when the piece is complete.

II

The stars dead heroes in the sky
may well approve the way you die
nor will the sun
revile those who survive because
for the dying and promising there was
these evils remain:

when you are dead and the harm done
the orators and clerks go on
the rulers of interims and wars
effete and stable as stars.

the stars in their fragile house
are the heavenly symbols of a class
dead in their seats,
and the officious sun goes round
organizing life; and what he's planned
Time comes and eats.

The sun goes round and the stars go round
the nature of eternity is circular
and man must spend his life to find
all our successes and failures are similar.

Wadi Natrun, 1942.

How to Kill

Under the parabola of a ball,
a child turning into a man,
I looked into the air too long.
The ball fell in my hand, it sang
in the closed fist: *Open, open*
Behold a gift designed to kill.

Now in my dial of glass appears
the soldier who is going to die.
He smiles, and moves about in ways
his mother knows, habits of his.
The wires touch his face; I cry
NOW. Death, like a familiar, hears

and look, has made a man of dust
of a man of flesh. This sorcery
I do. Being damned, I am amused
to see the centre of love diffused
and the waves of love travel into vacancy.
How easy it is to make a ghost.

The weightless mosquito touches
her tiny shadow on the stone,
and with how like, how infinite
a likeness, man and shadow meet.
They fuse. A shadow is a man
when the mosquito death approaches.

Tunisia-Cairo, 1943.

'*I Think I am Becoming a God*'

The noble horse with courage in his eye
clean in the bone, looks up at a shellburst.
Away fly the images of the shires
but he puts the pipe back in his mouth.

Peter was unfortunately killed by an 88:
it took his leg away—he died in the ambulance.
When I saw him crawling he said:
'It's most unfair—they've shot my foot off.'

How can I live among this gentle
obsolescent breed of heroes, and not weep?
Unicorns, almost,
for they are fading into two legends
in which their stupidity and chivalry
are celebrated. Each, fool and hero, will be an immortal.

These plains were their cricket pitch
and in the mountains the tremendous drop fences
brought down some of the runners. Here
under the stones and earth they dispose themselves
in famous attitudes of unconcern.

Enfidaville, 1943.

Elegy for an 88 Gunner

(Published elsewhere under the title 'Vergissmeinicht')

Three weeks gone and the combatants gone,
returning over the nightmare ground
we found the place again and found
the soldier sprawling in the sun.

The frowning barrel of his gun
overshadows him. As we came on
that day, he hit my tank with one
like the entry of a demon.

And smiling in the gunpit spoil
is a picture of his girl
who has written: *Steffi, Vergissmeinicht.*
in a copybook Gothic script.

We see him almost with content,
abased and seeming to have paid,
mocked by his durable equipment
that's hard and good when he's decayed.

But she would weep to see today
how on his skin the swart flies move,
the dust upon the paper eye
and the burst stomach like a cave.

For here the lover and the killer are mingled
who had one body and one heart;
and Death, who had the soldier singled
has done the lover mortal hurt.

Homs, Tripolitania, 1943.

Cairo Jag

Shall I get drunk or cut myself a piece of cake,
a pale Syrian with a few words of English
or the Turk who says she is a princess; she dances
by apparent levitation? Or Marcelle, Parisienne
always preoccupied with her dull dead lover:
she has all the photographs and his letters
tied in a bundle and stamped *Décédé*.
All this takes place in a stink of jasmin.

But there are the streets dedicated to sleep,
stenches and sour smells; the sour cries
do not disturb their application to slumber
all day, scattered on the pavement like rags,
afflicted with fatalism and hashish. The women
offering their children brown paper breasts
dry and twisted, elongated like Holbein's bone signature.
All this dust and ordure, the stained white town
are something in accord with mundane conventions.
Marcelle drops her Gallicism and tragic air,
suddenly shrieks about the fare in Arabic
with the cabman; and links herself
with the somnambulist and the legless beggars.
It is all one, all as you have heard.

But by a day's travelling you reach a new world,
the vegetation is of iron.
Dead tanks and gun barrels split like celery
the metal brambles without flowers or berries;
and there are all sorts of manure, you can imagine
the dead themselves, their boots, clothes and possessions
clinging to the ground. A man with no head
has a packet of chocolate and a souvenir of Tripoli.

Egyptian Sentry, Corniche, Alexandria

Sweat lines the statue of a face
he has; he looks at the sea
and does not smell its animal smell
does not suspect the heaven or hell
in the mind of a passer-by,
sees the moon shining on a place

in the sea, leans on the railing, rests
a hot hand on the eared rifle muzzle
nodding to the monotone of his song
his tarbush with its khaki cover on.
There is no pain, no pleasure, life's no puzzle
but a standing, a leaning, a sleep between the coasts

of birth and dying. From Mother's shoulder
to crawling in the rich gutter, millionaire of smells
standing, leaning, at last with seizing limbs
into the gutter again, while the world swims
on stinks and noises past the filthy wall
and death lifts him to the bearer's shoulder.

The moon shines on the modern flats
where sentient lovers or rich couples
lie loving or sleeping after eating.
In the town the cafés and cabarets seating
gossipers, soldiers, drunkards, supple
women of the town, shut out the moon with slats.

Everywhere is a real or artificial race
of life, a struggle of everyone to be
master or mistress of some hour.
But of this no scent or sound reaches him there.
He leans and looks at the sea :
Sweat lines the statue of a face.

On a Return from Egypt

To stand here in the wings of Europe
disheartened, I have come away
from the sick land where in the sun lay
the gentle sloe-eyed murderers
of themselves, exquisites under a curse;
here to exercise my depleted fury.

For the heart is a coal, growing colder
when jewelled cerulean seas change
into grey rocks, grey water-fringe,
sea and sky altering like a cloth
till colour and sheen are gone both:
cold is an opiate of the soldier.

And all my endeavours are unlucky explorers
come back, abandoning the expedition;
the specimens, the lilies of ambition
still spring in their climate, still unpicked:
but time, time is all I lacked
to find them, as the great collectors before me.

The next month, then, is a window
and with a crash I'll split the glass.
Behind it stands one I must kiss,
person of love or death
a person or a wraith,
I fear what I shall find.

Egypt–England, 1943–44.

Thomas Eastwood

The Draft—Cairo, 1942

Fifty men standing in line of threes
    On a station square.
Fifty names typed on a list,
    And not one there
Who knew what the Western Desert was like,
Or was yet sufficiently trained for the fight
    That awaited him there.

The list I held in my hand was long,
    And glancing down
I read such ordinary English names
    As Robinson, Brown,
And a host of others, which I forget,
That carried a breath of Cockney air
    From battered London Town.

I called the roll, and they clicked their heels
    And answered: 'Sir!'
And my Sergeant marched them across to the train
    That awaited us there.
Rifles and packs were stowed away
And we settled down in the heat of day
    To the flies and the dusty air.

Just twenty-four hours or more
    And Mersa Matruh—
Lying in the sun by a sea
    Of dazzling blue—
Told us we'd reached the forward base
Which held for the men in the desert waste
    Supplies that were then too few.

We left the train and I marched them down
    To the Depot Camp by the shore;
And I halted them there and stood them at ease
    And called the roll once more;
And the sound of each name was a clarion bell
(As I finally ticked them off to Hell)
    Resounding to England's call!

I can see them now in the searching glare
    Of the noon-day sun;
Knowing they were set on their way to take
    Their crack at the Hun.
Thinking, perhaps, of death or renown,
Or of girls they'd left in English towns
    Till the battle might be won.

I do not know if they lived till the fame
    Of Montgomery's name,
Or fell in the flames that burnt the retreat
    To Alamein.
I did not lead them in battle's fear,
I passed them on to another's care,
    Whilst I (for shame!)
    Went rear again.

P. J. Flaherty

. . . But Not Forgotten

The hungry crash of guns, the charge of lean
Unconquered men, the rock-strewn sand,
The shivering in a dawn wind keen;
Facing the menace of a mine-pocked land
Sown thick with death, and hatred, fanned
To desperation by each defeat.
The long pursuit, first life-renewing sight
Of white farms placid in a lazy heat,
Green grass, green trees, and flowers that might
Have bloomed in English soil; the sky, soft light
Of new-moon rise on palm-tree bordered sea.
The sudden rain, and eucalyptus trees that weep
Their gusty tears in rustling reverie
For those who fought and won their last, deep sleep.

Ian Fletcher

Unquiet Lives at the Base

These are the soldiers whom the Base restrains.
A starched life wakes among the melancholic walls,
The strangled voice of gutters where it rains.

The soldiers whose heroic vacancy appals:
The flaccid cigarette that crowns the face;
The moon-blank eyes in sicksweet urinals.

And in each moment rears the sad disgrace
Of useless work, of labour without hope;
Limbs unchained, but lost the sense of space.

While the mechanical, drab horoscope
Is daily re-affirmed. In every place
They hug their deserts, and through deserts grope.

Egypt, 1944.

Trooper Tufty Trotwell sings at the Cockshot Cabaret

That girl with the egg-curved face and the serpent lips
will only ask Americans to cough:
in spite of my ginger moustache, my
money is not coloured enough.

I look at her rogue dress and sigh.
It flutters like a dimly feral
snigger, or as invitation
to the eye, to the pubic eye.

One woman who flopped on the stage
had pimpled legs. I was pleased:
Each breast like a greengage
with sciatica when she sneezed.

They wear top hats and they dance
with Americans behind a locked door :
I would sell my circumcision and chance
a sweaty of merging interests

with a giggling greengage whore;
but art and all that crap crap
is never quite enough so I go
quietly indignant, healthy
to where the moonslivered ephebes
chromosexual virgins glow

are still not enough and I go
cock virginal calm skinned
where the moon glazed Thyads,
Lamia, Lady Lise all the fatals

Simper arcanely confession
cats that have nicked the cream
propped on moist ankles . . .

G. S. Fraser

The Traveller has Regrets

The traveller has regrets
For the receding shore
That with its many nets
Has caught, not to restore,
The white lights in the bay,
The blue lights on the hill.
Though night with many stars
May travel with him still,
But night has nought to say,
Only a colour and shape
Changing like cloth shaking,
A dancer with a cape
Whose dance is heart-breaking,

Night with its many stars
Can warn travellers
There's only time to kill
And nothing much to say:
But the blue light on the hill,
The white lights in the bay
Told us the meal was laid
And that the bed was made
And that we could not stay.

Three Characters in a Bar

(Cairo, 1944)

One who wishes to be my friend,
One who at sight hates my face,
Drinking late at the same bar.

Lurching colonial character
Technicoloured and wired for sound:
'Why don't you hurry out of this place?'

Charming gentle bohemian
Last, last of the Jacobites
Lighting my countless cigarettes.

'Pleased to meet indeed, old man,
No one to talk to all these nights
About the prompters behind the sets.'

And there over behind the bar
A mirror showing my own face
That shows no love, that shows no hate

That cannot get out of its own place
And must hear me talking at night:
I drink to you, long-sufferer!

Christmas Letter Home

To my sister in Aberdeen.

Drifting and innocent and sad like snow,
Now memories tease me wherever I go.
And I think of the glitter of granite and distances
And against the blue sky the lovely and bare trees,
And slippery pavements spangled with delight
Under the needles of a Winter's night,
And I remember the dances with scarf and cane,
Strolling home in the cold with the silly refrain
Of a tune by Cole Porter or Irving Berlin
Warming a naughty memory up like gin,
And Bunny and Stella and Joyce and Rosemary
Chattering on sofas or preparing tea,
With their delicate voices and their small white hands
This is the sorrow everyone understands.
More than Rostov's artillery, more than the planes
Skirting the cyclonic islands, this remains,
The little, lovely taste of youth we had;
The guns and not our silliness were mad.
All the unloved and ugly seeking power
Were mad, and not our trivial evening hour
Of swirling taffetas and muslin girls,
Oh, not their hands, their profiles or their curls,
Oh, not the evenings of coffee and sherry and snow,
Oh, not the music. Let us rise and go—
But then the months and oceans lie between,
And once again the dust of Spring, the green
Bright peaks of buds upon the poplar trees,
And summer's strawberries and autumn's ease,
And all the marble gestures of the dead,
Before my eyes caress again your head,
Your tiny strawberry mouth, your bell of hair,
Your blue eyes with their deep and shallow stare,
Before your hand upon my arm can still
The nerves that everything but home makes ill:
In this historic poster-world I move,
Noise, movement, emptiness, but never love.
Yet all this grief we had to have my dear,
And most who grieve have never known, I fear,
The lucky streak for which we die and live

And to the luckless must the lucky give
All trust, all energy, whatever lies
Under the anger of democracies:
Whatever strikes the towering torturer down,
Whatever can outface the bully's frown,
Talk to the stammerer, spare a cigarette
For tramps at midnight . . . oh, defend it yet!
Some Christmas I shall meet you. Oh and then
Though all the boys you used to like are men,
Though all my girls are married, though my verse
Has pretty steadily been growing worse,
We shall be happy; we shall smile and say,
'These years, it only seems like yesterday
I saw you sitting in that very chair.'
'You have not changed the way you do your hair.'
'These years were painful then?' 'I hardly know.
Something lies gently over them, like snow,
A sort of numbing white forgetfulness.'

And so good night, this Christmas, and God Bless!

An Elegy for Keith Bullen

(Headmaster of Gezira Preparatory School, Cairo, and a friend to
English poetry and poets.)

A great room and a bowl full of roses,
Red roses, a man as round as a ripe rose,
Lying in a bowl of sun. And who supposes
Such a sad weight could support such a gay pose,

Flying his sad weight like a round baby's
Petulant balloon! He has blue pebbles for eyes,
Petulant, bewildered, innocent eyes like a baby's;
Like a great baby or a clipped rose he lies

In a white bowl of light in my memory;
And expands his tenuous sweetness like a balloon;
I shall die of feeling his dear absurdity
So near me now, if I cannot cry soon.

Keith was particularly Sunday morning,
Red roses, old brandy, was unharrying Time,
Was that white light, our youth; or was the fawning
Zephyr that bobs the gay balloon of rhyme,

He bobbed incredibly in our modern air;
With his loose jacket, his white panama hat,
As he leaned on his walking stick on the stone stair
He seemed a balloon, moored down to the ground by that.

As he leaned at the bar and ordered us pink gin
Or arranged a flutter on the three-fifteen
He seemed a child, incapable of sin:
We never knew him prudent, cold, or mean.

Or tied to the way the world works at all
(Not even tied enough for poetry);
All that he was we only may recall,
An innocent that guilt would wish to be,

A kind, a careless, and a generous,
An unselfseeking in his love of art,
A jolly in his great explosive fuss;
O plethora of roses, O great heart!

Alan Freedman

Overseas Soldier

This was a year! Across great seas,
The salt of living tang upon my lips,
Whipped, blown, spun to wind-gust,
Bent to steel rain or lying prone
In heat like the aftermath of passion;
Weather gone wild and days gone dizzy,
All things—
Bold, shy, bright or winsome sudden—
Flamed in me electrical.

After the stench of skin in hived kraals
How lovely the dusk suffused the valley,
Weird and soft athwart a thousand hills.
And then, climbing by crazy pathways,
The night peace of the garden under jacarandas.
So many hours to treasure,
Each in his own way finding it—on slopes
Looking across the city to the Southern ocean
And the ships waiting in the bay,
In food and friendship and new merchandise,
In local twang, or beer, or the rickshaw boys.
Through cool or calm or sick-sliding ocean heave
We cut with straight prows, the sharp destroyers
Low down and furrowing a lane for us.
In coloured ports with no quays
We anchored for a cargo or the hold's discharge.
In Sierra Leone the soldiers with malaria,
Natal the contraceptives for immediate use,
And for dusty, scorching, rock-clamped Aden
A present of two airmen raving with the heat.
But always there was friendship.
Even in the gulf between bronze mountains
There was the glow of like minds,
Always someone, from the grey lurch of the Atlantic
To the Red Sea glaze.

Coming over sand dunes, I remember
The health-drenched land of Palestine,
The blue water and the green, green, green
Of orange groves; those Arab children
Dirty and lithe and sun-quick
Blazing curses around the olive trees,
Cactus and vines and citrus fruit,
Quaint dress, quaint ways and half hidden things
In cobbled alleys descending to bazaars.
These filled me with delight,
Not the monumental falsity men worship.
Lies! Lies! Lies! Mine is no God
Sitting in synagogues and churches, festooned
And hung with riches, no God
To kneel before with incense and tapers,
No God to chant at and extol.
Mine is the glorious mongrel
Muscled in beauty and coated in sin,
The song of all things together
And the taste of the earth and the sky!

Then sand.
A city thrown down in the desert,
Barren of spirit and flaunting its corruption.
Sand! Back to the pleasure-spin
And the chirrup of rubbed glass
Which passes for laughter,
The smiling deceit, the clever facade,
The ledges of living.
Sand! Sand in the bones
And nagging at the will.
Sand and siesta and the cicadas.
Seeing loose lips and loose ways,
Prim barriers lifted, there was hot questing
Up stairs wet with urine to hot rooms.
Young hags, red lips devouring flung, seized, held,
And constantly the old woman, the hell begotten,
Sitting where the money was and twisting her slitted eye.
In cabarets, what did it matter?
Over smashed chairs and bottles and girls cackling,
What matter?

Or in quiet corners hiding passion
Beneath the blaring band.
What matter, what matter?
In lights and laughter is forgetting—
Till the spiritual vomit
And, of the fine beer, only the bitter residue.

But was this all?
We, upright and springing with youth,
Surely found more. There was dissonance,
Yet think of the brilliant harmony
Of strong men sprawled strangely,
Listening to music and discovering their souls.
Remember the thoughts bursting from khaki
And the conflict of words in tents, or in lorries?
Here on the anvil of war was shaping
The future, here where the hammering iron
Galvanized best from the worst.

This has time brought me
And I just one of a million
Living in history with simplicity
And dreaming of home.
In back streets of battle
Things seen, things done, we number up
In diaries—this good, this bad—
Yet never a total, for such experience
Works out in after living and is not
To be counted on the fingers of one hand.
So much learnt or wasted, built or broken down,
And out of it all, like clouds before sunrise,
A mood, a memory, and uncertainty.
That's all.

John Gawsworth

The Dead Pilot

O hasty World that would Man's steps outpace,
Hustling him on with you to reach an end,
Pause now one instant, grant me that small space
To think upon, commemorate my friend,
He whom you hurtled to a shadowed place
Beyond my powers of vision. I intend
No reprimand—how may I?—whilst his face
Still smiles rebukeless, still exhorts: 'Contend!'

What is one year, World, in your breath of Time?
So little to you, yet so much to me
Who now lack voice, and shoulder at my side
That made the avenging of a human crime
A deed of honour and necessity,
A venture of humility, not pride!

The Fallen

When they fall, men grasp at feathers,
Cheat the knowledge of their doom
With hot hopes, and see all weathers
Fine, not overhung with gloom.

They have failed, and there's no falling
Further. Uncrowned heads are light.
Ambition no more is calling.
Restlessness has passed with fright.

None but fools offer their pity
To the fallen who at last,
Driven from their tyrant city,
Into freedom have been cast.

Peter Hellings

Black Sunset

The bay shaped like a womb lies spread before me
Where childhood, like a false coin, was soon spent,
The guilt returning in doom of discontent
Beneath the salutary moon.
                              The sun grows stormy,
And distant people shift like a desert army:
The sombre girl in sandals at the tent
Of any scoundrel offering refreshment
Alone remains; nothing is left to charm me
Back into childhood:
                              neither the hellfire speeches
On Sunday evenings, halfway between the docks
And winking lighthouse, where a gay man preaches
Repentance, nor the drifting crowd that flocks
To flaunting music:
                              nothing is left that teaches
Silence or sadness, but the lamp that mocks.

The Exiles

Remember those warm evenings, when we drank
Our amicable bottles of Tokay
After long absence, and forgot the rank
Stench of authority.
                              Yet all that time decay
Remorselessly attacked our memories
And fed the bitter thirst we drank to quench,
Till we too, suffering some remote disease,
Stretched Beauty out like any human wench
And shared her, with no bicker of remorse
Or cries of cant;
                              and in her poetry read
Of pure corruption in the soil we ploughed
And intellectual lechery's intercourse
Over the table, till the gathering crowd
Awoke her, and discovered the sweet dead.

Hamish Henderson

We Show You That Death is a Dancer

For Captain Ian McLeod

Death the dancer poked his skull
Into our drawing-room furtively
Before a bullet cracked the lull
and stripped jack-bare the rowan tree.
Now flesh drops off from every part
and in his dance he shows his art.

The fundamental now appears,
the ultimate stockade of bone.
He'll neutralize the coward years
and all poor flesh's ill condone.
When we lie stickit in the sand,
He'll dance into his promised land.

Alamein, 1942.

FIRST ELEGY[1]

End of a Campaign

There are many dead in the brutish desert,
        who lie uneasy
among the scrub in this landscape of half-wit
stunted ill-will. For the dead land is insatiate
and necrophilous. The sand is blowing about still.
Many who for various reasons, or because
        of mere unanswerable compulsion, came here
and fought among the clutching gravestones,
        shivered and sweated,
cried out, suffered thirst, were stoically silent, cursed
the spittering machine-guns, were homesick for Europe
and fast embedded in quicksand of Africa
        agonized and died.
And sleep now. Sleep here the sleep of the dust.

[1] This and the next two poems are from *Elegies for the Dead in Cyrenaica*

There were our own, there were the others.
Their deaths were like their lives, human and animal.
There were no gods and precious few heroes.
What they regretted when they died had nothing to do with
     race and leader, realm indivisible,
laboured Augustan speeches or vague imperial heritage.
(They saw through that guff before the axe fell.)
     Their longing turned to
the lost world glimpsed in the memory of letters:
an evening at the pictures in the friendly dark,
two knowing conspirators smiling and whispering secrets; or else
a family gathering in the homely kitchen
with Mum so proud of her boys in uniform:
     their thoughts trembled
between moments of estrangement, and ecstatic moments
of reconciliation: and their desire
crucified itself against the unutterable shadow of someone
whose photo was in their wallets.
Then death made his incision.

There were our own, there were the others.
Therefore, minding the great word of Glencoe's
son, that we should not disfigure ourselves
with villainy of hatred; and seeing that all
have gone down like curs into anonymous silence,
I will bear witness for I knew the others.
Seeing that littoral and interior are alike indifferent
and the birds are drawn again to our welcoming north
why should I not sing *them*, the dead, the innocent?

SECOND ELEGY

Halfaya

(For Luigi Castigliano)

At dawn, under the concise razor-edge
of the escarpment, the laager sleeps. No petrol fires yet
blow flame for brew-up. Up on the pass a sentry
inhales his Nazionale. Horse-shoe curve of the bay
grows visible beneath him. He smokes and yawns.
Ooo-augh,
         and the limitless
shabby lion-pelt of the desert completes and rounds
his limitless ennui.

At dawn, in the gathering impetus of day, the laager sleeps.
Some restless princes dream: first light denies them
the luxury of nothing. But others their mates more lucky
drown in the lightless grottoes. (Companionable death
has lent them his ease for a moment).
        The dreamers remember
a departure like a migration. They recall a landscape
associated with warmth and veils and a pantomime
but never focused exactly. The flopping curtain
reveals scene-shifters running with freshly painted
incongruous sets. Here childhood's prairie garden
looms like a pampas, where grown-ups stalk (gross outlaws)
on legs of tree trunk: recedes: and the strepitant jungle
dwindles to scruff of shrubs on a docile common,
all but real for a moment, then gone.

        The sleepers turn
gone but still no nothing laves them.
O misery, desire, desire, tautening cords of the bedrack!
Eros, in the teeth of Yahveh and his tight-lipped sect
confound the deniers of their youth! Let war lie wounded!
Eros, grant forgiveness and release
and return—against which they erect it,
the cairn of patience. *No dear, won't be long now*
keep fingers crossed, chin up, keep smiling darling
be seeing you soon.

On the horizon fires fluff now,
further than they seem.

    Sollum and Halfaya
a while yet before we leave you in quiet
and our needle swings north.

    The sleepers toss
and turn before waking : they feel through their blankets
the cold of the malevolent bomb-thumped desert,
impartial
hostile to both.

The laager is one.
Friends and enemies, haters and lovers
both sleep and dream.

INTERLUDE

Opening of an Offensive

(a) the waiting

Armour has foregathered, snuffling
through tourbillions of fine dust.
The crews don't speak much. They've had
last brew-up before battle. The tawny
deadland lies in a silence
not yet smashed by salvoes.
No sound reaches us
from the African constellations.
The low ridge too is quiet.
But no fear we're sleeping,
no need to remind us
that the nervous fingers of the searchlights
are nearly meeting and time is flickering
and this I think in a few minutes
while the whole power crouches for the spring.
X—20 in thirty seconds. Then begin

(b) the barrage

Let loose (rounds)
the exultant bounding hell-harrowing of sound.
Break the batteries. Confound
the damnable domination. Slake
the crashing breakers-húrled rúbble of the guns.
Dithering darkness, we'll wake you! Héll's bélls
blind you. Be broken, bleed
deathshead blackness!
    The thongs of the livid
firelights lick you
    jagg'd splinters rend you
        underground
we'll bomb you, doom you, tomb you into grave's mound

(c) the Jocks

They move forward into no man's land, a vibrant sounding board.
    As they advance
the guns push further murderous music.
Is this all they will hear, this raucous apocalypse?
The spheres knocking in the night of Heaven?
The drummeling of overwhelming niagara?
No! For I can hear it! Or is it? . . . tell
me that I can hear it! Now—listen!

    Yes, hill and shieling
sea-loch and island, hear it, the yell
of your war-pipes, scaling sound's mountains
guns thunder drowning in their soaring swell!
—The barrage gulfs them: they're gulfed in the clumbering guns,
gulfed in gloom, gloom. Dumb in the blunderbuss black—
lost—gone in the anonymous cataract of noise.
Now again! The shrill war-song: it flaunts
aggression to the sullen desert. It mounts. Its scream
tops the valkyrie, tops the colossal
    artillery.

Meaning that many
German Fascists will not be going home
meaning that many
will die, doomed in their false dream
We'll mak siccar!
Against the bashing cudgel
against the contemptuous triumphs of the big battalions
mak siccar against the monkish adepts
of total war against the oppressed oppressors
mak siccar against the leaching lies
against the worked out systems of sick perversion
mak siccar
            against the executioner
against the tyrannous myth and the real terror
mak siccar

John Jarmain

At a War Grave

No grave is rich, the dust that herein lies
Beneath this white cross mixing with the sand
Was vital once, with skill of eye and hand
And speed of brain. These will not re-arise
These riches, nor will they be replaced;
They are lost and nothing now, and here is left
Only a worthless corpse of sense bereft,
Symbol of death, and sacrifice and waste.

El Alamein, 30th October, 1942.

Sand

We have seen sand frothing like the sea
About our wheels and in our wake,
Clouds rolling yellow and opaque,
Thick-smoking from the ground;
Wrapped in the dust from sun and sky
Without a mark to guide them by
Men drove along unseeing in the cloud,
Peering to find a track, to find a way,
With eyes stung red, clown-faces coated grey.
Then with sore lips we cursed the sand,
Cursed this sullen gritty land
—Cursed and dragged on our blind and clogging way.

We have felt the fevered Khamsin blow
Which whips the desert into sting and spite
Of dry-sand driving rain (the only rain
The parched and dusty sand-lands know,
The hot dry driven sand), the desert floor
Whipped by the wind drives needles in the air
Which pricked our eyelids blind; and in a night,
Sifting the drifted sandhills grain by grain,
Covers our shallow tracks, our laboured road,
Makes false the maps we made with such slow care.

And we have seen wonders, spinning towers of sand
—Moving pillars of cloud by day—
Which passed and twitched our tents away;
Lakes where no water was, and in the sky
Grey shimmering palms. We have learned the sun and stars
And new simplicities, living by our cars
In wastes without one tree or living thing,
Where the flat horizon's level ring
Is equal everywhere without a change.

Yet sand has been kind for us to lie at ease,
Its soft dug walls have sheltered and made a shield
From fear and danger, and the chilly night.
And as we quit this bare unlovely land,
Strangely again see houses, hills and trees,
We will remember older things than these,
Indigo skies pricked out with brilliant light,
The smooth unshadowed candour of the sand.

Buerat-el-Hsun, January 1943.

Bivouac

In my bivouac at evening lying close
Beneath the tent's low roof,
I steal this moment, quiet on my bed,
To let the dust and wind of day die down
And make still my soul as an evening pool.
Night draws about my head
Her breath of darkness cool,
And at my feet the moon comes palely in;
Like a wan cold field outspread
Is the pale and vacant sand,
Which was so hot and turbid all day long;
And the sky more mapped with light than any land
Is filled with all its stars;
The crooked scorpion low across the south
Lies in the tent's small mouth
Like a curled and jewelled snake
The wind and sand and sound of day are still,
Now is the desert by the moon washed clean
And pale in beauty shines.
This is the cool hour I wish to keep,
So I lean towards the moon to write these lines
Before I sleep.

El Alamein

There are flowers now, they say, at Alamein;
Yes, flowers in the minefields now.
So those that come to view that vacant scene,
Where death remains and agony has been
Will find the lilies grow—
Flowers, and nothing that we know.

So they rang the bells for us and Alamein,
Bells which we could not hear.
And to those that heard the bells what could it mean,
The name of loss and pride, El Alamein?
—Not the murk and harm of war,
But their hope, their own warm prayer.

It will become a staid historic name,
That crazy sea of sand!
Like Troy or Agincourt its single fame
Will be the garland for our brow, our claim,
On us a fleck of glory to the end;
And there our dead will keep their holy ground.

But this is not the place that we recall,
The crowded desert crossed with foaming tracks,
The one blotched building, lacking half a wall,
The grey-faced men, sand-powdered over all;
The tanks, the guns, the trucks,
The black, dark-smoking wrecks.

So be it; none but us has known that land:
El Alamein will still be only ours
And those ten days of chaos in the sand.
Others will come who cannot understand,
Will halt beside the rusty minefield wires
And find there, flowers.

Sidney Keyes

In Memoriam S.K.K.

Elegy

April again, and it is a year again
Since you walked out and slammed the door
Leaving us tangled in your words. Your brain
Lives in the bank-book, and your eyes look up
Laughing from the carpet on the floor.
And we still drink from your silver cup.

It is a year again since they poured
The dumb ground into your mouth;
And yet we know, by some recurring word
Or look caught unawares, that you still drive
Our thoughts like the smart cobs of your youth—
When you and the world were alive.

A year again, and we have fallen on bad times
Since they gave you to the worms.
I am ashamed to take delight in these rhymes
Without grief, but you need no tears.
We shall never forget nor escape you, nor make terms
With your enemies, the swift-devouring years.

The Expected Guest

The table is spread, the lamp glitters and sighs;
Light on my eyes, light on the high curved iris
And springing from glaze to steel, from cup to knife
Makes sacramental my poor midnight table,
My broken scraps the pieces of a god.

O when they bore you down, the grinning soldiers,
Was it their white teeth you could not forget?
And when you met the beast in the myrtle wood,
When the spear broke and the blood broke out on your side
What Syrian Veronica above you
Stooped with her flaxen cloth as yet unsigned?
And either way, how could you call your darling
To drink the cup of blood your father filled?

We are dying tonight, you in the aged darkness
And I in the white room my pride has rented.
And either way, we have to die alone.

The laid table stands hard and white as tomorrow
The lamp sings. The west wind jostles the door.
Though broken the bread, the brain, the brave body
There cannot now be any hope of changing
The leavings to living bone, the bone to bread;
For bladed centuries are drawn between us.
The room is ready, but the guest is dead.

Advice for a Journey

The drums mutter for war, and soon we must begin
To seek the country where they say that joy
Springs flowerlike among the rocks, to win
The fabulous golden mountain of our peace.

O my friends, we are too young
To be explorers, have no skill nor compass,
Nor even that iron certitude which swung
Our fathers at their self-fulfilling North

So take no rations, remember not your homes—
Only the blind and stubborn hope to track
This wilderness. The thoughtful leave their bones
In windy foodless meadows of despair.

Never look back, nor too far forward search
For the white Everest of your desire;
The screes roll underfoot, and you will never reach
Those brittle peaks which only clouds may walk.

Others have come before you, and immortal
Live like reflections. Their still faces
Will give you courage to ignore the subtle
Sneer of the gentian and the ice-worn pebble.

The fifes cry death and the sharp winds call;
Set your face to the rock; go on, go out
Into the bad lands of battle, the cloud-wall
Of the future, my friends, and leave your fear.

Go forth, my friends, the raven is no sibyl
Break the clouds' anger with your unchanged faces.
You'll find, maybe, the dream under the hill—
But never Canaan, nor any golden mountain.

Uys Krige

The Taking of the Koppie

No, it was only a touch of dysentery, he said. He was doing fine now
    thank you . . . What the hell were the chaps grousing about anyhow?
He was sitting on the edge of his hospital cot clad only in a slip with both
    his feet on the floor,
his strong young body straight and graceful as a tree, golden as any
    pomegranate but only firmer,
its smooth surface uncracked, gashed with no fissure by the burning
    blazing sun of war;
and with his muscles rippling lightly
like a vlei's shallows by the reeds touched by the first breath of the wind of
    dawn,
as he swung his one leg over onto the other.

He was telling us about the death of the colonel and the major
whom all the men, especially the younger ones, worshipped.
'The colonel copped it from a stray bullet. It must have been a sniper . . .
just a neat little hole in the middle of his forehead, no bigger than a tickey,
    and he dropped dead in his tracks.
The major was leading us over some rough open ground between the gully
    and the far koppie
when a burst of machine gun bullets smacked from the kloof, tearing him
    open;
he was a long way ahead of us all and as he fell he shouted:
'Stop! Stay where you are! Don't come near me! Look out for those
    machine guns! There's one in the antheap and one on the ledge . . .

Bring up the mortars! The rest take cover!'
Then he rolled over on his back, blood streaming all over his body, and
with a dabble of blood on his lips he died—Christ, what a man he was!'

The boy reached for a match box, then lighting a cigarette, he continued:
'We came on them about ten minutes later, three Ities curled up on some
straw in a sort of dugout
—as snug as a bug in a rug—and they were sleeping . . .
The two on the outside were young, I noticed. They were all unshaven.
The bloke in the middle had a dirty grey stubble of beard—and that's all
I noticed . . .'

As the boy stopped talking he moved, his hair falling in thick yellow curls
over his forehead, his eyes.
And as I caught the soft gleam of blue behind the strands of gold
I was suddenly reminded of quiet pools of water after rain
among the golden gorse that mantle in early summer
the browning hills of Provence.

'Then I put my bayonet through each of them in turn, just in the right
place, and they did not even grunt or murmur . . .'

There was no sadism in his voice, no savagery, no brutal pride or perverse
eagerness to impress,
no joy, no exultation.
He spoke as if he were telling of a rugby match
in which he wasn't much interested
and in which he took no sides.

And as I looked at his eyes again
I was struck with wonderment
at their bigness, their blueness, their clarity
and how young they were, how innocent.

Addis Ababa, May 1941.

Sorley Maclean

Glac a' Bhais[1]

Thubhairt Nàsach air choreigin gun tug am Furair air ais do fhir
na Gearmailte 'a' chòir agus an sonas bàs fhaotainn anns an àraich'.

'Na shuidhe marbh an 'Glaic a' Bhàis'
fo Dhruim Ruidhìseit,
gill' òg 's a logan sìos m' a ghruaïdh
's a thuar grìsionn.

Smaoinich mi air a' chòir's an àgh
a fhuair e bho Fhurair,
bhith tuiteam ann an raon an àir
gun éirigh tuilleadh;

air a' ghreadhnachas 's air a' chliù
nach d' fhuair e' na aonar,
ged b' esan bu bhrònaiche snuadh
ann an glaic air laomadh

le cuileagan mu chuirp ghlas'
air gainmhich lachduinn
's i salach-bhuidhe 's làn de raip
's de sprùidhlich catha.

An robh an gille air an dream
a mhàb na h-Iùdhaich
's na Comunnaich, no air an dream
bu mhotha, dhiùbh-san

a threòoaicheadh bho thoiseach àl
gun deòin gu buaireadh
agus bruaillean cuthaich gach blàir
air sgàth uachdaran?

Ge b'e a dheòin-san no a chàs,
a neoichiontas no mhìorun,
cha do nochd e toileachadh 'na bhàs
fo Dhruim Ruidhìseit.

[1] For English rendering see 'Death Valley' opposite.

Death Valley

Some Nazi or other has said that the Fuehrer had restored to
German manhood the 'right and joy of dying in battle'.

Sitting dead in 'Death Valley'
below the Ruweisat Ridge
a boy with his forelock down about his cheek
and his face slate-grey;

I thought of the right and the joy
that he got from his Fuehrer,
of falling in the field of slaughter
to rise no more;

of the pomp and the fame
that he had, not alone,
though he was the most piteous to see
in a valley gone to seed

with flies about grey corpses
on a dun sand
dirty yellow and full of the rubbish
and fragments of battle.

Was the boy of the band
who abused the Jews
and Communists, or of the greater
band of those

led, from the beginning of generations,
unwillingly to the trial
and mad delirium of every war
for the sake of rulers?

Whatever his desire or mishap,
his innocence or malignity,
he showed no pleasure in his death
below the Ruweisat Ridge.

Michael Martin

Electric Storm

El Alamein, 1942

A rumble of guns—not earthly ones—
A flicker of light on yon distant height,
And the beasts of the forest, the fish of the sea,
Come drifting, menacing, down to me;
A swordfish, a shark, with the fleece of a ram,
Elephants swimming in blackberry jam,
Crocodiles, camels, and unicorns too,
Helplessly barred in the Thundercloud Zoo

A mutter of fury
   And the bass drum's boom,
The flash of a thousand cannon,
   The rumble of Doom;
Electric light of curious source
Threading its fickle but forcible course,
Showing the path through the raincloud gap,
Traced like the routes on a railroad map,
Shaping fantastical carcasses there
Of a panicky, paralysed pet polar bear,
Anthropoid apes, and the Baskerville hound,
Witlessly perched on a feathery mound.

N. T. Morris

The Jeep

I'm the Colonel, the Old Man, the C.O.,
I'm in charge of the whole bally show,
    And to check up the Tanks
    And the cranks and the wanks
Do I ride in my Staff Car? Oh no.

I go for a ride in my Jeep
I've a driver but he makes me weep—
    And on matters internal
    A Lieutenant-Colonel
May drive himself round in his Jeep.

As Major and second i/c
A Jeep is allotted to me;
    Though Senior Major
    I'm no damned old stager;
I shake 'em all, A, C, or B.

As I go for a ride in my Jeep
In the enemy's country quite deep.
    I return from the blue
    With a panzer or two
Attached to the back of my Jeep.

Commanding a Squadron's some task,
—Oh the million of things people ask—
    There's a Conference at ten,
    I must rally the men,
You really have no time to bask,

So I have to ride round in my Jeep
And go off on an offensive sweep,
    All the crews get the jitters,
    I shake up the fitters
And tell them to service my Jeep.

It's the Captains who do all the work.
Do you think we could actually shirk
   From treating 'em rough,
   Or producing our stuff?
Well we've got a good Squadron clerk.

So we go for a ride in the Jeep.
I wish that this Jeep we could keep
   While the Major's away
   We can ride round all day,
Important as hell in the Jeep.

Oh it's sometimes a Subaltern's job
To hand out some dope to his mob.
   I don't like to snoop,
   Like a spy round the troop
So if there's a lift I can rob

   I like to drive up in a Jeep.
To attention the troop smartly leap.
   I just airily say,
   'There's a scheme on today,'
And drive off again in the Jeep.

The men with the rank R.S.M.,
—You'd better be careful of them—
   When you're stood to attention
   You daren't even mention
A sound like a cough or a hem,

But when he comes round in a Jeep
He is coming to have a quick peep
   At the hole, neatly tinned.
   Situated down-wind,
Before he drives off in the Jeep.

The Officer, Warrant, Class 2,
Has a hundred and one jobs to do;
   He must check the untidy,
   The leave list for Friday,
And tick off the cooks for that stew,

So he has to have loan of the Jeep,
Like a shepherd in charge of his sheep,
    Sweeping down on his flock,
    And reciting much cock,
Before he breaks down in his Jeep.

A sight seldom seen, we declare,
Are Sergeants who whizz here and there,
    They're seldom erratic,
    Apparently static,
But there have been occasions, yes, where

We've seen 'em zoom round in a Jeep,
With a scream which has shattered our sleep
    They drive round with zest
    On a thing called a test
Which just about wears out the Jeep.

A Trooper so wretched am I,
I feel I could have a good cry,
    For the car on my charge
    Is now roaming at large;
Hence the teardrop which starts from my eye,

'Cos I never ride out in my Jeep
It returns to me all of a heap.
    They lose all the nuts.
    They rip out all the guts
Of my eats-for-all, seats-for-all,
    See-for-all, free-for-all,
    Brew-up-some-tea-for-all,
                   JEEP.

It's Always Mealtime

Oh, they're queueing up for breakfast, they have rattled on the gong;
Hear the mess tins jingle-jangle. Let us go and join the throng.
There is porridge made from biscuits. There's a Soya for the fry.
There is tea that tastes of onions; there is bread that's rather dry;
And the cooks are looking browned off as they pass the grub along.
Oh, that look they get from cookhouses and drinking tea too strong.

Oh, it must be time for tiffin. What d'you think it is today?
Well, there's fish and meat and pickle mixed in some peculiar way.
There is yellow cheese as usual, and marg., and that's the lot—
Oh, help yourself to biscuits, 'cos the weather's —— hot.
And the cooks are looking browned off as a dollop each one deals,
The look they get from arguing and never eating meals.

You can tell it's time for dinner by the fidgets of the queue,
And it's world-without-end bully meat mocked up as pie or stew,
And if you're mighty lucky, there'll be flour in the 'duff,'
But the chances are it's rice again, and rice is . . . rough.
So the cooks are looking browned off, slightly woebegone and worn,
The look that comes from cards all night, and lighting fires at dawn.

Victor Musgrave

Song of Egypt

When Cheops
raised with 80,000 slaves
the stones of that historic, ancient pile
The Sphinx
surveyed the epic operations
without the vestige of a single smile

    Sitting in Saults in the winter
    (dreaming of the Med. at Alex in the summer)
    I watched a beautiful girl
    swaying gently to the rhythm of the drummer

    I watched her.
    And I never thought of home.

Alexandria, once great, was humbled
to ruin and decay
then rose like a phoenix from the ashes
to what she is today.

The dizzy dancing gharry lights
illuminate the street at nights
Neon, the Queen of Evening
Bows to the God of War
who put her behind a blackout trap
and closed the door.

The street-boys call;
trams shriek, horns blare, bells clang, dogs fight:
the noise of Armageddon fills the air
Under the moon in Cairo in the night.

It wasn't very far from here
Unless the history books have lied
Where Cleopatra lived and loved
And held her court and fought and died.

While at Gezira they're dancing and laughing
and swimming and playing games
we wander slowly, awed and silent,
through streets with long-forgotten names.

Immobilia
frowns down
and hides the moon at night
I think it is only in England
where the traffic keeps left
instead of right.

Have you read
of strange Hakim?
Who, when he was Egypt's king
turned night to day.
Then faced his horse
to the Mokattam Hills
And rode away.

And was never seen again.

I'm alone in Cairo.
I could dine at the YM
Find some audacious fem
Window-buy some sparkling gem
Drink till 12 p.m.
Or worse.
But I don't.
I've an empty purse.

My sense of touch, my sense of taste,
My eyes, my nose my ears:
Strange sensations push and pull
Surprises, pleasures, joys and fears
Bobbing tarbrush, barking dog
Imploring beggar, morning fog,
Odour of kebab and oil:
Outstretched hands symbolical of toil.

Saladin,
His ghost last night
Rose from the dead
And hovered haunting
Round my bed.

Once Egypt fought the mighty power of Rome.
Later,
The Fatherland and Britain
Strove hand to hand.
I found a book of Shakespeare
(To Gerald with love from Mum)
Half buried in the self-same sand.

But if it all
Gets sometimes just a little in your hair
Remember the pyramids
Have been thru a damn sight more than you
And they're still here.

John Papasian

Past Tense

I spoke of you today. Echoless words
looped to a knot the self same threadbare cords
upon which hung illusion crucified.
Silence tears most when words have died.

Festered the seconds we no longer share.
The nail bed bleeds. Moulding lips part to blare
their corrupt putrescence sick with despair,
polluting your stark pureness in mid air.

Gnarled is the laughter. Warped the livelong hour
that mars your face and turns earth's palate sour.
Days are a nightmare dead-end void of sense:
I spoke of you today in the past tense.

Desert Rats

The boys, flaxen hair sandy in the winds,
with twisted desert hearts and fire shot minds,
the boys have marched back torn with lice and fleas.
Mangled their souls. Their eyes greener than trees.

Ale soaked, their avid loins have moved and surged.
And against loins have they their hatred purged,
their newborn, their bloodstruck vengeful hatred.
They whose sea-bound land said love was sacred.

The boys have limped in poorer than the poor
and stormed against the painted brothel door
and retched and railed and raged and raped new skin.
For love and loth and lust are ever kin.

G. O. Physick

Lines without Title

The voice of One crying in the wilderness,
In the wind's cry, and in the crying of the sand;
Nor can you still that cry
For there is sand in your hair
And five rank deserts shift in your hand.

Wherever the dry sand shuffles and falls,
Wherever the weak wind flounders and blows
'Prepare' says the cry—
The terrible cry
Of one who cries out for the rose!

Think at this Time

Think at this time of the patient infantry
Far from your comfortable, lit rooms,
Where you sit talking about Victory
And listening to gramophones

Outside—oh, not in the books you read!—
Is the legend of wounds that bleed,
Story of the Sower and
The dragon-seed.

It is the harvest-time in no man's land,
And the big granary is being made,
The yawning, open grave
For casualties.

Who will be wrapped in blankets
When death puts out their eyes.

F. T. Prince

Soldiers Bathing

The sea at evening moves across the sand.
Under a reddening sky I watch the freedom of a band
Of soldiers who belong to me. Stripped bare
For bathing in the sea, they shout and run in the warm air;
Their flesh, worn by the trade of war, revives
And my mind towards the meaning of it strives.

All's pathos now. The body that was gross,
Rank, ravenous, disgusting in the act or in repose,
All fever, filth and sweat, its bestial strength
And bestial decay, by pain and labour grows at length
Fragile and luminous. 'Poor bare forked animal'
Conscious of his desires and needs and flesh that rise and fall,
Stands in the soft air, tasting after toil
The sweetness of his nakedness; letting the sea-waves coil
Their frothy tongues about his feet, forgets
His hatred of the war, its terrible pressure that begets
A machinery of death and slavery,
Each being a slave and making slaves of others; finds that he
Remembers lovely freedom in a game,
Mocking himself, and comically mimics fear and shame.

He plays with death and animality,
And reading in the shadows of his pallid flesh, I see
The idea of Michelangelo's cartoon
Of soldiers bathing, breaking off before they were half done
At some sortie of the enemy, an episode
On the Pisan wars with Florence. I remember now he showed
Their muscular limbs that clamber from the water,
And heads that turn across the shoulder, eager for the slaughter,
Forgetful of their bodies that are bare,
And hot to buckle on and use the weapons lying there.
And I think too of the theme another found
When, shadowing men's bodies on a sinister red ground,
Another Florentine, Pollaiuolo,
Painted a naked battle; warriors, straddled, hacked the foe,
Dug their bare toes into the ground and slew
The brother—naked man who lay between their feet and drew
His lips back from his teeth in a grimace,

They were Italians who knew war's sorrow and disgrace
And showed the thing suspended, stripped; a theme
Born out of the experience of war's horrible extreme
Beneath a sky where even the air flows
With 'lacrimae Christi'. For that rage, that bitterness, those blows
That hatred of the slain, what could it be
But indirectly or directly a commentary
On the Crucifixion? And the picture burns
With indignation and pity and despair by turns,
Because it is the obverse of the scene
Where Christ hangs murdered, stripped, upon the Cross. I mean
That is the explanation of its rage.
And we too have our bitterness and pity that engage
Blood, spirit in this war. But night begins,
Night of the mind; who nowadays is conscious of our sins?
Though every human deed concerns our blood,
And even we must know, what nobody has understood,
That some great love is over all we do,
And that is what has driven us to this fury, for so few
Can suffer all the terror of that love.
The terror of that love has set us spinning in this groove
Greased with our blood. These dry themselves and dress,
Combing their hair, forget the fear and shame of nakedness.
Because to love is frightening we prefer
The freedom of our crimes. Yet as I drink the dusky air
I feel a strange delight that fills me full,
Strange gratitude, as if evil itself were beautiful
And kiss the wound in thought, while in the west
I watch a streak of red that might have issued from Christ's breast.

John Pudney

Combat Report

'Just then I saw the bloody Hun'
You saw the Hun? You, light and easy,
Carving the soundless daylight. 'I was breezy
When I saw that Hun.' Oh wonder
Pattern of stress, of nerve poise, flyer,
Overtaking time. 'He came out under
Nine-tenths cloud, but I was higher.'

Did Michelangelo aspire,
Painting the laughing cumulus, to ride
The majesty of air. 'He was a trier
I'll give him that, the Hun.' So you convert
Ultimate sky to air speed, drift and cover;
Sure with the tricky tools of God and lover.
'I let him have a sharp four-second squirt,
Closing to fifty yards. He went on fire.'
Your deadly petals painted, you exert
A simple stature. Man-high, without pride,
You pick your way through heaven and the dirt.
'He burnt out in the air; that's how the poor sod died.'

Landscape: Western Desert

Winds carve this land
And velvet whorls of sand
Annul footprint and grave
Of lover, fool, and knave.
Briefly the vetches bloom
In the blind desert room
When humble, bright and brave
Met common doom.

Their gear and shift
Smother in soft sand-drift,
Less perishable, less
Soon in rottenness.
Their war-spent tools of trade
In the huge space parade;
And with this last distress,
All scores are paid.

And who will see,
In such last anarchy
Of loveless lapse and loss
Which the blind sands now gloss,
The common heart which meant
Such good in its intent;
Such noble common dross
Suddenly spent.

127

T. W. Ramsey

Eighth Army

We ploughed the sand with shell and burning bomb
And found few bones there where we left our own
Bleached by the drifting detritus of stone,
Bright in their busy many-fingered tomb.

Myriads of little hands there were to clutch
And hold us, when we lay down to our rest,
Quiet of the torn and sun-enkindled breast,
Hands that were feverish and dry to touch.

The papers called us heroes, but we knew
A hero is a visionary being,
Uncomfortable to live with probably—
In Greece perhaps you might find one or two.

We never liked them, and we hated sand
So loving warm, so thirsty for our blood;
But still they might have sent us into mud
A fathom deep—this was at least dry land.

But cold at night, a whisperer to the moon,
Where many of us with the dust of Kings
For coverlet rest from our wanderings,
Where even heroes are forgotten soon.

Waken, bright winds of Thebes and Assouan,
Wake up like little running messengers
And wake your metal-backed green scavengers
To contemplate the hieroglyph of man!

Who only knows his brotherhood in death,
Who only wakes when rising from the feast—
Bright crawling scarabaeus, you at least
Understand beauty set apart from breath.

You who have seen the Sphinx and Pyramid
Challenge in vain a million scarlet dawns,
You who have lived with kings and queens and pawns
And seen many a game end and the lid

Closed on the gathered pieces, carry these
A benediction, feathery light as love,
And softly spread the warm gold dust above
Those who sleep soundly through long hours of ease.

Crawl on the naked scapula and roll
Your ball of dung as the sun rolls his wheel
To the great socket of the noon, conceal
From that great eye these fragments of a whole.

These lived and were believed and did believe
In common pawns as well as queens and kings;
Let the dry burnish on your metal wings
Be bright in eyes life will no more deceive.

These loved and were beloved—give them yet
Between the glassy sky and burning sands
Reminder of the warmth of human hands;
As we remember, let them not forget.

John Ropes

Voluntary Ladies of the Town

The scene: Any soldiers' club in Cairo just before opening time. Three Cairene matrons are
seen putting the final touches to the tea tables. They sing:

VERSE:
    Though many years ago, we said goodbye to beauty,
    We've a most important duty to fulfil.
    Every Saturday at three,
    We serve the soldiers tea
    And put their half piastres in the till.
    And when the shadows lengthen, and the light begins to pale,
    We do a splendid trade in bottled ale.

CHORUS:
    We're voluntary ladies serving voluntary beer
    To voluntary soldiers compulsorily here.
      We try to do our bit
      To keep them fighting fit,
    Though we don't encourage any horseplay here.

We're voluntary workers selling voluntary eggs
To keep the men's attention from those voluntary legs.
    A lightly toasted bun
    Is just as jolly fun
As draining Passion's goblet to the dregs.

Some of the men are jokers, you can very quickly spot 'em,
They ask for fancy pastries when they know we haven't got 'em
And last Tuesday Mrs Smithers had a sergeant pinch her bottom
Because she's such a voluntary lady.

So if ever you want some ping-pong, some billiards or a bath
Without military policeman and a nasty aftermath
We'll try to keep your footsteps on the straight and narrow path,
We're the voluntary ladies of the town.

SECOND CHORUS:
    We're voluntary ladies serving voluntary food
To servicemen to whom we hope to do a little good.
    We dispense Egyptian bangahs
    To the heroes from the hangars
To distract their minds from Nature in the nude.

We're voluntary talkers to the soldiers as they eat,
The boys all like to talk to any girl that they can meet,
    Though a man the other day
    Took it quite the other way
And said a word I really can't repeat.

It's interesting to hear them and the stories that they bring,
I listened to a corporal for half an hour last spring
After which I much regret, he did a most peculiar thing,
He tried it on a voluntary lady.

But we never fuss or worry and we're none of us complaining,
After this evacuation, we're the only ones remaining,
And the fellows must go somewhere to complete their early training
With the voluntary ladies of the town.

THIRD CHORUS:
    We're voluntary ladies in voluntary clubs
    Keeping rather browned-off soldiers from the cabarets and pubs,
        When you've nothing else to do,
        Just come and have a brew
    With Merrie England's tea-dispensing tubs.

    We're voluntary ladies going voluntary gay
    Being rather free and easy in a voluntary way,
        Though we gaily love to flirt,
        We draw the line at dirt,
    And we leave at nine o'clock to hit the hay.

    All the same, its pretty risky if you see behind the scenes,
    They draw the rudest pictures on the backs of magazines,
    And the words . . . well, we can really only guess at what it means,
    Because we're such voluntary ladies.

    So whether you're from the desert or the greeness of the veldt,
    Australian, New Zealander, a Scotsman or a Celt,
    Play the game like British soldiers, and don't hit below the belt
    Of these voluntary ladies of the town.

You Mustn't Drop Your Aitches at G.H.Q.

    You mustn't drop your aitches at G.H.Q.,
    There are lots of things you really mustn't do.
    There isn't any chance of our ever being beaten
    If the D.A.Q.M.G. has been to Eton.

    You mustn't utter jokes about G.H.Q.,
    It's only helping Hitler if you do.
    For certain things are sacred, and you mustn't ever laugh
    At the educated efforts of the Staff.

        Don't think we never work,
        Don't think we mean to shirk
        If the enemy advances any nearer
        With our colours flying high
        We will fight and we will die
        In a fortified position in Gezira.

So if you have ambitions to retire to gilded bliss,
With mornings spent dictating to a blonde Semira-miss,
Your manners must be perfect, or your marks are very few;
You mustn't drop your aitches at G.H.Q.

You mustn't drop your aitches at G.H.Q.,
There are lots of things you really mustn't do.
You mustn't be a fusspot wanting action on the 'phone,
Just pass the file and leave the thing alone.

You mustn't reach the office at unfashionable hours.
You mustn't sign the bumph that comes in such depressing showers,
For hustle is a thing to which no officer will stoop
As a member of the short-range desert group.

> If you're desert-worn and hardy
> From a sojourn out at Maadi,
> And you want to go to Shepheard's on the spree,
> If a comely AT you know,
> It is strictly comme il faut
> To get your clerk to vet her pedigree.

You mustn't miss your Friday night's immersion in Amami,
You mustn't speak to boot-blacks, or to members of EIGHTH Army,
Your tunic must be spotless though your duties may be few,
You mustn't drop your aitches at G.H.Q.

James Walker

Libyan Cove

We burned the helm the last, and crouching there
Well-fed and quiet watched the encroaching moon,
And thought of home, and evenings there, and of
The mariner of this bescattered ship,
Whose boards had given us our cautious firelight
Here in the coral evenings of the cove.

Mariner, now, your ship is harboured here,
Becomes at last the loam from which it grew.
Your hands had held this helm within their grip,
Loving it as a man loves what he owns
Because he chose it. There were Vikings once
Who loved the sea and loved their ships so well
Their ship was made their pyre upon the sea;
Here, thus, for warmth, have we unwittingly
Made you a kind of Viking's funeral?

We turn the thought deliberately away.
It is no time, we think, to think these things.
The west is lambent with the last of day;
The dwindling air about us hums with wings.
Someone tells dirty stories; someone sings
Low, to beguile himself, the Song of Skye—
That song of all most tender of the sea.

Was she a good ship, Mariner, was she yare?
Whaled she the rough and swanned the summer seas?
Was there a lilt with her? Had she a flair
For nosing out a channel's subtleties,
All times but once? What mastered her, out there?

One sings. We make the tenderness our own
For a town hovel or a Cotswold grange.
But one says: 'Aw, for Christ's sake, wrap up, mate,
Or else sing something cheerful for a change.'
Meaning, for comfort do not sing of harbours.

The helm burns low. The foreign stars come out.
The swinging sea turns silver to the moon.
Jasmine and asphodel sharpen the night.
And habit in us hides the last firelight
From hostile eyes at sea, or in the air.
Tomorrow we shall camp some other where.
We feel time closing, multifoliate,
About us and about your jetsomed care.

Because you were not wrecked alone, my Mariner.

John Waller

The Ghosts

Daylight is a hoverer and diamond
A poor jewel for you. The brightness of eyes
Is what we remember, and the gay laugh
With which you left. The careless passionate glances
Over the shoulder, bravery for girls.

Magic made mazes where you walked
And it was Sunday and the weather fine
Walking that hill. And you said:
'Thoughts will last for ever.' And I replied:
'Like ghosts these moments will haunt.'

But nightfall came and wrapped us close
In each other's arms, On the soft couch
It was two children playing at love
On the first bright evening of the world.
Remembering that, I often embrace a ghost.

The moonlight shone across the room
As you left; and as you passed
The beam caught your face and held your hair
In a kind of fire. Then with a smile
The door closed. I heard your step on the stairs.

And next day the armies sailed;
I watched from a window the banners waving
And felt inside me the noise and the cheering
I could not hear. From that moment I was left
With memories of ghosts and ghosts of memories.

August

Flood-swift and brown with earth-break,
Rock-spun, bridge-cleft and clamouring,
In one great turbulence—thus the Nile.

Down to the arms of the aching delta
Swirls the green-wrack silently.
Yet, river entire, there is no quiet
For water is reft and the whole length
Surfaced with sail and flutter of birds.
But rarely now the weighted oars
And plash of fishnets dropping.
All things wait, feeling the turn
Of season and the coming up of cloud.
Enough and enough of heat and aridity!
Seep, pour, drench down the coolness,
Stride in the bluster of evening breeze
For this is the sign, the months develop
And soon the quick and the cold and the clean.

Underneath the mosque
The cistern cellar is splash
With flooding and still mounting,
While on the palms the tight date clusters
Redden and ripen.
Root sprung with roaring sediment
All things conceive.
Night after night the banks are mad
With multiple voices
And the maize fields yelling with frogs.
Pulse after pulse, like blood beat
Of desire, moves the strong life,
Beats upwards. This is the river
Whose autumn is a strange new spring.

John Warry

To a W.A.A.F.

Even that wretched uniform she wears
Cannot prevent her being beautiful.
I met her in the train, where as a rule
I travel second class with third class fares.
And now my heart is in need of repairs,
For she, part Greek and three parts Austrian,
Apparelled as a sort of ersatz man,
Seemed worthy of her warrior forbears.
And though the language of Themistocles
And that of brave Don John who sailed his galleon
Against the Turkish menace at Lepanto,
Are both unknown to her, she speaks Italian,
English and French. Nay, but her voice would please,
Though she could speak no tongue save Esperanto.

The Pyramid

(On being stationed near the Pyramids of Gizeh)

Alas, I never did
Conceive of such a hate
For aught inanimate
As for this Pyramid.

Behind the hill half hid,
Beyond the guarded gate,
I see him morn and late,
This cursed Pyramid.

Oh, how long must I wait
Before I may be rid
Of this vile Pyramid,
This symbol of my fate?

Nay, I shall always rate
The day on which they bid
Me leave this Pyramid
As a red-letter date!

Victor West

Drumhead

Four trestle tables in the sand
covered with issue blankets taken
from the tented hospital . . . The forms
pushed back, as though in hasty decision,
standing a solitary still-life
group in early morning sun.

The scene rises before me
and I people it in my mind.
Here, the President of the Court Martial
with the powder-puff pink
visage of his rank in contrast
to the dusty sunburn of the mountain
troop and the young parachutist Major.
On the other side, standing in casual
conversation, three officers like
three scabrous Graces.
But no grace here;
only short shrift to the accused
whose only crime that they are Greek.
A last, eloquent plea, translated
badly by the *dolmetscher;*
the Cretan in the white shirt
throws an arm around the youth
and flings a last, imploring gesture
for the old man, standing knees half-bent
by age in his black vraka.
But no pity here
for the 'Defending Officer'
has put his papers away and shrugs
off his defence with apologetic brevity.
Impassive, grey like sea-bleached
breakwater timbers—and with as much feeling,
the stolid guards stand close by,

starred with the pressed-tin edelweiss
like dead starfish. Down on the beach
wait the idle firing squad
ready for the verdict:
'Three more Greek bandits shot
for committing unspeakable atrocities' . . .

The scene has unfolded itself
and the figures vanish before my eyes . . .
only the horror remains
and that I cannot paint:
Four trestle tables in the sand.

> 29th May, 1941 'The Galatos Cage', formerly
> 7th British Tented Hospital,Calibes, Crete.

'La Belle Indifference'

I hate that which is changing me
to treat all my past friends
with cold, impersonal disinterest
Perhaps War makes inevitable
that false, local loyalty, only
to the immediate companions
of your own small circle.
One grows armoured like a lobster
against loss—can grow new limbs, claws.
Survival inhibits any feeling, save the joy
of survival. Your own miserable hide . . .
To hell with the Rest, England Home and Duty.

Take Terry, Company Clerk.
At Qassassin we shared spartan end of Coy. Office
shared Leave to Cairo, every darn thing
until I asked for a transfer to a fighting platoon.

A thousand miles later, up in the snows
of Florina Pass, just after the action
against the 'Adolf Hitler Leibstandarte' SS
the Coy. Commander comes over with, 'Your friend,

Lance Corporal Spears, has been wounded.
Took a Bren into the Railway Tunnel
so that you blighters could get out . . .
Caught it by blast. Both eyes.
Not likely to see again.'
                                        I say nothing.
Betray no reaction. Cannot feel. Terry BLIND!
I cannot even breathe, 'Poor bastard.'
Now heading south in complete dark
only able to finger head bandages
in a stinking Red Crossed camion
on that bumping, rotten road.
Either I have a character defect
or else my loyalties froze hard up there.
We eye what's pitifully left of 'A' Coy.
Shrug. Crowd round the steaming brew.
Only the Section counts.

Darrell Wilkinson

Drifting at Sea

Look! my beloved, the sea-waves are rocking,
softly the eddies hurry past the boat;
here are no moments, we are not caught
in the dance of hours, and are excused
the sounding of the chimes.

For there to be time there must be sense
and consequence; the perception that rotates
in the changing of the symbol;
the opening and closing of the flower,
the scent of honeysuckle drifting in the wind,
the swoop of predatory birds
and the interminable agonizing instant
drained of precision, when the ferret
comes slinking towards the rabbit.

Such is the time of landsmen; but here
is only the continuous indifference of the sea
and the inconsequential rocking
while the cold, tireless moon
reiterates her journey in the sky.

III

Previously Unpublished
Soldiers' Poems and Ballads

Ronald E. Bee

Before El Alamein

Dull, quiet and sand hills and a pallid moon,
A little young moon in a cloudy drift.
Small matter for a poem! I shall soon
Be old for rhyming; wonder's a child's gift
And this is no child's world. This sand is mined.
Planes wander like the ghosts of men who died
Without absolving priest. My easier mind
Finds pleasure wandering but is close tied
To this steel coffin, all due service said.
Quietness, but for a cricket's scrape
And the far sound of gossip before bed.
A dust plume travels on the distant shape
Of hills, where tanks are leaguered, without sound.
So, in far sand, be all day's echoes drowned.

Gordon Begg

Chanctonbury Ring

The Royal Sussex called it 'Chanctonbury Ring',
This hill the maps named Abu Shamla's tomb;
And as I lay there far too tired to seek the shade
Of trench or tent I thought of Easter Days
When we had driv'n there after church and stayed awhile,
Running past dew-ponds under gusty clouds
That bring soft April rain. But there are no clouds here
Only the black puffs of the Ack-Ack shells
That mark the sky's smooth countenance like some dark rash.
To me a lover of the Saxon South
The name of Chanctonbury brings back much; but it
Means not a thing to these stout Caithnessmen
From Lythe and Lybster, Thrumster, John o'Groats and Wick.
They only see a steepish mound of sand
That marks an Arab's grave. But looking south
I can see Storrington and Steyning and the sea.

The Western Desert, September 1942.

142

Bray

The Price

A voyage home from the Med., 1942

After night-hidden bombers' drone
Has drooled and drooped and groped and grown
Vast, and flares straight as street lamps bloom
And lap the tanker in gold gloom,
While stark in the dead stare of fate
Her crew give glance for glance, and wait—

After the four-inch crash and jar,
And crump which follows its swift star,
And Oerlikons' and Vickers' chatter
And spent shell-cases trickling clatter,
While tracers lobbed in dotted arc
Are strings of lanterns drawn through dark—

After the numbing flash, the boom
As torpedo strikes engine room
Where figures jerk in flame and steam
And lipless faces gape to scream
And through the rending, hissing din
Murderous ocean thunders in—

After the scattered fires unite
To one volcanic gush of light
Till the hull lifts, cracks wide asunder,
Ere dark drops down goes rumbling under,
And limbs awhile thresh bloody foam—
After this hell, men say at home,

'Petrol shortage? Not a bit!
You've only got to pay for it.'

J. E. Brookes

Bardia 1941

The first dead man I saw was one of ours.
We were advancing, rifles at the port.
I knew his name AND number for the powers
that be had made me check Grade 3. What sort
of war was this? Men ACTUALLY killed?
Men actually KILLED!? I looked and half
expected him to rise with no blood spilled
and none intended, look at me and laugh
and say 'I fooled yer that time Sport'. But not
without a head he wouldn't! There we were,
in line abreast advancing, not a shot
been fired in anger, suddenly a whirr
of something overhead and there he was,
a headless torso on the desert sand;
a name and number, that's all. Just because
some Eyetie fired a gun I understand.
Cause and effect. One moment he was there,
as large as life and looking in the pink,
but not the next. I did not stand and stare
(manners you know)—but well, it makes you think!

Tobruk 1941

His Company was in the second wave.
ADVANCE! Unfortunately something gave
him 'Gyppo Tummy', water melons p'raps,
and as a consequence occurred a lapse
of social etiquette if not the sin
of breaching military discipline.
Public Exposure! Desert Waste Defaced
By Private Soldier! Infantry Disgraced?

Then pulled his trousers up, pulled down his hat,
and checked his safety-catch. And after that
he caught the others up. To leave no doubt
in anybody else's mind about

the nature of the incident because
they might think he was shit-scared (which he was),
he started whistling *British Grenadiers*
as if he'd been a fighting man for years.

Ken Burrows

It's Churchill's Fault

It's Churchill's fault we're stuck out here,
With all the flies and sand,
Whilst he and all his cronies,
Live a life that's grand.

It's Churchill's fault we've got no beer,
Nor any decent grub,
I'd sell my soul to walk right now,
Into my local pub.

It's Churchill's fault we've got no fags,
Except for Victory Vs,
They're made from camel dung and sand,
Cigars for him, not these.

It's Churchill's fault we've no canteen,
To buy a razor blade,
We're on fatigues, because we are
Unshaven on parade.

It's Churchill's fault when things go wrong,
It sometimes seems a shame,
But it's always he who's at the top,
Who has to take the blame.

But when at last we win this war,
Bring the Nazis to a halt,
I've got a feeling deep inside,
It'll all be Churchill's fault.

1942.

C. Carter

My Mind

Patchwork and ragwork; bits of this and that—
Such is my memory, these the things I keep
Glowing like voltaged wires connected at
The point of waking, and the point of sleep;
And now so real the things remembered are
That past becomes the present, and the sense
Of well-known things recurring from afar
Triggers the pleasure, makes the joy intense.

Yet what is remembrance but the shrivelled leaves
Of faded sunshine, summer stored and cold,
No longer green, but like the corn in sheaves
Dead and ungrowing; fulfilled; and very old?
As water poured on water, so must I
Like them in formless time dissolve and die.

Graham Cawthorne

The Bend

It's a grim bend, a smooth bend, that's polished all the way
With galabeahs and baksheesh as all the guide books say,
The taxis do not know the town, the gharries do not care,
They'll drive you round and charge a pound, unless you tell them where.

It's a grim bend, a blue bend, and you go round too fast,
In Middle East where all is peace and panics all are past,
There's Groppi's and Gezira, and a visit to the zoo,
The lions pace their cages as impatiently as you.

A blazing bend, a humid bend that drains your life away,
And keeps you sweating on your bed throughout the long midday,
And every time you try to sleep, a buzzing fly will sit
On your wet skin—so cool to him—until you fetch the Flit.

A curving bend, a spiral bend that's strewn with washy tea,
Well stewed and dried, and stewed again for likes of you and me,
There's coffee and there's cocoa and harder liquor too,
And beer that foams like liquid gold—mighty heady brew.

A crazy bend, a daft bend that makes you laugh and roar—
If you're short of plates for dinner your saffragi goes next door,
The oven will not work again—but do not eat your hat
They'll cook the dinner just the same in someone else's flat.

A crowded bend, a bend that's full of weary lonely eyes
Of men too long from those they love—who says they like it—lies.
But everything must finish—and though you're round that bend,
You know that any time at all—The wretched bend will end.

Louis Challoner

Ballad of Young Sam Small

(Written for 'H' Battery Concert, Tmimi, Cyrenaica, February 1943)

You've heard of Samuel Small perhaps, that lad o' Lancashire,
Who faced the Duke o' Wellington without a sign o' fear,
And told him his opinion (but told him all in vain)
That them as knocks a rifle down should pick it up again?
    Now Sam's too old for t' Army but still he's working hard,
As an Acting-Unpaid Lance-jack in t' Rottenstall Home Guard.
    His grandson's in the Forces—a brave lad he is too,
And he's often heard the stories Old Sam tells of Waterloo.
How Grandad with his musket, and t' Duke of Wellington,
Helped only by the R.H.A. and t' 25-pounder gun,
Took on Napoleon Bonaparte—and what is more—they won!
    Young Sam is in the Gunners—giving old Rommel socks
That he's a lad of bulldog breed he showed in t'Knightsbridge Box.
    The enemy was shelling, when through the order come—
'We want a volunteer'—boys to go and fetch the rum.
'That is, if you're in need of it—!' The sergeant says 'I am!'
'So take this 'ere quart bottle, lad, and go and get it, Sam!'
Sam didn't need much telling and without a trace of fear,
He took the empty bottle and advanced—towards the rear.

147

The battle still were raging when he returned again,
They'd just fired ten rounds rapid and prepared another ten.
The G.P.O. were shouting 'Repeat!' and t'number four
Snatched t' bottle off our hero—and rammed it up the bore!
The tragedy were awful—but Sam his gundrill knew,
He had to keep his mouth shut—so he shut both eyes up too!
The shoot at that was ended and though without much hope
Sam shoved aside the number three and peeped through t' telescope.
He gave a cry of anger—it were more nor he could stand,
When he saw a big fat Jerry—with the bottle in his hand.
    That night when all were silent, and everyone a-kip,
With half a cup of char a man and not of rum a sip,
Sam crept out o'er the midan and through the Jerry lines,
He'd lived for years i' Lancashire, so he wasn't scared o' mines—
He crept up to the leaguer where the Jerries all were snorin',
And looked about for t' smell o' rum and a bloke as looked like Goering.
    At last he found the bottle and the Jerry, fast asleep,
Was clutching it, half empty, beside his slit-trench deep.
    Thought Sam, 'If I should take it, he'll wake as sure as hell:
To get the ruddy rum at all—I mun tek him as well.'
No sooner said than started—and, cutting t' story short
Sam soon returned with half the rum and t' Jerry he had caught.
    The Major were delighted, and said 'It's glad I am
'To have an 'ero in my troop!' 'And so am I!' said Sam.
'The rum should have a medal, and that without a doubt,
'For though I brought the Jerry in, 't wer't rum as knocked him out!'

Song: The Royal Horse Artillery

Tune: *Chattanooga Choo Choo*

Get mobile, boys! We are the Royal Horse Artill'ry—
The old R.H.A.—and we're coming this way.
We've got the guns—for we're the Royal Horse Artill'ry
Enough to get through—and to keep moving, too.
We have kicked our heels in Cairo and the Alamein line
But now we're chasing Rommel and we think it is fine—
Nothing we won't tackle, to force him into battle—
On to Tripoli to keep that date with the mayor!
When you see the quads come rattling over the rocks,
Then you'll know the R.H.A. is giving 'em socks—
Mussolini banished—all his empire vanished—
Nothing left but Italy—and we'll be there!
Then we may see all the friends we left behind us
In Greece and in Crete—won't reunion be sweet!
Roll on the day that brings us news that victory is won
Then—Royal Horse Artill'ry—our work will have been done!

Ralph C. Chopping

They Had Only One Idea

When on leave in Cairo in Gezira swimming-pool,
Drinking beer and immersing self in the waters cool,
I met a fair young maiden, never fairer did I see,
And a tale of woe and trouble she began to tell to me.
'Life' she said 'is very boring, such a frightful strain, my dear,
Your Service boys may all be heroes, but you've only one idea'.

Once I met a boy from Malta who in a Hawker Hurricane
Did many a deed of deathless glory, shot down many a German plane,
Though he fought like a Crusader, he was no St George, I fear,
Resolute in the offensive, he had only one idea.

Then I met some bomber pilots, far and wide did they roam.
One especially caught my fancy, he had just come out from home.
True he'd talk of home and beauty, but when one forced him, 'twas but clear
Steering straight towards the target, he had only one idea.

Then I met a silent sailor, very fine in navy blue,
Here, I thought, is someone different, here at last is someone new.
I will charm him from his silence, and when he is at his ease,
He will tell me of adventures sailing o'er the seven seas,
Swiftly was that silence broken, sailors are not dumb, no fear,
But when he cleared decks for action, he had only one idea.

Then I met a big and burly six foot six South African,
Fresh from off the rolling bush veldt where a man's a real he-man
His red tabs meant he was willing to leave home and fight up here,
But red also stands for danger, he had only one idea.

So I sought out some one older. Someone from the gilded staff. Laugh.
Complete with tabs and crowns and buttons, glamour suit and Poona
Very smooth and very wealthy, played his polo once a week,
Took me out to dance at Shepheards in a staff car smooth and sleek,
But at Mena in the desert I cut short his smooth career,
Though he talked a lot of riding, he had only one idea.

Oh the R.A.F. talk of many things and the Army talk of tanks,
The Navy prefer action and confine themselves to thanks,
But whatever their rank or service, it is always all too clear,
Whatever they may talk about, they've only one idea.

She ceased and looked for comfort, but in her hour of need,
I very much regret to state I proved a broken weed.
Saluting I arose and said 'Farewell I cannot stay I fear'
For just like all the others, I had but one idea.

Michael Croft

Leaving the Med.

We came this way before
In different ships
Which knew no casual watch.
The hills rose crimson from the brooding coast
As at the guns we watched the light's last span
Shrink with the fatal sun
To night, and eyes the night concealed
Peering from black waters.

Historical islands
Familiar as midday bombers
Pass, known by their battle names,
Islands with the dead we once had watched
When dawn was shell plunged
Dragged by gaunt islanders down jagged graves
Or buried in torn groves.

Now leaves are green and ruins are arranged
To soothe the tourist on the languid cruise;
Bored elegance can gaze,
Admire the luscious view, the beach,
And ask, when guides are hired in hills,
Which bones are which.

We have raced periscopes
Slanting for murder
From neat waves, seen water lap blood's blue serge
From gun decks when ships screamed,
And when night's bombs had ceased,
The sick convoy, limbs floating in loose scarves,
And bobbing aimless caps.

Soon even the love we learnt will be lost,
Blotted from memory like the ports of Egypt,
Buried in obscure images of distant poetry.

This was our way.
We know faith's private history
Alone defines a way.

                                December 1945.

Sailor Song: Back to the Andrew

(After a rough night in Sister Street, Alex.)

There are seven ways to heaven
     And I've slipped on every one,
Now the pearly gates are closing
     And I haven't strength to run.

The angels up in heaven
     Are saying prayers for me
And all the choirs in heaven
     Are singing mournfully

For the soul that missed the moorings
     And took the road to sin
For the whisky and the women
     And the devil sealed within.

But after all the choirs
     Have harped upon my fate
I begin to feel impatient
     With the angels at the gate.

For how the angels got there
     Was never made quite clear,
Or by what rare promotion
     They should punish men down here.

Whatever power created us
     Did not divulge the plan,
And all who loved or hated us
     Saw each a separate man.

There are seven ways to heaven
     And every one's a snare,
So angels up in heaven,
     Don't waste another prayer
On a sinner not for salvage,
     Who doesn't even care.

The Andrew was slang for the Royal Navy and Sister Street the
brothel area of Alexandria.

D. M. Davin

Elegy I

Their bones are our memorial. We are theirs.
The night breeze strokes the desert hills.
But no breeze placates, no night consoles
Sullen ashes and abandoned fires.

Lonely as the whirlwind twirling its lost heart
Under the blazing day or Libyan moon,
These ghosts unlaid must call unheard
On other comrades lost, too late, too soon.

Elegy II

No water ever in this wadi's bed.
Its ripples are the wind's, and sand.
The long dawn shadow's silent tread
Darkens no wet grasses and no joyous land.
Only the winds are mirthful in this sand.

A beefbox cross: 'Italian dead.'
'Serves the buggers right. Waste of bloody wood.
Aussies should know better,'
We coldly said.

This at the wadi's end. The late wind sang
Through the rocks. Our long shadows fast
Followed minds elsewhere, as the last boot rang.

Yet the mind that wakes in this night's bed
Broods on that wadi where the wind and sand
Mock the tethered shadow's cross-bound tread,
The cross marking time in that sombre land,
The dupes who were men and now are sand.

Libya, December 1942.

Cairo Cleopatra

No mighty Caesars helpless gasp
In these lubricious thighs.
Plain soldiers in their practised grasp
Grunt inexpensive sighs.

Simple and short her shift,
Cheap is her price.
All that she has in gift
Is pubic lice.

You who have sobbed above
This mortal core,
Cast off your agonied love
On this jetsam shore

Recall to your coward heart,
Remind your despair,
This used Egyptian tart
May also ask where,

Where is there peace at last,
Peace from all lust?
The quiet of the womb long past,
What of the dust?

Or worse, no questions sear
This public flesh.
Enjoying each desperate dear,
She is content in the mesh.

Cairo, July 1942.

Egyptian Madonna

On the kerbstone of this iron-hearted street
Wearily she sits,
The baby's head against her wrinkled teat,
And tender fingers search his head for nits.

At the brown breast sucks the infant mouth.
Uncertainly the hands
Grope the sunk slopes, poor slake of vital drouth,
Oasis in this city's hungry sands.

Dear nostrils of this infant god
Dribblingly ooze snot,
Nectar to the clogging flies which wad
The future of his brief beloved lot.

At the corners of her loving smile
Sluggishly the flies
Suck and trample sticky feet. Meanwhile
That is pus that was her eyes.

Obliviously she hears us pharisees
Pass on protected soles,
A crucified child at the height of our knees,
Our eyes on more lofty goals.

Cairo, July 1942.

Grave near Sirte

No poppies bleed above his blood.
His diary closed before last spring.
Upon his cross there greens no second bud.
He feels no more the sandstorm's sting.

The sweating dew upon his helmet's steel
Dries through each day to rust.
Caressing sand he cannot feel
Has blanketed his lust.

Eyes look no longer to the sea
His hope had often crossed.
Rocks shade his bones, and no dark tree,
No thaw for this death's frost.

Not British and not German now he's dead,
He breeds no grasses from his rot.
The coast road and the Arab pass his bed
And waste no musing on his lot.

December 1942.

A. Dunn

A Soldier's Lament

In a little bivouac, lying sweating on their backs;
In this hot and filthy clime, where the sun shines all the time
And the sand storms fill your eyes; make you blast those ruddy flies,
Snakes and centipedes on the floor, bites from mosquitoes in galore,
Can you wonder we're all crazy! six a.m. we hear reveille;
There the sergeant goes again, shouts Wakey! Wakey! there you men,
Weary boys sit up in bed—Blast this tent I've bumped my head!
Crawling out on hands and knees, we shake off all the ants and fleas
From our shirts and pants and vests, there's no time to take a rest,
Hurry! get the small wash tin, there's a pint of water in,
Plenty there for you and me, sieve it quick and make some tea;
Then at last with kits outside, every man must take a pride—
Fold his blankets nice and neat, now it's time to go to eat.
What's this! Soya links again; the very thought drives me insane,
If you think that we are barmy, since we joined this blinking army;
When at last this war is o'er and we return to blighty's shore—
Say a little prayer—a little prayer!

Donald Everett

Envoi

The show was over, we did not know
how long it had been over.
There was a slow drift from shelters,
some thought we were dead, all knew
that we were mad. The oaths were strong
the sullen stub was lit, but sleep
soon re-assumed
its overweaning power.

We awoke as the dogs licked our faces—
dawn was a woman in violet
wearing a red sash—
we worshipped her.

Ian Fletcher

Soldiers at the Base

Among lupine faces on the rabid posters
'V.D. is dangerous to the Family' and
'Buy National Savings Now', in their blunt postures,
Ranked, numbered, moved, removed, the squaddies stand.

Those who past polemical terrain
Bumbled by tank and lorry to the front
But hazard if their day may bloom again
In quiet-keyed living, the menial stunt.

Others in flycapped kitchens, office and hutment, band,
Dressing the sick sweet altars of the Latrine;
Outflanked by boredom, sliverings of sand;
Sensed, the high rigours of the lost campaign.

So I, raw poet, notionally quite least
Of such uncompassed travellers, come
By war, all langour, on this middling east
And jeopard in survival's trivium.

A carrier, standing for its convoy;
I talk to a serious trooper. All these ends.
O Predellas, Aumbries, Archlutes, arcs of joy;
Over there, up the Blue, is freedom, death and friends.

Base, all base, in our off-coloured dreams,
Clawed not those waxed infantas, dimly kind;
But divas in frot velvet, whose bare screams
Skewed us like shot. *We have fallen too far behind.*

Geneifa, January 1944.

Brian Gallie

War's Benefit

We had not heard the music in men's laughter
Until we heard them crying as they died.
All their proud beauty, glory of glance and mein—
We only saw these after,
When they slid overside
At dusk, into the rushing of the wake.
Silence and Peace were words until we'd been
Shipmates with noise and danger, and could take
No respite. Were there colours to the sea?
Did beauty dance or dream
In ever-new perspective, shade and shape
Of cloud? And did it seem,
Before, that there could be
A measure of the distance to a star
Within the brain that wandered—
Behind the eye
Seeking in sea and sky
For death—and found escape
In gardens of strange beauty, where it pondered
On this strange gift of War?
This bounteous giving
To sense and ear and eye . . .
Our youth took fire, and flamed with the wonderful living
We only learned when we were asked to die.
So, for the spell allowed us, we have laughed
The louder for the crying;
Thrown back our heads and quaffed
A sparkling magic, gulping, naked-throated,
Divine, insidious wine. There's no denying
The taste once learned; for to be so elated
Is worth all danger—even what we'll find
If the Gods show they love us, and are kind.

H.M.S. *Hyperion*, November 1940.

Intercepted

'One damaged, one shot down' the signal read.
'I hope they don't get back to base' he said,
'I hope they don't get home!'
                              And then he laughed.

                    Somewhere they launched a raft
Their last, wild hope—a bubble, bubble-light,
On wild, black water in the lowering night;
Numbed by the lash of wave tips curling-down—
And took God knows how many hours to drown . . .

To a German Airman

Who flew slowly through the British Fleet

Perhaps you knew not what you did,
That what you did was good;
Perhaps the head I saw was dead,
Or blind with its own blood.

Perhaps the wings you thought you ruled,
With sky and sea beneath,
Beat once with love for God above—
And flew you to your death.

Perhaps: but I prefer to think
That something in you, friend,
No inch would give to land and live,
But conscious chose the end.

That something in you, like a bird,
Knowing no cage's bars,
Courage supreme—an instant dream
Of mind beneath the stars:

Misguided, arrogant, or proud,
But—beyond telling—great,
Made you defy our fire and fly
Straight on, to meet your fate.

Steel-capped, we cowered as you went,
Defiant and alone;
A noble thing, we watched you wing
Your way to the unknown.

You passed us, still a mile from death,
Rocked by the wind of shell;
We held our breath, until to death
Magnificent you fell.

Whatever comet lit your track—
Contempt, belief, or hate—
You let us see an enemy
Deliberately great.

B. D. Garland

Groppi's, 1st January, 1943

What if the sun should send a gleam,
To kiss your golden hair,
engendering such a living flame
of harmony that he himself must stare?

Would all the room, the house, the town,
caught in the red unearthly light,
expand, explode in a triumphal sound?

It might.

Eric B. Gill

'Old Butch'

For ever remember 'old Butch'
   and the confident smile he wore
He never had doubts at all
In those fitful days of May and June
   when we were on the run
He inspired us all with his old tune
   that soon we'd see the fun
But days passed on and grim the fight
   it seemed that Jerry had won
But still 'old Butch' from morn to night
   just smiled and said 'who's done?'
And then one night I heard the news
   'old Butch' was 'in the bag'
But three days later out of the Blue
   after trudging twenty mile
Who should stroll in with a 'How do you do?'
   and his old perpetual smile
His face was gaunt and haggard too
   for want of food and rest
He'd gone through Hell as we well knew
   but he'd stood up to the test.
We crossed the wire and came at last
   to El Alamein to stand
Determined no Hun should ever pass
   that stretch of barren sand
And as we watched the men and guns
   and scores of mighty tanks
'Old Butch's' face was joy to see
   as they daily swelled our ranks
It was the 23rd of October a full moon in the sky
   when we let Hell loose
And advanced to win or die
For days and nights that battle raged
   no human flesh and blood
Could stand for long the war we waged
   our fire was like a flood
And then the enemy broke and fled
   the slaughter it was such
They left behind them scores of dead
   alas we left 'old Butch'.

Clive Gimson

28th March, 1943—Somewhere near Mareth

I'll tell you a tale of what you can see
On an average day in a gunner O.P.   (Observation Post)
You get up at five when you can't see at all,
(At least an hour early the guard's sure to call
Since his watch is a Wog one; he got it bakhsheesh): (Free)
Still you get up at five and mutter 'Maleesh'. (Don't Worry)
The object and aim, or so we've been taught,
Is to send back by wireless a First Light Report.
The First Light Report is really a guess:
Your eyes are so bunged that it's Nuts Monkey Ess (No Movement Seen)
But as it gets lighter you realize slowly
You're in a position completely and wholly
Impossible: full in the view of the Hun:
And now it's too late for aught to be done
So be very still and see what you can.
You'll first see a bush—but it's really a man
And then, when the sun rises up in the sky,
So will the bushes or men—perhaps fly—
And soldiers or bushes will hazily swim
Across the horizon. Now send back to Tim (Adjutant)
And say that the Jerries are moving their men,
Or their bushes, about in square 70, 10.
At this comes the signal for all to get ready
To blaze willy-nilly upon the Don Freddy. (Defensive Fire)
And as it comes down with the hell of a din
You are asked quite politely if you would look in,
And see if the shelling and gun-firing pushes
Back all the masses of Jerries—or bushes.
So long as you're careful and sensibly wary, a
Message goes back that it's in target area.
And now you can probably find out the gen
As to whether the target was bushes or men.
And so you go on in a similar mode
Reporting, and checking map sequence code,
And asking for 'boxes' or 'drink' or 'octane'
Until in the evening you come round again
To the be-all and end-all, for so we've been taught
Of an O.P's existence the Last Light Report.

E. F. Gosling

Mechanization

Only seven months have passed but what a change they've made.
Remember how it used to be when troops got on parade?
'See those bits are fitted right!
See those girths are tight!
Mind you shake the blankets out before you put 'em on!'
How the nose-bands caught the light, how the steel-work shone!

All that's very different now. We dress like garage hands;
Gone now the clink of bit and spur; no trumpets now, no bands.
'Petrol, oil and water right?
All the wheel-nuts tight?
Did you check the levels up before you got aboard?'
No more, alas, the head-tossed foam, the fretful foot that pawed:
Oh glory that was Tetrarch's might, oh drabness that is Ford!

Hamish Henderson

So Long

(Recrossing the Sollum Frontier from Libya into Egypt, 22nd May, 1943,
in a lorry carrying captured enemy equipment.)

To the war in Africa that's over—goodnight.
　　To thousands of assorted vehicles, in every stage of decomposition,
　　littering the desert from here to Tunis—goodnight.
To thousands of guns and armoured fighting vehicles
　　brewed up, blackened and charred
from Alamein to here, from here to Tunis—goodnight.
To thousands of crosses of every shape and pattern,
　　alone or in little huddles, under which the unlucky bastards lie—
　　　goodnight

　　　　　　　　　Horse-shoe curve of the bay,
　　　　　　　clean razor-edge of the escarpment,
　　　　　tonight it's the sunset only that's blooding you.

Halfaya and Sollum : I think that at long last
　　we can promise you a little quiet.

So long. I hope I won't be seeing you.

To the sodding desert—you know what you can do with yourself.

To the African deadland—God help you—and goodnight.

R. Hildgard

Tobruk

　　To that sweet wadi mist the dusty wastes,
　　Where grew green bushes in March suns,
　　Came the golden Oriole and the azure Roller,
　　Where I lived in a square sandy cave.
　　And all the days were filled with song and scents,
　　And all the nights with stars and breeze.
　　While far away the quiet enemy
　　Prepared his fierce, victorious blows,

And not a fearful breath reached us in the soft airs
That came across the yellow rolling sands.
And every day I strolled in sunshine, admired
The birds, descended to the fretted shores,
Bathed in blue warm waters,
Laughed, read and dreamed of Poets;
Till one dawn we rose and drove out
From that sweet wadi to be drenched
In agony and blood where dreadful strife
And toil were waged, friends fell, where
Death and pain marred all that charmed air.

W. G. Holloway

South of Alamein

When they're talking now of Russia and the moves of war-like states,
I just can't forget the last one, with its death and bloody hates
And I often think of chummies on that last, long desert scout,
When the news said front was quiet and there were no Fritz about.
We were right out in the desert, to the south of Alamein,
And the distant hump of rock mounds were the guardian terrain.
And the heat was harsh and shimmering from off the desert bed,
And our pennants were a-flying as we swiftly southwards sped.
Then we were going down escarpment, if mem'ry serves me well,
When these Stukas came a-diving, like some denizens from 'ell,
But there were no Bofors banging as we dived into the sand,
'Cos they didn't have the gunners for our tiny little band.
I remembered as it 'appened, with the black smoke rolling round,
And there was nothing glorious as writers make it sound.
And I could hear the crying as the blokes around were hit,
As I grovelled in the desert, just a-chewing of the grit.
And when the tumult and the shouting, it 'ad died, as poet says,
We then started a-digging of the graves to rest the dead,
And last memory of Gordon, and of Charlie and of Ross,
Were the silhouette in evening of the tiny desert cross.
And later on in leaguer when we listened to the news,
The bloke said front was quiet, but they were just 'is views,
And all the time he's talking we were thinking of the loss
Of the boys just under desert and a tiny sand-blown cross.

Night Barrage, Western Desert

The cannons' bloodshot eyes
Blinked out their murderous message
Through the night,
And the soaring Very lights
Climbed up to peer
At spectator stars.
And the thump of guns
Found fearful echo in the frenzied
Beating of the heart.

Peter R. Hopkinson

Maleesh Aforethought

We're soldiers in North Africa
Avoiding being shot.
The natives rob us right and left
And murder like as not.
Which goes to show we might as well
Be back in Aldershot.

The sand is all surrounding us
To very large extent.
It fills our boots, our food, our guns,
It takes up half the tent.
Oh God, let us advance before
They bring up the cement.

The bombing and the shelling tend
To liven up the day.
Those shells cost fifty quid apeace,
Or so the gunners say.
If I fired off a cartridge would
They stop it from my pay?

Our General don't drink or smoke.
He's full of vim and zest.
He says, P.T. and training schemes
Are what we need the best.
I hope I die and go to hell.
I need a bit of rest.

The German Erwin Rommel though,
So say some friends of mine,
Is normal and informal and
His soldiers think he's fine.
I'd put in for a transfer but
My Deutsch is rather klein.

We're going on a mission soon
Which may be suicide.
A peck of dirt we all must eat
They say, before we've died.
I'm ready Sergeant-Major.
I've just now qualified.

We British have a spirit force
That helps us through the war.
The favourite expression that
We use, *Esprit de Corps.*
The other troops don't need it.
They're paid a dam sight more.

Why are we in this desert hell?
Why are we so accursed?
Because in hearts of free-born men
The principle is nursed
To save the democratic way
For King Farouk the First.

Leslie Howe

Desert Madness

Have you ever seen a locust on the desert breeze?
Have you ever had a scorpion crawling on your knees?
Have you ever watched black beetles rolling balls of dirt?
Have you ever caught a sand-louse exploring in your shirt?

We make a pint of water do our washing for the week,
Folks, *you* have a try, but watch the basin doesn't leak,
And don't forget that in that pint you also ought to bathe,
Brush your dentures, wash your hair and have a ruddy shave.

And then there is the question of sand sauce in your stew,
Mix the sand in good and thick, it will clear your system too
And add a dash of petrol to flavour up the pot.
But that's done for you already, so do not use a lot.

We could tell you quite a deal about this desert heat,
How it burns our flesh, makes us limp and rots our aching feet,
Then before our fevered eyes a mirage will appear
And dancing in the air we see pink tankards full of beer.

You should see the wretched sandstorms, that come in from the dunes
When the wind screams round our lorries, playing funny tunes,
And the sand gets in our food, our clothes, our eyes and hair
Through our kit bags, in our packs, in fact just everywhere.

And then the C.O. toddles round, 'Pack up boys, look slick'
And all our stuff is on those trucks, you bet, in half a tick
'Cause Jerry's just along the ridge—we will give him hell.
Tho' tyres be flat, for in the loads a ton of sand as well.

And driving on the desert is not a pleasant ride,
For bumping over rocks and scrub plays pop with your inside
And shovel for an hour or two, by gosh, it beats the band.

Thus we live, day in, day out, they never send us back
I guess when peace returns once more, they'll leave the poor Ack-Ack.
And we'll grow old and dodder round with beards all long and white
Telling camels gory tales of how we fought the fight.

Barbara Howroyd

Thoughts on Spring in England

Should bird song stab us with the ache of spring
And should the gaiety and joy of trees that sing
And should the dance of live air start a flame
In us, that spring has come again?

Should spring come fearfully from winter's grip
To steal into our hearts and gently strip
All our habitual thoughts of war and pain
And whisper, 'I have come again?'

Should beauty come to us who live when others die,
Should we be blessed by winds that sweep across the sky.
Should we kneel down to worship God in vain,
Because the spring is here again?

Should I then laugh with joy when primroses are blown
By sea-borne breezes launching drift of foam,
Should everything we knew and loved be still the same
When spring comes slowly in again?

                                        Alexandria, 1944.

V. J. Locke

Tobruk

We're all heroes I've been told
'Cos we did our bit to hold
The Jerry in a place they call Tobruk.
And no matter what we say
Contradict them as we may
They call us heroes. We who held Tobruk.

Tho' the truth we've told folks oft
But their hats to us they've doffed.
You're heroes! Don't you know you held Tobruk.
You tell us a different story
Modest lads you're dodging glory.
You're the heroes of the age, you held Tobruk.

Now I think it would be best
If the world would let it rest
Let us forget that we were in Tobruk.
We thank you from our hearts
For applauding us our parts
But please let us forget about Tobruk.

16th I.B.

Infantry Brigades 16th for the use of-one.
Let's look up your record and find out what you've done.
You started out in Palestine quelled many an Arab riot
Then chased off to the desert to feed the Eyeties on lead diet.
You did this well you gave them hell and came out on your feet
Nothing else to do m' lads but pack you off to Crete.
In this fair isle there wasn't much that supermen could do
But looking thro' our battle lists we found the job for you.
Syria needed lessons for she'd let the Jerries land
Let them use her aerodromes and gave a helping hand.
So then we put you on the job to round up Colonel Dentz
Packed you in your vehicles and told you to get hence.
You finished that job on schedule which proved you knew your stuff
So we shipped you into Tobruk which we knew was rather rough
But when this war is finished and we have our victory feast
Your country will remember you? Hell! They're still out in the East.

Calvin Makabo

Desert Conflict

Written by Sgt Calvin Makabo 1946 Coy. A.A.P.C. (Basuto), on the occasion of King
George VI's visit to the Western Desert in 1943 after the defeat of Rommel. Sgt Makabo
was drowned west of Tripoli later in 1943. Translation by Sgt Alexander Qoboshane.

Cast your eyes and look over to the ocean and see ships.
It is far, you cannot see with your naked eyes.
Had it not been so, you could see the track of a big sea snake.
It is dusty, it is where the sea dogs play.
Raise the waves and hide yourselves, for you see the country has changed.
England and Berlin are in confliction.
It is where we saw bulls in a rage,
Each one being proud of its equipment.

A woman left the baby and ran away,
The women up north are crying,
They cry facing towards the east,
And say 'There our husbands have disappeared'.
Keep silent and listen to the war affairs.
Year before last in September,
There were great flashes towards the west.
It is there the enemy were troublesome.
The Resident Commissioner heard from home,
He heard about great deeds done by Africans,
He heard they were victorious.
Rommel neglected his duties.
The son of Makabo has taken part in those deeds.
The Chiefs at home heard—Chiefs Theko, Litingoana, Seele Tane and
    Mahabe

You always deceive us and say that
His Majesty King George VI is not seen.
A telegraphic message was sent from England to Tripoli.
It was received in the morning,
And delivered to the companies on Saturday, 21st June.
All Companies according to their race and colour
Coming to cheer the King.
There were those with three stars on their shoulder,
And those who had a crown in their hands.

The General Lyon[1] went down by the main road being silent.
There was wireless round his motor car,
And cannons guarding him on all sides;
Then the soldiers cheered the King as he passed and shouted HURRAH!

[1] 'General Lyon' was the code name for the King.

Dennis McHarrie

Luck

I suppose they'll say his last thoughts were of simple things,
Of April back at home, and the late sun on his wings;
Or that he murmured someone's name
As earth recaimed him sheathed in flame.
Oh God! Let's have no more of empty words,
Lip service ornamenting death!
The worms don't spare the hero;
Nor can children feed upon resounding praises of his deed.
'He died who loved to live,' they'll say,
'Unselfishly so we might have today!'
Like hell! He fought because he had to fight;
He died that's all. It was his unlucky night.

J. G. Meddemmen

L.R.D.G.

He threw his cigarette in silence, then he said:

You can't predict in war;
It's a matter of luck, nothing less, nothing more.
Now here's an instance. Darnley copped it in the head
His third day up the blue although he'd seen the lot
In Dunkerque, Greece and Crete—
The sort that went in tidy and came out neat;
He copped it when the going wasn't even hot.
And there was little Pansy Flowers,
Machine-gunned through the guts; he bled
(And not a murmur from him) for hours
Before he jagged it in.

                    And you remember Bowers?
Bowers got fragmentation in the lungs and thigh;
We couldn't do a thing: the moon was high
And a hell of a bright
On that particular night.
Poor sod, he won't kip in a civvy bed.

It's queer . . . I've even laughed
When blokes have chucked it in and gone daft.
I remember one that scarpered bollock-nude
One midnight, out across the dunes, calling for Mum;
You'd have thought him blewed.
He wasn't seen again—not this side of Kingdom Come.

One job that I really funked
Was when Fat Riley bunked
From a Jerry leaguer on a getaway.
We found him blind, with both hands gone.
When we got him back inside the lines
He'd only say,
Over and over, 'the mines, the mines, the mines'.
It's the lucky ones get dead:
He's still alive. I wonder if his wife understands
How you can't even shoot yourself without your hands.

March 1942.

Peter M. Moulding

Peace

Once in a blue and golden land
A young man lay on the burning sand:
The sand was gold and gold the sun
And the blue of the sea and sky were one.
He lay as only youth can lie
A smile on his mouth, a dream in his eye,
And brown limbs stretched in easy grace,
A world of happiness in his face.
Fanciful thoughts danced in his mind
Like smoke from his pipe in the playful wind,
And each sweet thought was as free from care
As the flecks of sunlight in his hair.

A sailing-ship across the bay,
Cleaving the waves in a glory of spray,
Quivered and checked some two miles out
And preened herself as she went about.
Nearer at hand where the sea began
In the warm white shallows a small child ran;
With spade and bucket he played his fill
And talked to himself as children will.

There in his worldly paradise
The young man, stretching, blinked his eyes
And awoke from the depths of his reverie
To the kiss of the breeze and the scent of the sea.
The song of the waters filled his ear;
The sun was friendly and warm and near . . .
. . . Peace, in a heart that knew no fear.

Alexandria, 1940.

A. F. Noble

Egypt

(Advance in a sandstorm)

Look to your front the sergeant said
You'll take the brunt an' you'll be dead
If you're careless of your front.

How far is the front the soldier said
we can only see one yard ahead
Tell us how far is the front.

The point of your bay'nit the sergeant said
You'll see his belly before his head
That's how far is the front.

But sand's in my eyes the soldier said
an' all I see is coloured red
That's what the soldier said.

Get sand in your guts the sergeant said
finish 'em off with your rifle butts
that's what the sergeant said.

So it's sand in your guts and sand in your hair
sand in your rifle everywhere
hole of sand for a bed.

But the point of a bay'nit holds no sand
it's polished an' bright an' rather grand
an' holding it steady an' making a stand
is just what the sergeant ordered.

So we looks to our front, keeps our head
doing all what the sergeant said
an' some stay alive, but the sergeant's dead.
Just as the sergeant ordered.

G. C. Norman

Night Raid

Martin stood up; a wafery arc of moon
Cast evanescent shadows, dimly seen
Against the scrub and sand.
                              He listened.
                                        Soon
The measured tread of sentries and the sheen
Of moonlight on steel helmet marked his man.
I tapped his leg. He walked a dozen paces.

The sentry is approaching and I can
Distinguish his white face.
                              He turns and faces
The two of us, I sink down.
                              'Halt! Wer da?'
'Kamarad,' says Martin, 'Oberleutnant Wehn.'

He speaks quite softly; voices carry far.
Besides, his accent will not bear much strain.

The sentry pauses; Martin lifts his hands.
I raise my Remington, take aim, and squeeze.
No noise: The German drops dead where he stands.

The laager is quiet. Martin is on his knees
Removing tin hat and rifle. Faintly now
Grey outlines shape themselves, with here and there
The glitter of steel turrets in a row
Of trucks and cars. No movement anywhere
Gives sign of wakefulness, and we resume
The sentry's beat along the laager edge.

Unconsciously I notice a perfume,
Some flower that recalls a hawthorn hedge
Sharpened by rain.
                        Sometimes my mind will turn
Unbidden on some small forgotten thread
Of past existence.

'Listen. Is that Hearn?'
Says Martin. I crouch down. A muffled tread
Approaches. Martin halts and clicks his bolt.
There comes an answering click, and now we see
That Hearn has been successful, too, and Holt
Comes close behind.
            'O.K. lads.'
                    Silently
We go our ways. I take the eastern side
As prearranged. Our men are closing in
From north and south, and noiseless shadows glide
Between the vehicles. I pull the pin
From my grenade. A six-wheeled armoured car
With turrets open looks an easy prey.
A rubber-footed Indian Havildar
Creeps to a bivouac some yards away.

A Very light goes up. That is the sign.

Out on the further side there is a roar,
And great red sheets of flame. A Teller mine.
I pitch my bomb into the turret door
And slam it shut. That one has seen the last
Of war in Libya. As I leap away
The ammunition goes sky-high. The blast
Blows out the roof.
                It is as light as day—
Someone has fired the petrol.
                    Now and then
A Tommy-gun is barking feverishly.
I drop a bomb into a tank again;
The turret splits and crumbles curiously.
Two Indians run among the bivouacs
With hand grenades; there is no opposition.
A corporal from the Rifle Corps attacks
A tractor with traditional precision:
There must have been a man inside.
                    A tent
Is smoking like a factory chimney stack.
I drop a petrol cocktail through a rent;
It turns dull red and blows up.

                              From the back
Of an open truck there comes a burst of fire,
But not for long. Lacey can throw a bomb
From forty yards.
                        The flames are mounting higher
From blazing trucks and oil. Some officers come,
Hands raised, out of a car. This is no time
For prisoners. Who makes a rule for war
Is playing tag with death.
                              Some ghastly crime
In Poland is avenged.
                        A big Mark IV
Is being started up. Some Germans run
Behind it for protection. Someone throws
Two flaring bottle bombs. A lucky one
Bursts on the driver's slits and petrol flows
All down the front and sides. The engine stops.

The group of Germans start to show some fight,
And fire behind the tank, till someone drops
A bomb on them. The tank is well alight.

Some yards behind me I can hear the crack
Of Johnson's Mauser, paying off old scores.
A German is hit and rolls upon his back
Half-wearily to die.
                        There is a pause.
The Germans have been taken by surprise,
Quite unprepared for battle. In the dark
Some half-dressed officers try to organize
A tentative defence line, and the bark
Of German automatic guns is heard.
I blow up two more lorries with Mills bombs
Thrown in the driver's seat. More than a third
Of them are blazing now.
                              A German comes
Towards me, rifle raised. A lean Pathan
Blows off his head.
                  I whistle.
                              That was near.
Red flares go up, and I unloose the can
Upon my back. The rest are getting clear,

And Martin is beside me.
                                    'All O.K.?'
'O.K.'
            He disappears.
                                    A dozen fires
Are burning and the place is bright as day.
Quickly I set the mine and join the wires,
Then race away towards the rendezvous
Where Hearn and Martin and the bantam wait.
We roar away. Jerry does not pursue.
In two more minutes it will be too late.

There is a burst and crackle of explosion
That shakes the truck and, as we race away
Towards the dawn the east is tinged with crimson,
Like the foreboding of another day

Morning in Abbassia

The sunlight on the D.I.D.
    Is gathered in a single eye
That molten and unwinking stares
    The starlight out of countenance,
And with its artless alchemy
    The sun transmutes the leaden sky
To amethyst and ancient jade
    And coral of transparent hue.

The sombre NAAFI building wears
    The yellow smile of sycophants
And rooftops on the Sergeants' Mess
    Are fired with corrugated gold.
Light fingers on long shadows laid
    Comes morning and her motley crew
To clothe anew in fancy dress
    The odd, the ugly and the old.

The sleepers on the sunken sand
    Awaken softly; in their eyes
The soldier's stoic sadness sits
    And solemnly surveys the world.

179

Acacia trees on either hand
  Whisper old secrets: nervous flies
Swarm up at footfalls. On the square
  A mongrel dog forlornly roves,
And where the twilight taper flits
  The sky is with soft tissues pearled.

Cookhouses stir: doors are unbarred:
  Thin columns waver in the air
From tall cigars of Soyer stoves.
  A bugle sounds: stand down the guard:
The day begins in Abbassia.

J. Nugent

The Path of Memory

The smell of new paint, of oil, and of guns,
Of exhausts and diesel oil drums,
The smell of ammo and brass shells in racks,
Of new bogies, snug in their tracks,
  and the smell of the desert too.

The smell of the fire as they rest for the night,
Of a fag and 'The old man's pipe',
The smell of M. and V. and corned beef stew,
Of strong tea, the tank man's brew,
  And the smell of friendship too.

The smell of battle, of the dust and smoke,
Of cordite fumes that choke,
The smell of hot engines, and screeching gears,
Of sweat and growing fears,
  And the smell of heroes too.

The smell of silence, the smell of the night,
The smell of that 'There's something not just right'.
The tank stands silent, the cold wind sighs
And the crew lie inside with sightless eyes,
  And the smell of DEATH came too.

The Bay of Tears

Twenty miles from Mersa, down where the wild waves roar,
I chanced one day on a windswept bay,
   and a man stretched on the shore,
He lay as if perchance he slept,
   Face down in the glittering sand,
A good ten yards[1] from the water's edge,
   He'd won, he'd made the land.

       He'd won, and lost, for in his sleep
       As exhausted there he lay,
       Dreaming perhaps of a far-off land,
          With a sigh he'd passed away,
       He was just one of the Italian dead,
          Swept up on this lonely shore,
       From a crowded troopship I reckon,
          That would sail the seas no more.

       Something made me stop, and think,
       For whatever race he might be,
       Somewhere a mother was praying,
          For her soldier boy over the sea,
       Maybe he had a sweetheart too,
          A sweetheart like you or I,
       Maybe she was writing him letters,
          And wondering why he didn't reply.

       He was just one of the many missing men,
          That never will come home,
       He'll be lying there still, in the bleaching sun,
          Ten yards from the wild waves' foam.

[1] The tide is only between one and two feet in the Mediterranean Sea.

Brendan O'Byrne

Incident at Suez

On seeing a German P.O.W.

I saw a superman today
   Who once walked deep in Europe's blood
With arrant pride and slavish heed
   Of tenets dimly understood
Who once with whip and knout and hose
   Cowed lesser breeds with brutal joy
I saw that superman today
   Salute the Captain's cabin-boy.

Geoff Pearse

At Sea

After the attack
In the warm blue seas
We lazed and lolled
Floating at ease
As the long waves rolled
But men in the morning
Bomb blasted sea choked
Floundered and gasped
In these same blue seas
Some dead some drowned
Some rescued maybe
But we the killers
Lazed and lolled
Floating at ease
As the long waves rolled

1943.

Frank Pike

Storks at Khanaquin

We saw the storks at twilight overhead,
White gleaming as they winged their homeward flight,
And from your voice I knew that dreams long dead
Had for a while returned to mortal light.

How well I understood your mood, my friend,
And shared with you a measure of your pain.
I felt your spirit soar aloft and wend
Its homeward way to Poland once again.

We saw the storks, and I who sympathize
Saw what you saw: forgotten was the sand
Of this wide desert place. I saw the skies
And blessed things of your dear native land . . .
We saw the storks, and I who love you well,
Wept in my heart for you as darkness fell.

Mick Quinn

The Strollers

I sometimes wonder who they were
And why the fates had led them there.
I'd watched them wander into view,
Along that tree-lined avenue.
The Arab, and the little lad
Whose tiny hand clung to his dad.

For two whole days we'd ceased to rove,
Encamped within that olive grove.
Our movements hid from prying eye,
Of Hun-filled danger, from the sky.
A chance to rest, and scrub, and clean,
To dream ALAS! what might have been!

Then WHAM! All merry hell broke out,
As sirens wailed, midst din and shout.
The Stukas dived, their guns ablaze,
Bombs screamed and burst, in smoke-filled haze,
As sudden death did pay his toll,
The Hun zoomed up, in victory roll!

So peace again, as off they sped,
Their pride elated, ego fed.
And there, his blood-soaked body lay,
Bomb-blast had blown his head away,
Unlucky strolling Arab dad,
With lonely, lost, and sobbing lad!

John Rimington

God of the Flies

Mundy, McCall, and Browne, and Saul,
Mulholland, Geer, and Snoddie,
Porton, Horton, and Heptonstall
Are dying in the wadi.

Charlie and Fred are already dead,
And Sergeant Crisp is sleeping
His final sleep beside the jeep . . .
His wife will soon be weeping.

But tell our wives that *Life* survives,
For God is mighty clever.
While He supplies eternal flies
The desert lives for ever.

Yes, tell our wives that *Life* survives.
A clever fellow, God is,
For He supplies eternal flies
To populate the wadis.

The Flap

It pains me deeply to relate
The sad and truly frightful fate
Of James Augustus Livermore,
A driver in the Service Corps.

One day they sent him down the road
Instructing him that he must load
A Honey tank at Alex. Docks
And take it to GAZALA BOX.

Now James Augustus it appears
Had been a soldier several years,
But up to now had failed to see
A sign of any enemy.
He set out, then, with courage high,
Resolved to DO THE JOB or DIE!

He drove by day, he drove by night—
And not a German came in sight.
The nights were cold, the days were hot—
And no one fired a single shot;
'Pooh-pooh' said Driver Livermore
    'If this is called a *total war*
'The thing will last for fifty years . . .'

Now, at that moment, it appears,
The German Field Artillery,
(Who'd shaved, and washed, and had their tea)
Decided that they might as well
Stand To, and fire another shell;
Alas! For James Augustus came
Precisely on their point of aim!

He heard the bang, he heard the whine
And, fearing he was in the line
Of fire, and that he might be trapped,
He did the only thing—HE FLAPPED!

As fast as a homer he shot past ACROMA,
Past MONUMENT CROSSING as quick as a flash.
The road that he took brought him straight through TOBRUK
Where he nearly removed a policeman's moustache!

He was very soon put on the road to GAMBUT
And tore up the road past the Y.M.C.A.
And as he drew near to the town of BARDIA
He nearly wrenched one of the bridges away!

Then he put down his foot, so the men in CAPUZZO
Were hardly aware that he'd come, when he'd gone!
Going down HALFAYA, he burst a rear tyre
But the others stayed up—so he went flapping on!

A few saw him zoom round the bay of SOLLUM,
And he entered the straight with a deafening roar,
And at SIDI BARRANI, not giving a darn, he
Went straight by a Redcap at seventy-four!

He very nigh flew into MERSA MATRUH
The dust fairly blinded the onlookers' eyes
And passing through FUKA, an enemy Stuka
Was left far behind, to the pilot's surprise!

At DABA his load tumbled off on the road.
But, not stopping, he let the thing lie;
And the only thing seen as he passed ALAMEIN
Was a dust-cloud, two hundred feet high!

As he passed EL IMAYID his engine backfired.
HAMMAM went by in a shake.
As he came to the DELTA, the people took shelter
From stones that flew up in his wake!

Then he came to the town; he began to slow down.
And he put on his footbrake at last.
Drawing into the side. 'Good old ALEX!' he cried
Convinced that the danger was past . . .

But my tale is not o'er: as he opened the door
He slipped, and fell out on his head.
The R.A.M.C. brought him hot, sweetened tea,
But too late! James Augustus was DEAD!

Fear

They tell us that the worst we have to fear
Is fear itself. I know no greater lie.
I fear not fear. I fear no fear of fear.
I fear one fearful thing—*I fear to die.*

R. M. Roberts

Old and New

Confusion of the lost days,
Lost the fragments of a dream,
The long dusty marches
On the rolling jolting wheel,
The changing crews,
The actions met and broken
By sudden night retreat,
The endless waiting on unknown sands,
Missing trucks and guns,
Collecting and the losing of the fighting tanks,
The hoarding of the fuel,
The dwindling ammo and the rations,
The losing of the water truck,
Thinning columns and fewer men,
The mockery of the roll
Calling on the names
Of the faces that we knew.
The thirst and the panic
The hunger and uneasy sleep
The dysentery and the fever
Of the sick at heart,
The soldier orphaned from his company.
Now we wait
On the barren sands at Alamein,
Bewildered remnants
The wreckage of our brigade,
Knowing not the reason or the plan
Or what the hour does hold.

There is no future
And the past is gone
Yet the troops that pass through our lines
Are fresh and pressing west.
The spark of hope
In each and every breast
Brings a light to tired eyes
And surges warm the soul
Someone asks
'Is it now July?'
No one knows the date:
Sufficient unto the day.

Charles Robinson

Air Raid

'Aircraft! Stand still you bloody fool.'
Too late. He's seen the movement and glittering in the sun,
The Messerschmidt swoops down with flame-tipped guns.
Around your sprawling form the deadly bullets splatter,
And lying tense fearful of the hideous chatter,
You feel Death's haunting figure stalking near,
Sweat, cold about your body, tingling with fear.

And now the plane has turned to its patrol.
You rise and fingers trembling light a cigarette.
One man lies groaning, arm smashed by a cannon-shell.
You pad a splint and bandage the jagged hole;
Now for the morphine, tell him not to fret,
He's bloody lucky he got off so well.

Alf Samson

Back to the Beginning

Inspired after our cook had been jilted.

Again the same old story
   Of the girl that's left behind,
When her fellow has to go off to a war,
   She writes for him she's yearning,
Living just for his returning,
   But the waiting, it really is a bore.
So just to stop her fretting
   She goes off to a dance,
When the cat's away, the mice will surely play,
   Meets a chap who is most charming,
Makes her heart beat most alarming,
   After that she sees him nearly every day.
Her letters then get scarcer
   To her man across the sea,
He blames the post and swears like bloody hell,
   Then a card he gets to say,
'Darling, let's call it a day',
   He's been jilted and he knows it very well.

Is he sad and broken-hearted?
   Well at first he feels depressed,
But time soon heals the aching pain,
   On his leave he meets a girl,
She sets his heart off in a whirl,
   After that he sees her time and time again.
Now this girl too, had a lover,
   Who sailed across the sea,
To help the mother country fight a war,
   She was the apple of his eye,
But to him she writes goodbye,
   And he knows she doesn't love him any more.
He says his life is ruined,
   For him it is the end,
Until one day he meets a pretty dame,
   No longer he feels blue,
He is sure this one is true,
   After all, *all women really aren't the same,*

And the pretty dame she sighs,
　　As she writes a letter-card,
To a boy, who thought that he and she would wed,
　　She explains her life's her own,
And as he had to roam,
　　There was nothing more between them to be said.
. . . BACK TO THE BEGINNING . . .

Peter A. Sanders

Tripoli

I've a mouth like a parrot's cage
And a roaring thirst inside,
My liver's a swollen, sullen rage—
Last night I was blind to the wide.

Canned as an owl, last night,
Drunk as a fiddler's bitch,
Oiled and stewed and pissed and tight,
Sewn-up, asleep in a ditch.

I can't remember much
And I wouldn't remember more
For vino gave me the golden touch
And a wit like Bernard Shaw's.

I'm rather weak at the knee
And not too strong in the head
But last night angels sang to me
And the world was a rosy red!

NOTE: Military historians are agreed that Eighth Army took Tripoli at its last gasp—we were out of food, cigarettes, tea and almost out of petrol—though it came as a surprise to us to be greeted as 'Liberators'. What historians have tactfully ignored is the sudden introduction of wine in unlimited quantities to men who had existed for months on an inadequate ration of brackish water. The result was the most glorious binge enjoyed by every man from Trooper to Brass Hat, excepting only Monty himself who was wise enough to look the other way.

Thomas Skelton

Seesaw Desert: Back and Forward

We are to withdraw, we are getting out.
You are to proceed to that place there, now!
You are to set up a camp for one hundred bods.
The planes will be in with you almost at once;
When that is done fly back here and happy landings.
We will hold a line just here, this calls for speed.
You will set up defences and defend that front, all round,
Air and ground. Sign here for ammo and petrol!

The heavy planes loaded, bombed up, revved up
Set off with the deep and determined roar,
Clouds of dust, desert throbbing, moving,
Blowing ground crews heads bent against the blast
All for the war of death and noises.

The rattle of trucks and transport
Moving for the flying craft
Servants of the war birds.
Some going, some waiting, and some blown up.

It's on to trucks and convoys off and on again to new places.
Back or forward, it is not retreat, it is withdrawal
Until we advance again. Press on
There is another sand dust bowl in another place.

Alan Smithies

The Mosque

Slim, silver minaret, on fire
Beneath this night of dark desire,
Shimmering in haze throughout a day
Where the world fights, and children play,
Gaunt, ragged, legless, armless, bright
With eyes that scan this mosque tonight,

There is this alien atmosphere,
The sense of some strange secret here
Which keeps these Arab children full
Of craft and mischief, never dull

But equal to most odd occasions,
Parades, strange uniforms, invasions,
Whispered or threatened on the long wave:
They do not care, and Hitler's rave
Means little to them, if at all:
Can this strange mosque hold them in thrall?

I sweep these errant thoughts from me,
Recalling English history;
Was there not here a fair exchange,
The vault for the pier? In spite of change,
This fact is evident. I view
Gothic and Moslem art: these two

In perfect trend and synthesis,
Redeem those fierce Crusades, a friend
Instead of hostile foe, stands here,
Rising into the stars, a spear
Aimed at the crescent of a moon
As Gothic spire at the sun at noon

In an English city, village or town,
And both shall aspire till the sun goes down;
Till the very stars break into space,
Mosque and cathedral, in incredible grace,
Shall still survive, to remind this age
That peace, not war, is our pilgrimage.

Let this tall minaret, this spire
Always reach up, golden as fire
While in our England, Lincoln and York,
Ely and Exeter together talk,
Using the same, immortal speech
As this slim Mosque beyond my reach . . .

Its beauty shall not be surpassed
Till Time, the last iconoclast,
In silence, sweeps its grace away:
But that is another, graceless day . . .
Tonight it fills the eastern skies
With magic, gentling each surmise,
Seeking to echo Christian hope,
While we below strive, guess, and grope . . .

Heliopolis, Egypt; summer evening, 28th June, 1942.

Sidney Stainthorp

To an Unseen Child

Your notion of daddy is still a bit dim,
Though Mummy has told you a lot about him!
I am sorry I have to be so far away,
But I'm doing my best to work for the day
When I help you to learn all those beautiful words
Like seaside and swimming and mountains and birds,
My hope and my prayer are that you never may
Give some words the meanings that we use today,
You'll think of brick walls when you hear the word mortar,
And tanks will be vessels for storing up water,
A line will be something you use with a rod,
And shelling mean taking the peas from a pod,
If this can come true I shall think it worthwhile
To have spent so much time in the land of the Nile.

—Daddy, 1943.

Theodore Stephanides

The Empty Road

The Road is empty now along the coast,
The Road that knew for years the pounding beat
Of tyre and track, the never-ending host
Of marching and of counter-marching feet.
The Road is empty now and, empty,glow
The lifeless sands that shimmer through the haze;
A long black streak its vacant length displays,
Straight as an arrow from a Titan's bow.
The desert stretches in a tawny plain,
An inland twin to ocean's blue domain,
And, taut, between them runs the empty Road.

Empty? Who knows? Perhaps the jackals say:
'We see on moonlight nights a pale array,
A stream that ever flows as once it flowed.'

Gambut, Western Desert; January 1944.

Tobruk: 21st January, 1941

The climbing plume of smoke
That churns into the skies
Proclaims to land and sea
That here a city dies.
A drift of dingy soot
Sifts black in every street,
And the reek of burning oil
Is the incense of defeat.

Trochee to Anapaest

(On board H.M.A.S. *Perth*, South of Crete; 31st May, 1941)

Down in the bowels of the speeding ship
A hoarse loud-speaker droned its dull refrain:
'Warning yellow . . . Warning yellow . . . Warning yellow . . .'
  It babbled on, again, again, again.

Until it was with actual relief
We hailed the change of rhythm when it said:
'Warning yellow . . . Warning yellow . . . Warning yellow . . .
  Air-raid red!'

Western Desert—Two Years After

The ancient melancholy of the moon's
Pocked face peers earthwards with unhoping eyes;
The moon—a tragic mask hung in the skies,
Pale mirror of a myriad buried noons,
Dead light from a dead world. The world below
In that dead radiance lies a lifeless sea,
Its long low swells of immobility
Congealed to silver silence. In that glow
All is pure whiteness rolling to the round
Eternity of the horizon's rim
Ringed by the galaxy's eternal haze.

All is pure whiteness, save alone where strays
One blackness on the sands: the shadow slim
Of a lone cross on a forgotten mound.

Tobruk, 1944.

Duologue

(Between two graves side by side on the battlefield)

'Did *you* slay me, or did *I* strike you dead?
In that mad welter who could ever tell!'
—'It matters not, O Brother, how we fell,
For now we share in concord the same bed!'

E. Storey

The Northumberland Fusiliers

They came from the North of England, where men are strong and free
They came to fight on Libyan sands to defend democracy.
Just a small, but gallant band of men who overcame their fear
'Till now the whole free world proclaims the Northumberland Fusilier.
From Mersa to Agheila they fought the Eyetie host, till overwhelmed by the Hun
They drew back down the coast.
At last they came to Tobruk Bay where they made that gallant stand
And there they fought with hearts so brave till their names rang through the land.
The next great task allotted them was in Bir Hacheim Box
They fought till many dead Fusiliers lay scattered round the rocks.
Again at Fort Capuzzo their name crops up once more,
Again the Germans heard the snarl of the Vickers song of war.
At Alamein they stood at last, though their ranks were sadly depleted,
But you see, they come of English stock, and an Englishman's never defeated.

And so they'll fight on till this war ends, till treacherous
Dictators have ceased to rant,
Then they'll return to their homes and friends
Until then their motto's
>   *Quo Fata Vocant*

>   El Alamein, 1942.

Edward Thoms

Desert Funeral

We wrapped two blankets round him
On a broken cookhouse bench
And with kindly hands we laid him
In a shallow four foot trench.

The Padre was a stranger
And he gabbled hurriedly
Then he departed in his gharry—
He was late it seemed for tea.

We stood a moment silent
While the khamseen whipped the sand
But we came to no conclusion
Though we tried to understand.

We built a mound above him
Which the wind forbade to stay
And laid petrol tins together
To keep piard dogs at bay.

And we left him to the quiet
Of the sand and camel thorn
In the only peace that he had found
Since the day that he was born.

September 1942.

N. J. Trapnell

One Day—Farewell

Land of heat and sweaty pores
Sandstorms, flies and desert sores
Streets of sorrow, streets of shame
Streets without a blinking name
Clouds of choking dust that blinds
Drives the fellows off their minds
Scorching heat and aching feet
Gyppo-guts and camel meat
Arab's heaven—soldier's hell
Land of Pharaohs, fare-thee-well.

Anonymous[1]

Cairo Love Song

Now Johnson joined the Army not so very long ago
    They sent him out to Egypt right away.
He didn't like it first because he couldn't quench his thirst,
    At least he didn't get that rate of pay.
Now one fine day in June, he thought he'd like to spoon
    So to a little Gippo bint he cried:

    Saheeda bint, I love your charming manner
    To walk with you would be my pride and joy.
    Your dainty little yashmak, your finger nails of henna
    Make me say to other bints muskeen: mafeesh falloos.
    Two eyes of fire, that make me stanna swire
    I'd give the world to have you call me dear
      So I think I'll call you Lena
     'Cos I think it rhymes with talla heena
    You're my little Gippo bint, you're quois kateer.

Ali Baba Moorshead

Jerry had us on the run, the news was far from hot,
He had his feet in Egypt and the Sphinx was on the spot,
So Auchinleck despondent sent signals out in sheaves
To Ali Baba Moorshead and his twenty thousand thieves.

So Leslie called his officers and whispered in their ears,
And his message went to Auchy 'Have a spot and drown your fears.
We'll make that blinking Rommel think he's got the desert heaves,
With Ali Baba Moorshead and his twenty thousand thieves.'

So we travelled down from Syria by tank and truck and car,
Leaving Tel Aviv and Haifa and pleasant towns afar.
Both Cairo and Alex were also left to grieve
For losing Ali Baba Moorshead and his twenty thousand thieves.

[1] The following five poems are from unknowns and were circulated hand to hand in Cairo and the Desert.

So we came back to the desert, well known from days of yore,
And stopped the foe at Alamein close by the Meddy shore.
The Eyeties were pathetic, the Huns fell back like leaves
From Ali Baba Moorshead and his twenty thousand thieves.

Now Rommel's got a headache, his tanks can't take a trick,
His Afrik' Corps are not so hot and his air force makes us sick;
His dreams of looting Egypt are ditched and he is peeved
With Ali Baba Moorshead and his twenty thousand thieves.

We have Kittyhawks and Hurricanes and bombers by the score,
Dropping loads on Jerry's bases and rushing back for more.
And it's sure that Rommel's stonkered, whatever plan he weaves
'Gainst Ali Baba Moorshead and his twenty thousand thieves.

M and V[1]

M and V! M and V!
We all like M and V!
Beans, beans, next of kin
From a factory to a tin!

When I awake late at night
Dreaming like I do
It's Commodore Fritz
Giving us the shits
On a tin of M and V.

Oh he shelled us from Benghazi
He shelled us to Bardia
He shelled us from Benghazi
And he shelled us right back here.

M and V! M and V!
We all like M and V!
Beans, beans, next of kin
From a factory to a tin!

[1] M and V: staple diet of tinned meat and veg—liable to explode on heating unless lid pierced. Towel put over against accidents. Also associated with gippy tummy according to vintage. Unfairly?

A Tale of Tobruk

An Australian ballad from the first siege of Tobruk

This bloody town's a bloody cuss
No bloody trams no bloody bus
And no one cares for bloody us
Oh bloody bloody bloody

No bloody sports no bloody games
No bloody fun with bloody dames
This place gives us the bloody pains
Oh bloody bloody bloody

All bloody fleas no bloody beer
No bloody booze since we've been here
And will it come no bloody fear
Oh bloody bloody bloody

The bloody rumours make us smile
The bloody wogs stink bloody vile
The bloody Tommies cramp our style
Oh bloody bloody bloody

All bloody dust no bloody rain
All bloody fighting since we came
This war is just a bloody shame
Oh bloody bloody bloody

The bully makes me bloody wild
I'd nearly eat a bloody child
The salty water makes me riled
Oh bloody bloody bloody

Air raids all day and bloody night
Huns strive with all their bloody might
To give us all a bloody fright
Oh bloody bloody bloody

Best bloody place is bloody bed
With blanket over bloody head
Then they'll think we're bloody dead
Oh bloody bloody bloody

Leave, Compassionate, Children, Production, for the use of

At the end of the war Sir James Grigg, Minister of War, authorized leave for fathering children

In distant lands the stalwart bands of would-be fathers wait,
Certificates to join their mates upon affairs of State,
For para 3 (appendix B) will authorize a chap,
to reproduce, for scheduled use, the species homo sap.

When good Sir James takes down their names in files, to procreate,
This caveat the unborn brat must circumnavigate:
'All who have wives (past thirty-five) and children unbegot
And certified that they have tried, are able, and have not

'May stake a claim. But if their aim is not, or has succeeded,
we can't allow that here and now their services are needed.'
All who apply must certify that they can understand
What lies behind the subtle mind of the Middle East Command.

The Middle East has now released a gallant group of men,
Of future Dads, like Galahads, who have the strength of ten,
And every dame must be the same, for it is infra dig,
That they should dare a child to bear uncertified by Grigg.

1945.

B. Cole

Anniversary

(Many Years Later)

Sadly Alf lifted his glass,
'I don't half feel a silly arse,
What made me come? I don't know,
One more drink, then I'll go.'

'Last year, there was Harry and Fred,
Now one's in dock, the other's dead.
Neither one seemed to have ail'd,
Time's done them where Jerry failed.'

'A damned good mob in forty-two,
Of four platoon us six came through,
When it was over we made this vow,
We'd meet every year in the "Old Dun Cow".'

'I don't suppose I'll come here again,
The last survivor of Alamein,
Don't seem no point in it now,
Drinking alone in the "Old Dun Cow".'

Last lunch with Keith Douglas

Strangely it was only a few days before D-Day, as I discovered later. He had perhaps brought that morning some extra drawings I had commissioned for us as epigraph, shoulder piece or tailpiece for a typical PL[1] illustrated book of his poems and yet another holograph fine copy of a poem I particularly liked, for possible use in the magazine—the last finished poem he wrote, and which he copied on special hand-made paper: 'On a Return from Egypt' was published on the inside back cover of PL 11—and, maybe, another watercolour or additional drawing for his war diary, *Alamein to Zem Zem*, which was also to be published in the PL wide-bodied format I had used for collections of poems illustrated by Barbara Hepworth (Kathleen Raine) and Graham Sutherland (David Gascoyne). I believed in Keith's considerable talents, and he had been awarded the full-blown 'top-drawer' PL treatment, as far as it was possible during those wartime years.

Months back, when he had pulled out from his wallet some photos of frescoes he had vented on the walls of a typical Cairene bistro (I have one of these snapshots, still, somewhere), I had suggested he try his hand at illustrating his two books in colour and black-and-white. His calligraphy evolved into more fluidity and expressiveness over the months (compare Keith's draughtmanship on the cover of Desmond Graham's biography with his frontispiece for *Alamein to Zem Zem*), and he made beautiful drawings and watercolours for a great many poems and his prose work *Alamein to Zem Zem*, an entrancing symbiosis of author and artist.

We had had some sessions over this period discussing the presentation of his poems to a wider audience (he had previously published in Oxford periodicals, two undergraduate anthologies and *Personal Landscape* magazine in Cairo, as far as I was aware) and I had finally convinced him it was best to publish first in several issues of PL—circulation 10,000 per issue at that time—include a selection of his army poems in *Alamein to Zem Zem* and follow up, to make the best impact, with a selection, *Bête Noire*, representative of the best from the juvenilia, Oxford and Army poems. One of my favourite pieces among the juvenilia, written when he was sixteen, concerns Ono-no-komache, the poetess, who sat on the ground among the flowers, in her delicate patterned dress, dreaming of the beautiful Lord Daikoku, and was suddenly confronted by the rotund and drunken Lord in the moonlight, with his round, white paunch:

> But the poetess sat still
> holding her head and making verses:
> 'How intricate and peculiarly well-
> arranged the symmetrical belly-purses
> of Lord Daikoku.'

---

[1] Poetry London.

That morning Keith had also brought all the poems he wished to preserve, in a folder. The several editors he has had (there are three editions of his two books, the first from Editions Poetry London Ltd, the second from Faber and Faber and the third from Oxford) speak of emendations and alterations by other hands than the author's. I feel quite sure this statement is correct since as he hovered, tall over my shoulder at the desk, making suggestions for alternative readings, deletion of entire passages, the welding of several poems into one unit (examples: the two lengthy poems 'The Offensive 1' and 'The Offensive 2' in the O.U.P. edition into one poem, with deletion of the last six lines, and the three poems 'Landscape with Figures 1', 'Landscape with Figures 2' and 'Desert Flowers', in the same edition, into the single unity of 'Desert Flowers', as I had it in the poetry section of the PL *Alamein to Zem Zem*), I had taken the unusual precaution of initialling each suggestion Keith made, after making a note of it. There was a sense of hurry and urgency and after a recital of the names of people who had read his poems, Keith said (I must record, quite immodestly, in view of the present terrible muddle over his poems), 'You are the only editor I can trust.'

He was not satisfied with the state of his poems and for the months he had been in England, in between the Middle East and Normandy, he had slipped out of camp each day in a race against time, working on his poems, never satisfied, arranging every detail. He could always polish and improve; he honed every word; he hated pretence and literariness in his poems. Keith was always his own commander, fighting his private war—even taking over a tank at El Alamein against orders. Now he was finally 'dumping' the entire unfinished business on me. In view of the frenzied creative state he was in, with foreboding of things to come, we had agreed that I would make the final selection for *Bête Noire*, while he settled down to illustrating the poems and diary and writing the title poem for the *Bête Noire* selection which he never completed. As a substitute he handed me that day, three sheets of closely written foolscap, ruled paper on the projected poem which he wanted as a 'Preface' and not 'Note on Drawing for the Jacket of *Bête Noire*' which Desmond Graham has in the text of the Oxford *Complete Poems*. (I took back these three pages of manuscripts, which included passages from *Bête Noire*, to Sri Lanka, since I assumed I would be putting together *Bête Noire* and editing the *Collected Poems* for PL, and later stored them in the basement of Bataan Faigao's house in Mount Vernon, New York with all my remaining books and papers. About four years later when I wished to collect some of my possessions, I was told by Bataan that his entire basement had been flooded. I am still hoping that some of my papers and books, including Keith's manuscripts, have somehow survived, although I was told of total destruction.) This incubus of Keith's urgency had hovered over me for weeks and finally settled on me when he handed over a copy of 'On a Return from Egypt'. I am a rather vague person, who moves by instinct and, being impressed, I simply asked him for a holograph fine copy of the poem:

> . . . For the heart is a coal, growing colder
> when jewelled cerulean seas change
> into grey rocks, grey water-fringe,
> sea and sky altering like a cloth
> till colour and sheen are gone both:
> cold is an opiate of the soldier.

And all my endeavours are unlucky explorers
come back, abandoning the expedition;
the specimens, the lilies of ambition
still spring in their climate, still unpicked:
but time, time is all I lacked
to find them, as the great collectors before me.

The next month, then, is a window
and with a crash I'll split the glass.
Behind it stands one I must kiss,
person of love or death
a person or a wraith,
I fear what I shall find.

We had our lunch at a Polish restaurant in Oxford Street opposite Selfridges. We ate borsch, his favourite dish, and drank Scotch and some grappa. When we had finished he said to me: 'You know, you are going to make a lot of money out of these two books, Tambi.' He knew the money would be passed on to his mother, Jo. He wanted her to be taken care of. That was his chief concern. (When the war was over I gave the original manuscripts to John Waller to sell to the British Museum. The money went to Jo.) On Oxford Street, Keith a rugged, tough man in his officer's uniform, shook me firmly by the hand and looked directly into my eyes. His was always a firm handshake. That was, alas, our last meeting. He disappeared to take part in the Normandy landings and was killed in action, three days after D-Day, while returning from reconnaissance under heavy German mortar fire. A vivid description of the action in which he took part, by Lt John Bethell-Fox, is on record in PL 10.

I kept to my arrangement with Keith and published him in every issue of the magazine, while I had control, and brought out *Alamein to Zem Zem* with many illustrations in black and white and two in colour. The snuffing out of an outstanding talent, the finest in the armed services (there was Alun Lewis also) prompted me to include a larger selection of his Army poems than we had intended in an appendix, in the finalized versions Keith had entrusted to my care.

On my way back to Sri Lanka to raise more capital for Editions Poetry London, the project of Keith's *Collected Poems* was still a distant one. More immediately there was the selection for *Bête Noire* and the proper use of his drawings for the book. My Ceylon trip, however, was a failure. My uncle, who had been negotiating with John Roberts for a majority share holding in Nicholson and Watson, was no longer interested. The war with its big profits was over and he thought it would be more appropriate for him now to subsidize publishing from Sri Lanka.

I went to India seeking capital. Months sped by and I cannot blame my partner, Richard Marsh, for publishing Keith's *Collected Poems*, without consulting me. Cancer had been diagnosed and he had only a few years to live. Keith's *Collected Poems* was the last PL book he published. Nevertheless, I was distressed when, without forewarning, the book arrived in Colombo, although Richard had done the proper thing, reviving interest in Keith's work, and paving the way for the Faber version edited by John Waller, G. S. Fraser and J. C. Hall and the O.U.P. *Complete Poems* edited by Desmond Graham.

And I am grateful to Desmond Graham for the total dedication and hard work he put into the 295 pp. biography *Keith Douglas* (O.U.P.). But the editing of Keith's poems is another matter. Although he gives the impression that he consulted me in preparing *Complete Poems*, in actual fact he had showed me but a single page of typescript with my initialling on it for a change Keith had suggested that morning. Had he produced a xerox of the Douglas manuscripts in the British Library, there would have been no need to bring out an edition of the 'Collected Poems of Keith Douglas' in which 'virtually every poem differs significantly from the form in which it has previously been published,' as the blurb states, a unique event in literary history!

I feel I have betrayed the trust Keith placed in me. An edition of poems in the two books we had envisaged is now overdue, with the inclusion of his illustrations for *Bête Noire*. I invite Desmond Graham, whose intention, I guess, was to preserve all the extant Douglas writings in print, to collaborate with me in publishing a definitive edition of *Complete Poems*.

As you well know, Desmond, I first wrote to T. S. Eliot on this subject in 1947 when the PL edition came out and later to Peter du Sautoy, Chairman of Faber's, on several occasions. You have the scholarship but one must also have poetic sense. The head isn't enough. I won't bore you or the readers of this book with your misreadings of Keith's texts, but here's an example of the way I can help. I reprint one of the pieces from your edition of *Complete Poems* with Keith's emendations. It speaks for itself.

> ⁊ The stars ~~are~~ dead *heroes* ~~men~~ in the sky
> *may well approve* ~~who will applaud~~ the way you die ⌠
> *nor will* ⌷ the ~~easy~~ sun
>   ~~won't criticize or carp because~~ *revile those who survive because*
>   ~~after the death of many heroes~~ *for the dying and promising there was*
> ~~these~~ ⌷ evils remain(.)
>
> lc. When you are dead and the harm done
>   the orators and clerks go on
> ⁊ the ~~fishlike~~ rulers of interims and wars
> ⁊ ~~are as~~ effete and ~~useless~~ as stars. *stable* ⌷
>
> ⁊ The stars ~~are people~~ in ⌷ a house ~~of glass~~ ⁊
> *are the* ~~representatives and~~ heavenly ⌷ of a class *symbols* ⌷
>   dead in their seats,
> *and* ⌷ *officious* ⌷ ⌷ the ⌷ sun ~~officially~~ goes round
>   organizing life; and ~~all~~ he's planned *what* ⌷
> *comes and* ⌷ Time ~~subtly~~ eats.
>
>   *goes round*
> The sun ⌷ ~~the sun~~ and the stars go round
>   the nature of eternity is circular
> *and man must* ⌷ ~~take as long as you like~~ to find
> *spend his life* ⌷ all our successes and failures are similar.

TAMBIMUTTU

(For Keith Douglas's text see pp. 81–2.)

A Tribute to Keith Bullen

K. B. Bullen was not in the Armed Forces and so none of his poems appear in this book. He was, however, the founder of the Salamander Society, without whose help *Oasis* would not have been published. No account of the literary life of Cairo during the 1940s would be complete without due tribute being paid to Keith.

Kinsman of the great Elizabethan scholar A. H. Bullen (1857–1920), Keith dedicated to him his own *Bells on the Breeze and other poems* (E. Menikidis, Cairo, November 1940). Keith himself was also an Oxford man, and numbered among his Jesus acquaintances Lord Louis Mountbatten and Lord Birkenhead. His early promise, encouraged by Lord Northcliffe, was not fulfilled, but his poetry was in full bloom when, as Headmaster of the English Preparatory School, Gezira, he kept open house for his friends and writers in the Forces. Then it was that the Salamander Society was born. A Chestertonian figure, he presided over its Sunday morning meetings with *bonhomie* and taste. The patriotic ring of his wartime sonnets—and he was a master of this exacting verse form—was epitomized in 'We Stand Alone', published in 1942 together with ten other sonnets, including 'Malta' and 'Stand Fast'.

Perhaps Keith's greatest achievements and the best examples of his scholarship are his finely wrought translations from French poetry. His most substantial book is *Charles Baudelaire (Un Poète Maudit)* which contains translations of thirty poems from *Les Fleurs du Mal* and excellent notes, published in 1941. In November 1942 came an evocative translation of De Musset's *Souvenir* and in October 1943 the poems of Albert Samain, the poet of eventide and the dying fall. Keith was preparing a book on Verlaine and working as co-editor with John Cromer on the miscellany *Salamander* (published in London in 1947) when news was received from Cairo of his sudden death on 30th July, 1946.

JOHN BRAUN

Vignettes

Almendro (Denis Saunders)

Action in the Desert

I remember the rain . . . one could hardly say rains . . . and a short while after the whole desert erupted into an incredible display of wild flowers. This was sometime in April 1942 and I was with 40 S.A. Squadron at El Adem. It was a time when very little seemed to be going on; the occasional skirmish along the front, the occasional strafing around El Adem; a time when the sight of the second Lady Tedder's nurses speeding along the Coast Road toward Tobruk caused great excitement. After all, they were the only women we saw in some thirteen months in the desert.

But all the while this euphoria was being indulged in, Jerry was moving men and material way down south and behind our lines. Our reconnaisance planes actually saw these convoys, but Jerry used to cover up the swastikas with coats and wave like mad at the plane so that those who should have known better, thought that these convoys were our own. Then when Jerry struck at Knightsbridge, there he was right behind us as well.

All that day I watched our tanks being pushed nearer and nearer toward us from the rear until at nightfall they were a few yards from my bivvy. I walked over to the line where a young officer, out with his revolver, wouldn't allow me any nearer. I thought him a bit overwrought but since he appeared to have most of his thumb shot away I suppose he was, understandably, irritable.

Next morning our tanks began to push and eventually succeeded in driving Jerry back so that we were able to evacuate the Squadron down the Coast Road. We used to call that road the Switchback. However, some thirteen of us were left at El Adem with two recce planes. We were outside Gen. Gott's 'box' which occupied part of the escarpment and thus entirely on our own. For fourteen days and nights we were subjected to intensified bombing attacks without Jerry doing any real harm to anyone or anything.

One night, the bombing stepping up and machine-gunning sweeping through the camp, I went into the slit-trench. A plane was strafing and the bullets were zing-zing-zinging over my back. I looked up and saw what I thought was a block of flats, from which a rear gunner was firing rearwards. It was a Focke-Wolf 90. But this seemed impossible because Jerry started the war with, I think, six of them. Three had been destroyed by this time and the remainder were supposed to be operating in Europe or the Atlantic. However, I reported the information to H.Q. by 'phone . . . though I doubt anyone believed me. Fortunately, the Australians shot this Focke-Wolf down a few miles south of El Adem during this raid, and that was my vindication.

At the end of fourteen days, we got a message from H.Q. to prepare to run to Tobruk in the morning. They said there would be an attempt to open the road between us and the harbour. This was successful and we all managed to get through. It was a beautiful morning. Those who remember Tobruk will remember the wreck in the harbour to which we used to swim.

One morning while I was in the ops tent, there was a loud commotion of aircraft and rushing out to see what gave, I saw a Spitfire hotly pursued by three Messerschmitts. All were low down on the deck and as they passed overhead one of the Messerschmitts broke off the chase and began a circling climb. I heard only one shot from the anti-aircraft guns and saw the shell penetrate the cockpit and the plane began to smoke. I could clearly see the pilot struggle on to the wing and jump. His chute opened immediately, but he was so low that he was swung violently into the ground and knocked out. We ran toward him and were able to prevent some of our Cape Coloured Corps from driving a pitchfork through the unfortunate pilot, a young Italian who had lately been decorated for bravery by the Germans. He came from Milan, was twenty-one and although he lost the leg through which the shell had passed he survived the affair and was evacuated to Alexandria by Red Cross ship. I got a picture of the event and wrote an article which was published in *Wings* magazine.

It was here at Tobruk, too, that we were first introduced to the whistling bomb. This had a greater psychological than physical effect. But, it sure could make one sweat! I remember nights in the underground palace of the photographic unit with whose members I was particularly friendly. We would get together for tea, cake, and sausages—always the food and the chatting, chatting, chatting. Then along would come the bombers. You could hear them from a long distance away, and finally the whistle of the bomb coming down from 30,000 feet. It took quite a time and you always knew that, if you heard it, it wasn't for you. Nonetheless, the chatting would stop and fists would clench up, the nails digging into the skin of the palm, and the sweat would start coming. Then the sigh of relief as the bomb burst somewhere else, perhaps on someone who hadn't heard it.

We hadn't been at Tobruk overlong when Jerry began his new push and it was decided to evacuate Tobruk of the soft-skin stuff and, keeping only necessary personnel to go into siege. I was asked to remain behind and my colleagues left. This was somewhere about 2 p.m., but by 6 p.m. the Brass had decided to abandon Tobruk and I was informed that I could leave and make my way to my Unit's H.Q. which was at Sidi Azeiz, some eighty miles back. I got into my small L.D.V. and made for the road leading out of Tobruk. It was jammed bumper to bumper with equipment being evacuated. However, I managed to get on the off-side of the traffic and made my way quite quickly toward the intersection with the Coast Road which was also jammed full with stuff coming back from the front. As I arrived at this junction I saw twenty-seven Stukas in formation, like lazy seagulls out for a loll, approaching. What an incredibly beautiful sight the airborne Stuka was.

The Stukas obviously intended to bomb the traffic jam at the intersection and prepared a dive. Fortunately they released their bombs just too soon and these exploded without doing any harm. Had they waited a while, they could have done disastrous damage. Anyway, I persisted with my retreat and through the night I drove—in the dark, of course. Alongside of me I could hear other transport and we were riding off the road across the desert just 'getting away from it all'. At about midnight I ran into a roll of apron wire. It could have been a minefield, but it turned out to be the perimeter of the airdrome used by 24 S.A. Squadron. Well, I didn't know this until morning, and being tired I decided to lay me down to sleep. This was probably as dangerous a decision as any, as dangerous as going through a minefield what with all the transport riding hell-bent without lights every whichway. But I was young, and, as I said, tired, and in spite of all the noise and the bombing I slept the sleep of innocence quite unaware that I was participating in the making of history, that I was taking an active part in the Great Gazala Gallop, an event that would one day stand side by side with Thermopylae, Hastings, Waterloo, Delville Wood and a host of other victories and defeats with which man has endangered, but also enriched, his life.

David Burke

My Personal Oasis

It was my own happenstance oasis—an occasional escape from the steamy and aromatic afternoon streets of Cairo—that brought me, happily, to the real *Oasis*, the one contained within the covers of this book.

I met Denis Saunders—Almendro in verse—and Victor Selwyn. They, and some of the poets whose work is published here, would gather on quiet afternoons at a cool cafeteria in the Victory Club to drink coffee, munch on sandwiches, smoke Cape to Cairo cigarettes—which the South African Army introduces to the Middle East —and talk.

These were delightful interludes during which the war, the noise and smells and frustrations of Cairo—and some of its pleasures, too—seemed as far away as do the searing sands and blazing sun in the shady coolness of a desert oasis.

We rarely talked about our extra-oasis activities. The exceptions were happenings that soared above the banalities of shop-talk to raise a chuckle or chill a spine, experiences that deserved to be shared. I can recall only one of mine that genuinely deserves retelling—a minor exploit, in fact, but one which left behind a question I still hesitate to answer assertively.

The time was the edgy days before the El Alamein assault, with Rommel and his Afrika Corps leaning heavily upon the gates of Alexandria. Egypt was technically a neutral country which had been press-ganged into Allied service. Its Western Desert had already long been a battlefield, criss-crossed by Allied advances and retreats. But the German threat had never come so close to an Egyptian city.

The people, by and large, remained loyal but Egypt had started to crumble from the top. King Farouk, our intelligence had learned, had been planning to flee to enemy asylum, helped by some of his ministers. The British reacted sharply. Tanks ringed Abdin Palace, in Cairo, to lock Farouk in, and Prime Minister Ali Maher Pasha had been flung into gaol *pour encourager les autres*.

I had not been long under Major Sansom's command, 259 Intelligence Section, when I was assigned to maintain surveillance on Ali Maher's brother-in-law, Thoma Pasha. I was told: 'This is only a precautionary measure. We have no solid grounds for suspecting Thoma. All the indications, indeed, suggest there are no grounds at all. But we have to make sure of everyone who might be involved in the conspiracy.'

Our section was too thin on the ground to set up the kind of round-the-clock surveillance practised by MI5. But we used to regard MI5 as rivals and would go to almost any lengths to handle cases ourselves and pass on completed dossiers. Thoma Pasha was a case Sansom felt we could handle.

I was to tail him whenever he left his home—ironically, a villa only a few hundred yards from our own in Garden City—and report on every place he visited and everyone he met. My cover for this assignment was that of a British merchant seaman on leave in Cairo while his ship underwent minor repairs.

This was my first surveillance, my first opportunity to put into practice the training we had had at Matlock. But once again any illusions about becoming a James Bond prototype were soon dissipated.

Thoma Pasha, a well-dressed, distinguished aristocrat with a thick head of greying hair, left his villa every morning at ten. His chauffeur would drive him to the broad downtown Fouad-al-Awal boulevard—the Champs Elysees of wartime Cairo—and leave him at the same sidewalk café near Opera Square. A marble-topped table was reserved for him permanently and galabieh-clad waiters would hurry to greet him at his limousine and see him seated.

The morning newspapers of the day would already be awaiting him at his table, and beside it, a naghilé, the water-pipe much favoured by Egyptians. As soon as Thoma Pasha sat down, a waiter would bring him a tiny cup of Turkish coffee, and a galabieh-clad boy with a crocheted skullcap would busy himself with the pipe—attaching a new mouthpiece to the tube that snaked up from the glass water bowl, placing a chunk of tobacco into the cup atop the bowl, and lighting it with a red-hot coal as the pasha took the first satisfying pulls at the water-cooled smoke.

Then Thoma Pasha would read his newspapers, occasionally sweeping the surrounding kaleidoscopic scene with mild interest. His large brown eyes, above a straight nose and neatly-trimmed full moustache, were as gentle as a doe's.

At exactly 1 p.m., his chauffeur would arrive to drive him home for luncheon and his siesta. He never left his home till six, when the evening began to cool. And then he would be driven, on alternate days, to the Semiramis Hotel in Garden City or to famed Shepheard's Hotel, where he would go to his regular corner table in their elegant bars.

After sipping two Scotches with water and ice, he would return home for dinner. About once a week, he would dine at the home of one of several friends.

That was the limit of his activity. It made surveillance both simple and difficult.

The first day, seated in my Austin 8 a little distance from his home, I followed him through the hooting, darting traffic, overwhelmed with self-gratification for the brilliant way I was carrying off my assignment. When his chauffeur dropped him off at the Fouad-al-Awal café, I swiftly parked around the next corner, watching him in my rear-view mirror lest this was some trick to shake his tail.

Pleased that I had succeeded with Phase One, I found myself a table from which I could watch him—I hoped—unobtrusively, and spent a listless morning sipping six sweet coffees to his one, pretending to be fascinated by a street scene I already knew by heart, feigning indifference, and waiting for something to happen—the subtle courier bringing a message, the contact passing a signal, anything that would put some meat into a report.

But despite my eagerness to be suspicious of the slightest sign of a contact absolutely nothing happened. I had to rule out the waiters, the *naghilé* boy, even the newspapers which were at Thoma Pasha's table before his arrival.

When his limousine collected him, I followed him back to Garden City and spent a dreary, sweaty afternoon in my car far enough from Thoma's corner villa to be out of sight, near enough to watch the gates, ready to move off immediately. But there were no visitors, no movement at all, until the limousine took him back downtown for his evening Scotch.

He was obviously known at both officers-only bars—the Semiramis and Shepheard's—as I myself was. For these were two of the bars our section spot-checked for British officers involved in careless talk—another routine duty that took up much of our time.

After three days I was convinced of two things: first that I could hardly continue turning up at the same places at the same times every day without Thoma Pasha getting suspicious of me and thus making surveillance pointless; second, that our potential suspect was living a quiet and innocent life. There seemed to be only one way to continue watching him without arousing Thoma's curiosity, and I felt it might work.

I suggested to Alfie Sansom that instead of keeping up this farcical tail, I should try to find an excuse for a direct approach and getting to know him. Sansom thought that, properly handled, my plan might work. I was allowed to give it a try.

Next morning I made my opening move. After following his car downtown and parking my own, I kept him under observation for some fifteen minutes from across the street, then walked over to the café terrace. Deliberately, I walked slowly past his table as he looked up from his newspaper, caught his eye, smiled, and wished him a good morning. He smiled back and returned the greeting, in English, with only a trace of the gutteral Egyptian accent.

'Excuse me, sir,' I said earnestly, 'but haven't I seen you here before?'

'Oh, yes,' he replied, 'I come here every morning. And you have come here also the past few days, I believe.'

My heart tightened as I shifted into higher gear. This was precisely the situation I had hoped to force. How it worked out would depend on how well I played the game. I promptly moved into my cover story, explaining that I was a British merchant seaman off a cargo vessel held up for repairs in Port Suez. My skipper, I said, had allowed me a few days leave in Cairo, and I mentioned a pension not far away as my temporary abode.

I was not surprised when he invited me to join him at his table and called the waiter to bring me a coffee, having first asked if I wished it sweet, medium or without sugar. Soon we were talking about Cairo and how little I knew the city, of how fascinating I found it, and how much I enjoyed sitting at this café terrace just watching the colourful city parade pass.

My plan could not have worked out better. Despite the twenty-five or thirty years difference in our ages, he appeared to enjoy talking to me and even told me he enjoyed young people. As we chatted I gave him many openings for expressing his feelings about the war, the Western Allies, the Egyptian king and his imprisoned brother-in-law. If he genuinely were involved in Ali Maher's conspiracy, I reasoned, sooner or later some clue would emerge.

When his chauffeur collected him for lunch I politely asked if he would care to join me for dinner.

'I always eat at home with my family,' he told me. 'But it is my habit to take a Scotch or two after sundown. I shall be honoured if you will join me.'

I watched him drive off, then drove my own car back to Garden City. Sammy was in his office and I reported on my morning. He was as pleased as I, and it was agreed that I would actually move into the pension I had named and use taxis in future instead of the car, which did not quite fit my cover.

For the next week, Thoma Pasha and I met morning and evening by appointment, the most agreeable tailing job I have ever had. We grew extremely friendly as the days passed, and our conversation ranged over the broadest of spectrums. At the same time, I managed to keep an eye on his home to make sure there were no suspicious contacts outside the hours we spent together. Soon, there was no longer any reason to doubt his loyalty. On one occasion, he even deplored Farouk's attempt to flee and the disgrace of his brother-in-law. I noted this fact, but showed no undue curiosity. Every opening I gave him to probe for information about my imaginary convoy duties, my feelings about the war, or other sensitive matters, he simply ignored.

Neither Sammy nor I felt there was any longer the slightest reason to keep Thoma Pasha under observation, but he was still a prominent Egyptian and a useful contact. And I was enjoying the hours I spent with him more and more.

He suggested places he thought I would be interested to visit. He offered me his limousine for a run out to the pyramids. One night he graciously accepted an invitation to dine with me. Ours had become a friendship and it grew steadily.

Too soon, in many ways, it reached a climax. We were sitting on the café terrace one Friday morning when he exhaled a plume of tobacco smoke, looked me straight in the eyes, and asked:

'Tell me, Mr David' (as he called me), 'what are your feelings about marriage? Have you ever considered it?'

A little taken aback by the earnestness of his question, I mumbled something banal about there being a war, my youth, the fact that there was plenty of time for me to worry about making lifelong pledges.

'That depends,' he said, smiling. 'I was about your age when I married, and I have never regretted it.'

He let me change the subject but I should have known him better than to believe him guilty of idle curiosity. Just before we parted he said something which, at the moment, I considered innocent and quite unconnected.

'Do you have any special plans for tomorrow afternoon, Saturday?' he asked, and when I said I had not, 'Then will you do me the honour of coming to my home for tea?' I thanked him, and he added with a smile, 'I have a surprise for you.'

I continued to suspect nothing unusual although I realized the invitation to his home was a major compliment.

At the appointed hour next day I climbed out of a cab at his villa and was let in by a servant. Thoma Pasha was in the hall, hand outstretched, to welcome me and lead me into a cool sitting room traditionally furnished with multi-cushioned couches, low, beaten-brass tables, thick carpets, and glass-fronted cabinets filled with collector's pieces in marble, jade, porcelain, ivory and precious metals.

He led me to a couch, sat at another placed at right-angles, and we were immediately served tea by a tall, be-fezed Nubian in a striped silk *galabieh* with a broad scarlet sash at his waist. A few minutes passed and an attractive, elegant woman in her late forties and dressed in high European fashion swept into the room. Thoma Pasha and I rose to our feet and with old-world courtesy he introduced his wife. I had been in Egypt long enough to realize how high a compliment this was. Indeed, I assumed that this was the surprise he had referred to. It could easily have been.

But I was wrong again. The three of us exchanged small talk for a while. Then Thoma Pasha turned to his wife, smiled almost boyishly, and said: 'My dear, I think it may be time to present Mr David with his little surprise'.

Mme Thoma chuckled musically, excused herself and whisked out of the room. Two minutes later she returned—her arms around the shoulders of two of the loveliest creatures I had ever laid eyes on. Both had shoulder-long jet black hair, enormous lustrous brown eyes, alabaster complexions, young but slender and shapely figures. For a moment I was overwhelmed.

The two girls smiled at me without embarrassment. In fact I sensed that they were amused by mine. Suavely, Thoma introduced them as his nieces, sisters, home for the holidays from one of Switzerland's exclusive finishing schools. They were, he said, sixteen and seventeen years old.

Mme Thoma and the two girls sat on a couch facing mine and accepted cups of tea. Nibbling on sweet biscuits, they launched into a lively conversation about many things in general and nothing in particular. I could not recall the details that night and my memory is even cloudier now. I was overwhelmed by their bell-like laughter, the melody in their young voices, their incomparable sophistication, their charm and wit.

We were together perhaps for fifteen minutes, although when their aunt indicated it was time to leave and we all stood up and shook hands it seemed they had passed in a subliminal flash of mini-seconds' duration. Thoma Pasha and I were alone again and we sat down.

'Beautiful, aren't they?' he purred. And when I expressed my breathless agreement, he went on to extol their intelligence, their fluency in five languages, the gentleness of their characters, the liberal but traditional upbringing they had had.

And then he subtly changed the subject, and we talked of other things until it was time for me to leave.

The following morning we met as usual on the café terrace at Fouad-al-Awal. For days, he had given up reading his newspapers from cover to cover. He would put them aside when I arrived and, I guessed, read them at home in the afternoon. And we would talk.

Today, he opened the discussion with unusual pointedness.

'Well, Mr David,' he said, his eyes twinkling, 'have you given any further thought to the subject of marriage.'

Guessing what was to come, I started to stammer but he gave me no chance. He returned briskly to the attack.

'I am referring, of course, to my nieces,' he said. 'I can think of no better future for them than to become British subjects.' And when I opened my mouth to speak he stayed me with a raised hand. 'I don't expect an answer here and now. But I urge you to give the matter careful thought. They will, I am certain, make excellent wives and companions. Moreover, each has a dowry of five thousand pounds.'

Still gasping under this onslaught, I said the first convincing thing that occurred to me, and which I prayed would not give offence.

'They are beautiful and intelligent,' I said. 'And I am deeply honoured by your offer. But there is one difficulty that seems insurmountable.'

He raised a bushy eyebrow and asked what that was.

'I would never be able to decide which one to choose,' I said.

'My dear Mr David,' he said smoothly. 'First of all, should you marry my nieces you would naturally be expected to convert to Islam. You see, you are not being asked to choose. I am suggesting that you marry both of them.'

Except for the wild pounding of my heart, the wild thoughts that chased each other like Cairo traffic through my fuddled brain, the story ends there.

I promised, hypocritically I am afraid, to consider and let him know. Instead, I hurried back to Sammy, told him the story—to his unwelcome, uproarious amusement—and requested that I be relieved of the Thoma Pasha assignment. This was granted, and I never saw Thoma again, except from a distance—a distance I was careful to maintain.

But still today, all these years, countries and lives later, I still recall that tea-time meeting as vividly as though it had just taken place. I still recall my youthful embarrassment at the pasha's offer.

And I still sometimes wonder, in moments of fantasy, whether the decision I took in Cairo was right or wrong.

Louis Challoner

With the Guns[1]

On 28th May, 1942, we camped within sight of Halfaya Pass and crossed the Pass on to the Axis Road the following morning. This area must have been held by Italians and taken from them by South Africans and New Zealanders. We deduced this from the souvenirs we picked up by the roadside or in the slit-trenches we dived into when enemy planes attacked the traffic strung out along the road. If German or United Kingdom troops had been here they had taken everything away with them when they left.

We saw no evidence of recent rain but there was abundant vegetation close to the

---

[1] These are extracts from his war diary.

sea and among the rocks at the sides of the Pass there were masses of red, purple and golden flowers. Crouched beneath a rocky outcrop I found a long-spurred violet which I picked and pressed between the pages of my pocket diary. It was my wife's birthday.

Of course, Jerry was not unaware of the fact that troops were on the move and his bombers visited our lines in the night. Luckily we had kept strictly to the instructions given to us before we left Almaza[1]. No lights at all were to be shown, spacing of vehicles was adequate and even moving about kept to a minimum. Our A.A. unit put up a reassuring barrage and we suffered no damage at all on this occasion. After all the excitement, we pulled the blankets over our heads and slept well.

★   ★   ★

Our record-breaking dash across the desert had sadly depleted our supply of water, and on the morning of 1st June everyone who could be spared was sent off in two three-tonners and with every available container, to find a well. According to the map it was not more than thirteen miles away, but the officer leading the column got somewhat lost and before noon we were in a hopeless position, miles apparently from where we should have been and bogged down in a blinding sandstorm. The wind was blowing violently and the sun was obscured with a fine white dust which made it appear, when we could see it at all, like a pale blue disc. Skin, as well as eyes, began to smart and painful tears cut rivulets in the caked sand on one's cheeks. The flying dust charged the metal parts of vehicles with electricity so that if one touched them there was a disconcerting shock. Worse still, shorts became frequent and some engines stopped and refused to start. The radio, with which we had intended to keep in touch with Battery H.Q., packed up altogether.

It was five hours before the wind dropped and slowly the airborne particles descended sufficiently for us to see where we were. A number of tanks were close by and the commander of one of them directed us to the waterhole. It was less than four hundred yards away. Two days ago the well had been in the hands of the Germans and none of the working parts had been left intact. The masonry had been broken and tumbled down the shaft so it was necessary to climb down to clear out the debris and then to lower four-gallon cans by a rope, fill them and haul them up again by hand. The water was cloudy and brackish but definitely better than none at all. At the moment none at all was the only alternative. There were smashed Jerry tanks nearby and a disabled anti-tank gun with an unburied dead gunner lying alongside. 'We're lucky they didn't drop his body down the well,' said someone, 'they dropped a dead camel down one near Agheila—God, didn't it stink!' 'Camels stink, even when they are alive,' said someone else and no one disagreed with him.

When they got back to their own lines, the water was distributed at the rate of four pints to each man and the drivers were soon preparing an extra brew-up to take to the gun crews. The tea was most acceptable although something in the water caused the tinned milk to curdle and sink to the bottom of our mugs into a gummy mass.

For tea 'mashing' two non-returnable four-gallon petrol cans had been made into a

---

[1] Royal Artillery Base, Cairo.

'kettle' and a fire-bucket[1]. The kettle was cut down to about eight inches deep, the sharp edges turned in and a piece of wire hooked into opposite corners to serve as a handle. The fire-bucket was also cut down to about six inches and pieces of the sides turned in to provide a platform for the kettle. Several holes had been made in the sides to provide air and half a shovelful of sand douched with a small quantity of petrol was the usual fuel. Theoretically wood, twigs and branches of camel-thorn only were supposed to be used and on at least one occasion a memorandum was received from H.Q. that in the interests of economy, petrol was on no account to be used in this way. If a memorandum was issued suggesting possible alternatives it did not catch up with our Battery.

★   ★   ★

The enemy attack did not materialize after all, but on 5th June we were heartened to see a Brigade of Light Tanks move into the Box and take up positions to our right. They were the rather high Stuarts, noisy vehicles of American make and called 'Honeys' by the men. We did not envy their crews as, even to our inexperienced eyes, they did not appear to afford much protection against armour-piercing ammunition. Also they were quite high and Mr Peters showed some anxiety until they had taken up position well below the crest and to our rear. In spite of this their arrival had not passed unnoticed by the enemy and he proceeded to plaster the area with H.E.[2] No damage was done and we replied on and off all day. The O.P.[3] reported successful shooting, but we noticed that no claims were made that we had hit any guns or anything else of importance. Actually the 105 mm guns that Jerry was using were well out of range for the 25-pounders, and we had no super-charge ammo. at this stage. From fifteen thousand yards he could land shells in our wagon-lines with impunity and it was remarkable that he had so little success.

★   ★   ★

June 14th, 1942: It was hard on the drivers but we kept going after leaving the last position and kept to the desert until within reach of Tobruk where we formed up on the road in 'column of route'. The going was much smoother now and we bowled along merrily, some chaps actually nodding off to sleep. About two miles outside the town, however, we suddenly came under attack from four Stukas which swooped down on the column out of the newly-risen sun and took us by surprise. Luckily the drivers remembered the drill devised just for this emergency and scattered off the road to widely separated stations among the rocks and stones. The bombs came down on a bend in the road further forward, and we escaped scot free.

We now understood why the older hands among the officers preferred to travel across the desert in open formation rather than keep to the road. It was uncomfortable, wasteful of petrol and energy, and much slower, but it was safer by far! The Stukas, or any other enemy aircraft, had only to line up on the road and swoop down on us from behind or out of the sun and scoring a hit was merely a

---

[1] The 'Benghazi cooker'.
[2] H.E. = High Explosive.
[3] O.P. = Observation Point.

matter of letting the bombs go at the right moment. The worst places to come under attack were where the road ran through an area of soft sand. There the vehicles were likely to shudder to a hopeless stop as soon as they ran off the tarmac and there was nothing the crew could do except jump out and scatter among the dunes. When the danger was past, and it rarely lasted more than a few frantic moments, we ran back to the quad, threw down the shovels and sand channels and by every means at our disposal got the vehicles, limbers and guns back on the road or on to firmer ground.

Molly Corbally

Nursing in a Sandstorm

A picnic on a beach is rather fun, and the gritty taste of sand in the sandwiches is all part of the holiday. Sand in one's sandals is a velvety lining, and sand trickling down one's bare back is a soft, delicious tickle. I can enjoy a picnic on the beach as much as the next person, but the gritty taste and feel of the sand brings back memories of the Egyptian desert.

While our men were up in the desert fighting Rommel and his Afrika Corps, at the Base Hospital we were fighting our own war, against death and disease, heat and flies, and sand. Most of the time, the sand stayed put, and on it we pitched our tents and built our huts, and in it we dug our air-raid trenches. But, from time to time, a high wind would blow across the desert, whipping up the sand, which swirled and eddied, a thick yellow cloud. It rendered visibility as poor as a thick London fog. It penetrated everywhere. One breathed sand, one swallowed it, one's eyes and ears and nose were filled with it. One's hair was matted with sand. One's face and arms were yellow and sore from the tiny gritty particles which penetrated the pores of the skin.

These sandstorms would last, on and off, for weeks at a time, until the sand was inches thick in every corner of the hospital buildings, had penetrated every cupboard and drawer and suitcase, had seeped into mattresses, books, watches, and had discoloured all the linen, scratched the furniture, and eroded the metals. The hospital, at such times, was full of sick and wounded men. Men with injured lungs breathed in sand with the hot fetid air of the *khamseen*. There was no way of protecting them. Throats became inflamed, and eyes infected. Irritated skin lesions broke down and ulcerated. Raw wounds remained untouched. We didn't dare take down the dressings, but padded and packed and rebandaged as the pus and blood oozed through. Miraculously they healed, and we learnt to leave dressings alone for a few days, even in clement weather. If we knew a sandstorm was brewing up, many injured limbs would be encased in plaster as an added protection against the infiltration from the enemy.

Sandstorms came with the hot winds of summer, and the cold winds of winter, but the worst one we experienced was in 1940, just before Christmas. I was on night duty, and the storm had been teasing us, on and off, for weeks. That night it reached gale force, and tore through the hospital, blowing down tents, smashing huts like plywood, tents and huts full of ill and wounded men. They lay, unprotected by even the canvas walls against the swirling sand and the bitter cold, endangered by the weight of the sagging canvas and falling tent-poles. Hurricane lamps were blown out, and we struggled in the dark, falling over guy-ropes, enmeshed in flapping canvas. While a working party secured a few tents in the more sheltered part of the compound, we wheeled beds and chairs and stretchers through the blizzard, guided by torches. By torchlight, the worst of the suffering was alleviated, injections given, oxygen administered, blood transfusions checked, eyes swabbed, and dressings repacked, although there was hardly room to move in the overcrowded tents. All the oil heaters had been turned out as soon as the tents started to disintegrate, so extra blankets were found for the most needy, and hot drinks were brewed to counteract the cold and thirst engendered by the chill sandy trip across the camp.

The storm blew itself out before dawn, and daylight revealed the extent of the devastation. It also revealed row upon row of yellow-skinned, sandy-haired men, buried in sand, like a close-packed holiday crowd on Brighton beach. It wasn't long before the roar of jeeps and the sound of hammering announced the arrival of a working party from the Base Depot. Then the day staff arrived, comparatively clean and fresh, and we stumbled, weary, bruised, and dejected across the calm desert, to find our own beds sagging under their load of sand, which we were too exhausted to remove.

After all, a great many people pay a great deal of money every summer just to stretch out on the sand, and go to sleep!

Erik de Mauny

Silver Fern Leaf up the Blue

A few random recollections.

The first is of arriving at Suez with a mixed convoy of New Zealand and Australian troops, after several blissfully unmemorable weeks over seas where dolphins frolicked, and then a long, parched, jolting train journey across the desert to the New Zealand base camp at Maadi, a few miles south of Cairo.

By the time I reached the Middle East, the 2nd N.Z. Division was fighting a fierce rearguard action in Crete and suffering heavy casualties. Survivors who reached the coast were evacuated by the Royal Navy. But many were still straggling down from the mountainous interior and had to take refuge where they could. Cretan villagers gave them shelter and on suitably dark nights, sent them off in *caîques* and small fishing boats. Many of them eventually made their way back to Egypt and to the base at Maadi, where a special interrogation unit, of which I was briefly a member, questioned them about their experiences, our aim being to pinpoint the German positions and possible areas of future resistance. They were full of praise for their Cretan friends and tended to shrug aside their own part in these otherwise unchronicled escapes.

I mention this episode only because, in retrospect, I see in it the first foreshadowing of what later became for me the dominant image of the New Zealand Division in the Middle East. With its silver fern leaf emblem, it was not quite like any other division.

Others undoubtedly fought as hard in the various campaigns in the Western Desert, 'going up the blue' as it was called, although I think only the Desert Rats of the 7th Armoured Division spent as much time there. But the New Zealanders' approach to the conflict was, to say the least, informal. They had a deep-rooted distaste for the ceremonial and formality of life at the base, with its kit inspections and square bashing, from all of which the eddying fortunes and dizzy improvisations of the desert war provided welcome relief; indeed, one sometimes got the impression that New Zealand front line units were fighting a private war entirely for their own private gratification.

Of course, as the war dragged on, it produced its inevitable toll of the maimed and the disabled, the sand-happy and the shell-shocked. But in general, I think the Kiwis continued to draw deep satisfaction from this image of themselves as being somehow apart. They took pride in being totally self-reliant, and it was by a process of natural gravitation that a number of them managed to wangle secondments to such unconventional formations as the Long Range Desert Group, with its extended forays far behind the enemy positions.

Many years later, Montgomery remarked that the chief characteristic of the New Zealanders was their craving for the wide open spaces. It is said that when he paid his first visit to General Freyberg at N.Z. Advance Headquarters, two soldiers sauntered by without a blink of recognition. This brought a tart enquiry from the newly-arrived C-in-C Middle East: 'Don't your men ever salute?' 'Not often,' replied 'Tiny' Freyberg, 'but if you wave, they sometimes wave back.'

Apart from a small nucleus of regular officers, the 2nd N.Z. Division was entirely composed of volunteers. Most of the men knew each other personally, coming from the same farms and small country townships, being drafted into the same units and remaining with them throughout the war: all of which made for a close-knit, family atmosphere.

Against this background, I felt myself to be something of a rootless cosmopolitan. My first posting, in 1940, was to a medical unit, the 7th Field Ambulance, with which I spent some months in the Pacific. Arriving in the Middle East, I transferred to clerical duties at the Maadi Base H.Q., an agreeable interlude since the work was unexacting and left plenty of time for exploring the mysteries of Cairo. Then, back to the medical corps again, this time to the 1st N.Z. Casualty Clearing Station, which had its own emergency operating theatre, blood-bank and dispensary, and followed closely behind the forward troops in the advance from Alamein.

In Tobruk, we came to a halt, encircled by a ring of Rommel's armour. The harbour was full of sunken ships. We dug slit trenches on the escarpment, shivered through the cold nights, and subsisted on a monotonous diet of bully beef, hard tack biscuits and chlorinated water. After two or three weeks of this, I went down with severe jaundice, was despatched back to Alexandria on the hospital ship *Somerset* (later sunk by enemy action), and left the New Zealand Division altogether for more than a year, on a secondment to G.H.Q. Cairo, where I ran the French section of the Radio Monitoring Service. So it was only after the division had moved to Italy, and after the great battles of the Salerno and Monte Cassino and the Gothic Line, that I rejoined it once more, this time to work in the Intelligence Section, interrogating German prisoners, as we slowly pushed northwards over the river barriers of the Adriatic front.

In the Casualty Clearing Station at Alamein, as a theatre orderly, I watched the New Zealand doctors perform prodigies of battle surgery while the ground quaked under the impact of incoming high explosives and the light from our mobile generator danced and dimmed over a shambles of gaping wounds. But wounds were only one form of attrition in the desert. Flies descended in plagues of biblical proportions, heavy chlorination made the water ration almost undrinkable, and when the *khamseen* blew, its fine dust infiltrated the body's most intimate recesses, setting up colonies of desert sores. A favourite site for these was under the foreskin, which was not only painful for the sufferer, but effectively put him out of action. As a result, many units found themselves seriously under strength, and urgent demands for a solution began to flow in from Divisional Headquarters. Finally, one young M.O. decided on drastic action. Equipping himself with a sharp scalpel and an ample supply of novocaine, he set up a trestle table outside the R.A.P., and invited the members of the daily sick parade to step forward for immediate circumcision under local anaesthetic, proving that this was not such a fearsome operation as it sounded by first performing it on himself. I was not present on that memorable occasion, and owing to the prudent foresight of my parents would have been in no danger of becoming a participant, but it certainly has an air of complete authenticity. Some of the Kiwis I knew were capable of even more intrepid gestures.

I have singled out some of the distinguishing features of the New Zealand Division (without even mentioning the special ice-cream factory at Maadi, the barrels of *toheroa* soup for Christmas, the acute laconicisms of everyday New Zealand speech in which anyone showing unusual activity could be described as being 'as busy as a one-armed paperhanger with the crabs' and anyone nearing death's door as being 'a bit crook', or the matter-of-factly tender ministrations of the New Zealand nurses at the Helwan base hospital); but it was not, of course, exempt from the fate of armies everywhere, which is to endure long periods of intense boredom, interspersed with lurid flashes of intense action, to mutter mutinously about the general conduct of the war, to resort to every form of low cunning in the pursuit of creature comforts, and to fill the rare periods of leave with epics of debauchery.

The images that return, however, are not all of violence, of squalor and discomfort. There were also nights of music at the Victory Club in Cairo; memorable drinking sessions in congenial company in a certain Greek bar off Sharia Kasr-el-Nil, where a boy in a soiled *galabieh* would offer us *beqafiq*, baby quail, roasting on a red-hot brazier; long walks along the escarpment above Maadi where I would try in imagination to project myself back into the Egypt of the Pharoahs; Sunday sessions[1] of poetry and pink gin with Keith Bullen at the Gezira Preparatory School and the Anglo-Egyptian Union.

Wilfred Owen said the poetry is in the pity: but that was in another war. This later war was one of great distances and rapid movement, and for me the poetry came when least expected, in the interstices of a generally agitated existence, in the rush of sudden contrasts, and in the recognition that, whatever else changes, one's own mortality does not.

---

[1] The Salamander Society.

Norman Hudis
The Cairo-California Axis

Questions 1 and 2: Are they so alike? Was I drawn here to Hollywood as much by palm trees as by professional opportunity?

It is possible. To the British, for a few Pax-y generations, sub-tropical climate satisfied just that kind of double need. Out, walking his mad dog or no, in the noonday heat, the o'erseas, open-neck-shirt Briton simultaneously revelled in the contrast with Motherland mufflers, and in the manful burden of necessary exile—life seen from the tea-plantation bungalow's verandah, or through the pink-wall-slit of a McTaggart fort. Over it all, the sun never relaxed: a baking, steaming Empire—Maugham, noon and night.

Twenty-three years separate my landing in Egypt from my first touchdown at Los Angeles Airport. The similarities are considerably closer.

The boy of 19, bedraggled in R.A.F. boots, kneecap-chafing shorts, steel-rimmed bug-eye-glasses and ceremonial topee one-quarter size too big, gawked at the sand and the palm trees and sensed that Torquay would never look the same again. Doing a duty, taking a tiny role in a huge piece of history—yes: but ignobly, self-huggingly happy to be doing so *there*—so unmistakably *abroad*, so purely foreign and exotic. And hot. I bet they're freezing back in Blighty, Ginger, and look at us—walking on the shady side of Sharia Suleiman Pasha to keep cool. In November.

The 42-year-old, plumping and horn-rimmed, due to confer with real, live Hollywoodians, overtured this programme by gawking at the sand and the palm trees. Pursuing the elusive, capricious zephyr of Career, seeking to grow as a writer—yes: but already hoping it would all work out *here* because it was so undeniably foreign, and exotic. And hot. We'll have lunch in the garden, shall we, Rita? In February.

Certainly would I have gone, if sent, as gladly as anyone, to Norway or Northern Canada, in World War II. But it was for the Middle East that I volunteered. Such was the intensity of the pull toward its comfortably British-dominated brand of atmosphere and exotica.

If the world's commercial movie and TV production was centred in Lapland, I doubt not I would have wound up there eventually—but not with the same undignified glee and scrambling haste which I answered Hollywood's first, tentative, but sun-infused call.

Questions 3 and 4: Am I that trivial? Or worse, so reactionary—still seeking, in a wrenched-around world, at least some of the trappings of a colonial life of ease? Such are surely to be had in California now, in a stupefying magnification of Cairo then: the most determinedly material society the world has ever seen, the most breathtaking array of consumer goods, a choking superfluity of staple, junk and gourmet foods, and (still) a virtually helpless and limitless supply of comparatively cheap domestic labour—illegal South American and Mexican immigrants (1,000,000 in the Los Angeles area alone).

What the Americans call checks and balances are clearly in order now, by way of a fuller reply. The Middle East was not all Cairo and water-buffalo steaks at the Café

Riche—and neither were my four years in that war theatre. Likewise, California is not all the Beverly Hills Hotel and the Farmers Market. I think we knew more, however, of the poverty of most Egyptians, because Cairo is a small enough city for us to be able to *see* it. Here, it is not unkind to guess that most Los Angelenos had not even heard of Watts until it rioted and flared and made itself known to the whole world. It is that far away, physically and from the affluents' experience. There was a constant underside of violence in Cairo: it came close, too: a stabbing, night murder in the office next to ours at the Ministry of Information, a gentleman bloodied to death for staying late and writing a letter to his wife. Violence in America, Lotusland included, needs no elaboration.

And yet—it is something of an effort to recall and tabulate the seamy and the disturbing. Of Cairo, remembering mostly oneself when young, the mind summons Kasr-el-Nil, Bolanachi brandy, Nile-side-strolling lovers of all permutations, the lights, the lights by night, and the sun, the sun by day—urbane and unreal, vibrating Durrell-y in a sweating, ugly, combative, burning planet. Thirty-six years later, here, more adept at screening-out the dire and the frightening—and *still* mostly remembering oneself when young—my emigrant surroundings mean 31 flavours of ice-cream, Napa Valley vintage wines, Wilshire Boulevard and Rodeo Drive, Hollywood-sidewalk-cruising lovers of all permutations, and the lights, the lights by night, and the sun, the sun by day. Nothing to do with reality whatsoever, except the reality of making it, so as to survive and go on clinging to the unreality, in a sweaty, ugly, combative, burning planet.

'What it amounts to' said a writer-friend, told of the invitation to write this, 'is that you're gonna sit under a palm tree and remember what it was like to sit under a palm tree.'

Los Angeles, 1980.

G. C. Norman
My War

It was the ideal location for a war. Hundreds of miles of empty desert, uncluttered lines of communication, a perfect climate and a civilized back-up along the Nile—it was a tactician's paradise. And there was the added bonus that it was clean. There were no muddy trenches, no atrocities that I ever heard of, and no civilians to get in the way of the professionals, apart from the totally uncommitted Senussi tribesmen wandering freely with their flocks across the lines.

At times there was even a kind of camaraderie between us and the enemy. We used their water cans, they used our lorries. We seduced Lilli Marlene, they made comic parodies of 'We'll hang out our washing on the Siegfried Line'. Breaches of the tacitly accepted rules of the game were deprecated. I recall a front-line intelligence report of a complaint by a captured German officer about the unsporting behaviour of some of our troops towards enemy wounded. We replied, probably over the field radio to which both sides were privy, that some of their supposed wounded were getting up during an advance and shooting our chaps in the back, which was certainly not British and not really Afrika Korps either.

It was all a long time ago but at this distance—and this may sound strange—my principal impression now of the desert war is of the total security. We were encapsulated in a miniature Welfare State. Naturally there were the moments of terror, the dive-bombers, the night raids, the crunch of action, but always there was full logistical support, regular rations and cigarettes, sometimes even baked bread. I never recall feeling hungry or thirsty, not seriously. And after combat came the periods of inactivity for reading, talking, brewing-up, foraging for eggs and water, mobile baths and cinemas, all inside the tight little microcosm of the unit, and bounded by the familiar and reassuring stereotypes of the ubiquitous Busty and Smudger, Lofty and Mac.

And, if you were lucky, there was leave.

Life at the base, 'the rigours of the Cairo campaign' as the English language newspaper cartoonist put it, gave us our first real taste of the totally unreal life which was being lived back there, while we were 'up the blue'. Cairo was a dream world of music, theatres and opera, cafés and cinemas, museums and mosques, where we strode the crowded, unblacked-out streets like conquerors, accepting the homage of shopkeepers, dragomen and shoe-blacks as to the manna born.

I suppose we should hardly recognise it now. Is Groppi's bar still serving Tom Collinses and real Vienna truffles? Do cool hands still take 6 a.m. temperatures in the former 62 General Hospital, and sleek modern buses glide where the crazy trams used to lurch up to Abbassia, stuck all over with people like fly-papers? What strangers now dwell in 'Music For All', that astonishing wartime outpost of the arts? Who now inhabits the Victory Club with its immense, life-giving library and a dozen other establishments created especially for us, where, as exclusive guests, we could briefly forget the war and the desert over roast chicken and miniature eggs and chips? As I turn the yellowing pages of my copy of *Oasis*, snatches of 'Saheeda Bint' and the ribald version of Farouk's anthem echo in my mind, I taste again the medicinal Stella beer which never saw the hop, the acrid flavour of Victory Vs[1] and the hot, dusty, pagan smell of Cairo, unique and unforgettable.

I am not suggesting that there was not anxiety too, the pain of separation and the dark threat of the more terrible battles casting their shadow over Europe: but they were deep down, pushed out of sight and mind, except when an airgraph or air lettercard from home intruded momentarily into the fantasy. Now, in 1977, there is an air of unreality about all that past life. Did I really wander amongst the Pyramids in khaki shorts, lie fearful between bursting bombs in slit-trenches and watch, gin in hand, a stout belly dancer agitate her pelvis in some almost forgotten establishment called The Blue Melody? Was it all a dream, that bright cameo? Did it exist? These verses are real enough, but they captured moments from which the emotion has long since been drained. After thirty-five years all that has gone, only the shell remains, the colour and the excitement, the friendships and the humour. Time, the old falsifier, has washed it all clean.

---

[1] Issue cigarettes.

John Rimington

In Retrospect

'TOTAL WAR'. I often wonder whether we who served in the Western Desert between 1939 and 1943 ever really understood the true meaning of that phrase. Oh, yes, there were those men, tens of thousands of them, who lost their lives: for these, the ultimate victims, the desert war was indeed a total one. Death is, after all, as fatal in one field of battle as in another. And there were those other tens of thousands of poor devils who went home alive, but crippled and maimed for whatever length of life the surgeons had managed to save for them: I don't suppose that many of them felt especially privileged because they received their injuries in North Africa rather than in other theatres of war.

Nevertheless, amongst the hundreds of men who served and survived through the Middle Eastern campaign I know many who, like myself, still think themselves lucky that it was to that part of the world we were drafted, and not elsewhere.

We sometimes used to discuss it, leaning against our vehicles in the stillness of the desert nights. To think, right now, we might be hacking our way through some steaming jungle in the Far East, our legs alive with greedy leeches. We might be clinging for dear life, our hands frozen to a metal stanchion in the agonizing cold of the Barents Sea on our way to Murmansk. We might be fighting hand-to-hand through the rubble-strewn back alleys of a shattered town on the mainland of Europe, with terrified children clinging to the skirts of our khaki greatcoats . . .

No, even in our worst moments of homesickness and depression, we recognized that, by contrast, our war was somehow more civilized than the others: cleaner and, yes, more sporting.

The word 'arena' derives from the Latin for 'sand': and the million or more square miles of sand between the Nile Delta and Tunisia provided a clear, natural arena for the ebb and flow of mobile conflict. There were no crowds of helpless, hapless, homeless refugees to be caught in the crossfire, no towns or villages to be shattered by shells and bombs, no green acres of farmland to be ground into muddy ruts by the tracks of heavy tanks. Tough and relentless though it might be, the game was one in which only the players risked getting hurt.

Perhaps it was this that conditioned the attitudes of the combatants. Perhaps it was this that prompted Erwin Rommel, a hard and realistic general of the Prussian School, to take time out in the heat of battle and stop to gossip with an isolated group of wounded British soldiers and to see that they were given medical supplies before he moved on to catch up with the battle. Perhaps it was this that prompted me, after my unarmed 'soft' vehicle had been rounded up on the Trigh el Abd by a support unit of the 21st Panzer Division, and I had been held prisoner for forty-eight hours, later to report to a New Zealand battery commander that my captors had been *A bloody good bunch of blokes.* In what other theatres of war, I ask you, would it have been thought necessary (as General Montgomery found it) for an Army commander to send a printed circular letter to all troops under his command, pointing out that the opposing commander was not a romantic hero, but a ruthless enemy?

Perhaps, though, the best illustration of the special atmosphere of the desert campaign came from a German Officer whom I met, some thirty years after it was all over, at a business seminar in Switzerland. Finding that we had served on opposite sides during the campaign of 1939 to 1943, we compared notes over a drink.

'*So you finally won in Africa*' he admitted. '*But I always thought the whole thing was rather unfair. We should have changed ends at half time.*'

Victor Selwyn
Looking Back at Oasis

No one asked—can we do it? Do we need permission? Will it sell? Or the big question of a publisher in Britain today, will it sell in America?

This was the Middle East. It was war-time, and if you had an idea you got on with it. And anyway, who in the Army approved an anthology of poetry? If the idea worked, then higher authority would come in. That was the order of things. And it happened with *Oasis*. True we informed those who would be interested such as Lt-Col. Stevenson in charge of education for British troops in Egypt. But by then, we had started.

As told in the Preface, when we launched our appeal to the troops for poetry the highest rank amongst us was corporal. We had no official backing. Yet three thousand poems descended on us, the editors, from eight hundred contributors. We would only have space for one hundred and twenty-one! Paper was rationed.

Luck, and that instinct which so often seems to guide one to the right place at the right time, made an idea a reality. A month before we dreamt up *Oasis* at 'Music for All'[1] in Cairo, I had taken the manuscript of a book I had written on navigation and map-reading (subbed the night before by ex-*Daily Mirror* man David Burk, in a tent near the Suez Canal) to the chief military censor, Colonel Stephens (pre-war, *Financial Times*).

Before I reached his office I was attracted by a bicycle propped up outside the door of another office. This was no utility get-you-there machine but a sleek racing bike. That was how I met Johnnie Walker, a sergeant in General Staff Intelligence, formerly with Wavell's Thirty Thousand, and founder of the Buckshee Wheelers[2], a cycling

---

[1] 'Music for All' was a service club ran by Lady Russell Pasha, wife of the Cairo Police Chief. In those days music meant music, an art form demanding skill, study and application. It is an illusion one must downgrade the arts to make them popular. Troops in the Middle East packed concerts where performers like Solomon came to play, just as the troops when they moved to Italy filled the opera houses. They filled 'Music for All' where serious music could be heard any time of the day. or one could read books, play chess, participate in discussion groups or paint.

[2] Buckshee . . . something free or extra; a word beloved by quartermasters. The 'Buckshee Wheelers' merit a book on their own, for they formed a perfect example of the British delight in doing things on their own, with no direction, as in our voluntary services at

club that grew to nineteen clubs in the Middle East by 1945. He was a man who enjoyed the distinction of being the only one to whom Randolph Churchill would entrust the key of his drinks cupboard, being wary of the Fleet Street exiles who staffed G.S.I.

That chance sighting of a bicycle led to Johnnie Walker playing the link role in the *Oasis* story. For when we launched *Oasis* he passed it round G.S.I., and they put it on the map. It was still unofficial but through them our appeal for poetry was read on the Forces and Egyptian State radios every day for a week. Military and civilian press carried the story and units picked it up to publish in orders. So three thousand poems flooded in.

When the anthology was complete colleague John Braun took the Foreword down the corridor of G.H.Q. for the Commander-in-Chief, Middle East Force, General 'Jumbo' Wilson, to sign. (John Braun knew the General's son, Patrick, which helped) and the Senior General in the Middle East put his signature to the work begun voluntarily by three other ranks, meeting over coffee in a Cairo club.

The troops own NAAFI (equivalent to U.S. PX) finally distributed and sold the 5,000 paperback edition to make £250 profit (under U.S. $500) for the Red Cross. *Oasis* sold at 25 piastres a copy (25p or less than 50 cents U.S.).

Forty years on, I must thank Jasper Sayer, Jimmy Hayes (*The Times*), Geoffrey Edwards (*News Chronicle*), Archie Chisholm (BP Oil P.R.), and Peter Scott (Radio), for their help. If I missed some names . . . well, it was a long time ago.

History repeats itself. So many poems in *Return to Oasis* would not have reached us; The Salamander Oasis Trust itself would not have been set up, without today's publicity on press and radio.

The original *Oasis* took months to produce whereas *Return to Oasis* has taken years. But then, so much was possible in a non-commercial world where we were kept and fed, and even paid a little[1], whilst we wrote and produced books in between military duties.

Services mail brought the poems to the editors. Not only was it free, but it was efficient, even if it caused grumbles from the post corporal as he flung mail into my tent, dug into the sand, from the other side of the slit trench. I read copy by the light of a Tilley lamp hissing with menace. When we needed help we could always detail a volunteer.

In the end three thousand poems were whittled down to less than two hundred, and the final choice to one hundred and twenty-one was made by Denis Saunders

---

home. The 'Wheelers' had no official status, appeared in no orders. Yet their nineteen clubs operated a detailed racing programme for members of the Forces. How, or where their machines came from no one asked. Members rode gaily off to Luxor without a pass. One advantage was having so many members from the sergeants' mess where most things are possible, aside from not asking for official status! For that invites orders and restrictions.

[1] 'Little pay'. Those were the days. The corporal who played the pipes for the 51st Highland Division, enjoyed an extra 3d a day allowance (just over 1p or 2 U.S. cents). (He was also allowed to grow a beard, the privilege of a Pioneer Corps sergeant.) We had a Mediterranean allowance of 1/6 a day (7½p or 14 U.S. cents) in addition to our pay.

(Almendro), who remained in Cairo, and colleagues of the Salamander Society (military and civilian writers and poets) who finally published them.

We all took a lofty attitude to the poetry. We had little space and could afford to. I recall even rejecting John Pudney's contributions as not up to his standard. (We reprint some of his previously published poems in this book.)

Miraculously, when *Oasis* was finally printed it contained few literals. Miraculously because the Syrian printer knew no English and John Braun went backwards and forwards by cab, collecting and correcting wet proofs.

My *Oasis* story must conclude on a personal note. If I had been writing for a mass circulation tabloid I would have led with it. Quite simply, *Oasis* saved my life!

A month after *Oasis* was published, the Medical Officer of a camp outside Cairo where I had been posted came to see me. I do not know his name, but maybe he will read this. He wrote poetry and wanted me to read some of it to include in a possible *Oasis* reprint. He wasn't to know it was to be nearly forty years before we could!

After reading his poems I asked him to look at my throat. It had been sore for a week and each evening in the sergeants' mess (I had gone up a step) I eased it with a paint stripper called 'Cyprus Brandy'. It anaesthetized a layer or two but the throat stayed sore. He took one look and declared: 'Hospital you!' 'But they'll keep me there,' I said. 'That' he replied, 'is the general idea.' An hour later, my throat was swabbed. I was put into strict isolation, injected with a 'horse' syringe in the base of the spine, and forbidden to raise even my head. I had diphtheria from which two of the hospital staff had died a week earlier.

By their calculations I had thirty-six hours to go. That morning I had been knocking in tent pegs and kicking over a brute of a BSA 500 motor bike. The evening before I had held a two hour news talk in a crowded marquee and revealed that an Arabic language newspaper in Cairo (officially censored) had carried the story of spontaneous riots in Beirut twenty-four hours before it happened! Now I had to lie still and keep quiet. I lived on. When I left hospital they posted me to Italy.

Darrell Wilkinson

Upside-down in a Tree

After so long, it is only the event itself which is etched on the memory. What led up to this, what followed it, have been indistinct, their outlines weathered and corroded by time. We had our parachute training at Rabat David, near Bethlehem. I think I was the only naval officer there. Certainly, when it was all over, the regular 'brass' in Cairo looked askance at the parachute badge sewn onto naval battledress; that and the balaclava. But it was indiscreet, then, to ask too many questions. They knew they wouldn't get a straight answer. Not that it mattered very much, I suppose. But we enjoyed keeping them guessing.

Our base camp was on Mount Carmel. We didn't move out much; we had learnt to keep a low profile and to be as anonymous as possible. But one could sense a certain antagonism in the air. Later, this was to become more apparent, particularly among the young and educated; it was understandable, at the time. They were irritated by the restrictions on immigration and were gearing themselves to forge their national identity. The anvils were still hidden but the fires were lit. This apart, it was only the training that was eventful; how to fall, how to jump, how to land. We went to the training ground early in the morning, in an open truck. It was desperately cold, I remember; the night cold of the desert that belies the popular image of the shimmering heat of the desert. I wore a long sheepskin coat which was miraculously to survive the twists and turns of the next few years and to finish its life as a bedspread for my son. Did I say that the training was eventful? Only because doctors make bad parachutists; too much imagination, they said. One admired immensely those tough, highly competent instructors. They had great courage and an astute understanding of how to deal with men faced with a new and unfamiliar art.

Then, our bags packed, we moved away one night and waited for the call. I do not remember how long. Time has little meaning without events. But then we were on the desert road, far away from Cairo, jolting and swaying in the trucks again towards an airbase in North Africa. I recall the tents and the hangar where the parachutes were laid out, to be folded carefully and the cords arranged exactly, so that there would be no mistake when the jerk came. And it came soon. One day the moon was right and the signals were right and time had a meaning again. We were in the darkness of the plane, my assistant and I and the medical equipment and stores. I suppose we must have come on to Greece somewhere above Arta. Below the mountains of the Pindos would be gathering height. Between them and the open hole in the floor of the plane lay the enshrouding night. Very soon now we would approach the landing strip, a piece of ground more level than the rest, perhaps one or two hundred metres long, a valley set in mountains, an awkward terrace in a wild terrain. There would have been brushwood fires, lit only at the last moment; perhaps exactly when we were expected, perhaps only when those waiting below heard the thudding of the plane as the pilot sought his way between the peaks. I do not know how it was organized, only how well. But I could appreciate the superb navigation and the skill and courage of the pilot.

Now we had become automata, ready to slip into position at the edge of the hole, ears tuned only to the command that would come suddenly, to spring the tension and propel us out. I knew that we would only have a few seconds; then the plane would have to rise sharply and turn away from the menacing mountain tops.

Years later, the memory of that moment came back to me, most incongruously, at the railway station of Brive-la-Gaillarde, in France. Then, I was the controller. There were twenty-two people, of assorted nationalities, all with baggage, who had just finished attending a conference. They were to catch the 'Capitol', a crack train, back to Paris. The train glides in, on the minute, the doors open electrically, stay open for one minute and then close, irrespective of what may be in their path. The porter had stationed us exactly where a door would be—when it opened, the inevitable elderly French lady would descend, with care, grace and deliberation.

Twenty seconds gone. Then 'go'—the memory flooded back. All in, one after another, the gear thrown with or after. The last man was aboard; nothing was left; the doors closed; the train moved on again. It was like that. *But then we were going down; into the night. And we had no tickets.*

229

But just before we reached the dropping ground the instructor made a routine inspection of our parachutes, pulling the ropes, checking the position, tapping the central box which caused the whole apparatus to fly apart on landing. My box was at fault. Either it opened when it should not have done, or the reverse. All I know is that he made an instant decision. The pilot pulled the plane up and we were over and away and circling back to the Mediterranean and North Africa. Our tensions snapped, we became irritable, then angry, wanting to kick any cat that crossed our path. The airbase was the first. Dimly, I remember clambering out of the plane, expending useless and unreasonable fury in the early dawn. Then we slept. Back in the mountains they would have realized that something was wrong. The flames would have been extinguished and they would be waiting, patiently, for another signal. Soon it came, new parachutes fitted, a new goodbye, a new beginning.

But we were not professionals. We had been to the edge of the hole and had seen the darkness beneath. We were unnerved. If the box were wrong again? And flung us tumbling down into the night when the line pulled taut? But the professional was there with us again, a companion and a true psychiatrist. He joked us through the return path, as imperturbable as ever. And a swig from our flasks of naval rum helped.

The moment arrived again, the tension increased. If we were unsteady, it did not matter. We would jump or we would be pushed. So we sat and counted the seconds in the throbbing and shuddering of the plane. The red light came on. Out we went, arms to side, all training remembered. The cord snapped tight, there was a jerk on the shoulders. Then I floated. There was absolute silence. The plane had vanished, rising steeply over the dark-edged mountain one could just perceive. It was dark. I was conscious of nothing except the silence and the swaying. It lasted perhaps twenty seconds; it seemed infinite; and so it remains in my mind. It was a suspension of all life and all activity. Sometimes, in the short moments before falling asleep, when the body becomes weightless and the mind is adrift, I have the same feeling of complete incapability and yet of intense awareness. Is this what Nirvana is?

Then there was a sudden tearing and breaking and jolting, and a tugging and tearing of silk, and I was alive again, upside-down in a tree. I was told later that I was located easily because I was singing a bawdy North African marching song. That was certainly an exaggeration. Except for relief, perhaps. Sounds of people; small torches, discreetly used. A foreign language. I had been taught enough to recognize some of it. 'Etho! Ekei!' the searchers called out, tracing the tree, clambering up, pulling me down, disentangling the precious parachute. Tremendous excitement. Noise, running, laughing. My assistant had landed on a mountain ledge and had nearly followed his revolver, which had fallen over it. But all was well. We were shepherded, like lost sheep, with great acclaim and brought into the group of Andartes, village helpers and carriers, and the British liaison officer. It was still quite dark and, I think, cold. Black olives and sour goat's cheese were pressed on us, and wine, while they searched for the goods that had been dropped with us.

I was in a foreign country, cut off from the world, but among friends. We were safe. The tension was released. I went behind a bush and was sick.

Darrell Wilkinson was regularly parachuted into Greece as a naval doctor to tend the partisans and pulled out again to Cairo where he behaved as if nothing had happened.

MIDDLE EAST ANTHOLOGY

'Oasis': The Middle East Anthology of Poetry from the Forces.

The compilation of this book has been the spare-time task of three soldiers of the M.E.F., Denis Saunders, Victor Selwyn and David Burk. Over a period of about three months, they read through and considered more than three thousand poems, all contributed by members of the M.E.F. The anthology, published last month in Cairo, has a foreword by General Sir Henry Maitland Wilson, C.-in-C Middle East, and a preface by Mr. Worth Howard of the American University. There is also an introductory article, "Poetry Today" by Mr. John Cromer.

Poems Under Stress

The poems in "Oasis" were written by men under the stress of war in the desert, in the air and on the sea; under the impact of countries and people strangely new to them; during spells of hard-earned leave in the cities and towns of the Middle East. Many things have been their inspiration; battle, the longing for home, hope for the future, comradeship and sacrifice and death. It is noticeable how many have drawn from the splendour of the Orient sky; from the sunset on the desert, where this was their only beauty. Seas, the voyage out, African ports, Egyptian dancers, beer and the memory of England, all these have made their poetry.

By any standard, there are fine poems in this anthology. Some of them, while lacking technical accomplishment, show great promise. Almost all have the stamp and ring of complete sincerity. If there is sometimes a sameness about them, that is because they were written in similar conditions, under trials and experiences often very much alike; it should not be allowed to detract from their individual merit.

Mention should perhaps be made of two poems by G.S. Fraser, J.G. Barker's "Vision" and George Malcolm's "Lament." But it is impossible here to select for separate mention all those one liked very much. Readers will find their own favourites.

The anthologists have done a very difficult job very well indeed.

In his introductory article Mr. Cromer passes much adverse criticism on the poetry of the twenties and thirties. He has a strong dislike for "the poetry with a frown," but to some extent his dislike runs away with his judgment. Much of the work of the twenties and thirties was very good poetry; and it had plenty to frown about. He has forgotten his own quotation from Hazlitt:

Fear is poetry, hope is poetry, love is poetry, hatred is poetry; contempt, jealousy, remorse, admiration wonder, pity, or madness, all are poetry.

— *K.*

Review in *Palestine Post*,
3rd November, 1943.

Tracing Oasis Poets

Oasis was published in Cairo in September 1943 and the contributors were all members of the M.E.F., mostly stationed in, near or passing through the capital of Egypt during the previous nine months. Some were Base-Wallahs, H.Q. Staff and so on, but many, perhaps the majority, were soldiers or airmen paying a brief visit or, reading about the anthology in the *Egyptian Mail* or a Service newspaper, sent in their manuscripts by post. Eventually there were fifty-one names on the contents list, but only a few were personally known to the editors or subsequently kept in touch with them through the Salamander Society or otherwise.

It was late in 1976 that I became aware that Victor Selwyn was trying to contact the original contributors with a view to organizing a reprint of *Oasis*. A mention on the B.B.C., paragraphs in several national or provincial newspapers had brought in some response but the address of barely a dozen were known to Victor and his colleagues when we met on 1st November and I undertook to try to trace as many of the others as possible.

From my battered but treasured copy of *Oasis* I made a list of names and commenced by looking them up in the London telephone directory. The task was deceptively straightforward. There might be two or three entries of the surname, one with the right christian name or initials. Half a dozen phone calls later I had my first success. With others it was a different story; there were forty-two columns of Jones but none with the christian name Dorvil. Darrel, Daniel or David, yes: a whole column with a simple 'D', but no Dorvil. The first suspicion that the task was not going to be easy forced itself into my mind. After all, the name Dorvil was unfamiliar to me; could it possibly be a misprint or a misreading by the Egyptian compositor from a hastily signed manuscript? Possibilities were endless. I moved on to less common names.

Meantime I visited Whitehall and the Ministry of Defence, as the War Office is now called, and asked for their help. They suggested a letter to *The Soldier* and gave me the address of the Army Record Centre. I was warned, however, that addresses would not be provided; if I could provide a man's full name and army number, his corps and date of demobilization also, if possible, they would forward my letter to his last-known address. The A.R.C. confirmed this information explaining that their small staff deals with many enquiries from ex-servicemen, widows and next of kin from all over the world and that my kind of enquiry was quite outside their terms of reference.

Anyone who has seen a copy of *Oasis* knows that the names of the contributors appeared without any details of rank or corps whatsoever. 'George Malcolm' might have been a gunner, a medical orderly, an airman, or even a naval officer attached to Intelligence in Cairo or Alexandria. The title of his poem, 'Lament', suggested bagpipes to me. Perhaps the poet was also a musician, a member of a regimental band? George Malcolm, the musician, was about the right age—I dropped him a line. My sincere thanks are due to Mr Malcolm who replied immediately to regret that he had not served in the Middle East, although during the war he had indeed served with a military band in the Far East and on the continent. Perhaps, he added, his namesake who had served with the Highland Division in the M.E.F. would be able to help. I would find his address in *Who's Who*. Sadly Lt-Col. Lord George Malcolm of Poltalloch who had indeed served with the Argyles in the Highland Division in North Africa in 1942 and '43 and who undoubtedly wrote 'Lament', had died in 1976.

Neither Whitehall nor the Army Records Office had told me of the existence of no less than fourteen Manning and Records Offices run by various branches of the Army. This I discovered for myself from *Whitaker's Almanac*, and they proved to be very helpful indeed. Given names only, they went through their files and, where possible, supplied me with army number and regiment of those who had served in their ranks. In addition, some gave helpful advice and I am particularly grateful to Col. C. G. K. Underhill of R.C.T. Manning and Records who gave me several useful leads and explained the difficulty of tracing others who had rather common names. To trace Dorvil Jones, for instance, it would be necessary to remove over 11,000 cards of different sizes and format, but all with that surname, from their racks and search various parts of the cards for the christian name or initial. All this for the R.A.S.C. alone!

Still, we are not finished yet: we have traced thirty-one *Oasis* poets. One day someone may recall meeting Dorvil Jones in the Salamander Club and remember that he was a gunner or a sapper or an airman perhaps, or that he had enlisted in Ceylon for instance. That would be enough to set me off on a fresh trail. Meantime, whatever happened to Arthur and Catherine Smithies? Stella Day, according to the R.A.F. P.M. Centre, now Mrs S. Sims, is also very elusive and I have still to hear from Max Bowden, John Bristow, Douglas Burnie, Dudley Charles, John Charnock, Hugh Laming, Norman Longhurst, Edward McHale, Bhag Singh, A. C. J. Davies, W. G. Graham, R. B. Lester, T. W. Louch and A. W. Marsden.

LOUIS CHALLONER

Biographies

The editors regret that they have been unable to include biographies of all poets due to lack of information. It is hoped to rectify this in later editions.

Juan ALMENDRO *see* Denis SAUNDERS.

J. G. BARKER *see* J. G. MEDDEM-MEN.

Ronald E. BEE, Royal Corps of Signals. With 8th Army Signals then 13 Corps Signals, Egypt, Sicily, Italy and Austria.

J. A. K. BONINGER, born 1911 in Germany, mother English, father German, correct name Baron James Arthur Kurt Boninger, but unused since 1937.

Educated privately and Berlin University. Left Germany in 1936 after a brush with the Gestapo and lived in Amsterdam before leaving for Kenya in 1937.

After a brief farming career, worked for the *Sunday Post* and *East African Standard* in Nairobi, then joined the Army in 1941 and was posted to the Middle East on Intelligence work connected with German prisoners of war at the Bitter Lake camps. Published first German newspaper for P.O.W.s, created Camp 'University' and lectured on democracy.

Demobbed 1946 in Kenya, farmed, sailed on a trading schooner, then joined Department of Information, Kenya Government as Provincial Information Officer. In this job he was responsible for press relations, visiting V.I.P.s, the running of vernacular broadcasting stations and created the first newspaper ever in the Masai language.

Returning to Britain in 1960 he married actress Dorothy Wheatley and joined the C.O.I., then the Ministry of Overseas Development, writing on overseas aid, contributing extensively to *Overseas Development*, a Ministry magazine. Retired April 1973 to concentrate on restoration of neglected houses. Lives in Sudbury, Suffolk.

Harold Ian BRANSOM, Brigadier-General, C.B.E., D.S.O., T.D., D.L., author of *Inferior Verse* and *Still Inferior Verse* published by James McAndrew, 14 Lyndhurst Road, Whitley Bay. President of the 124 (Northumbrian) Field Regiment R.A. (T.A.) Old Comrades Association. The members of the Association ordered the Brigadier to send his poems to us. Captured when R.A. Commander, 32nd Army Tank Brigade. Men sent his poems to be published under the title *Inferior Verse*. This raised money during the war to send parcels to men who were also P.O.W.s. Lives at Gosforth, Newcastle-upon-Tyne.

John Cromer BRAUN, O.B.E., writing as John CROMER, born 1916, lawyer. Two earliest poems published in school magazine *The Portsmuthian* 1933.

Private in Hampshire Regiment 1940. Egypt September 1940. February 1941 transferred to Field Security, Cairo.

Commissioned Intelligence Corps 1941 as Lieutenant, finally Major in Security Intelligence, Middle East.

Published in *Poems from the Forces*, *More Poems from the Forces*, and Cairo publications, *Sphinx, Orientations,* and Egyptian newspapers and reviews. Lectured, British Institute, and Anglo-Egyptian Union, several programmes on Egyptian State broadcasting network and contributor to *Cairo Calling*.

A co-founder of the Salamander Society with Keith Bullen. The Society published five issues of the *Salamander* and several slim volumes of poems by members including John Cromer's *The Battle*.

Back in law practice, still in uniform, called to Foreign Office for appointment as liaison officer to the South American delegations to U.N. Conference in London.

Magistrate, City Councillor, Chairman of Governors, Portsmouth College of Art. 1965 Secretary Advertising Standards Authority, and member of European bodies monitoring advertising standards. Moved to Brussels 1974 as Head of Consumer Protection Division in E.E.C. Commission and awarded O.B.E. Back to England 1977.

He is now a Consultant in European and Consumer Affairs; Vice-President and European Adviser, Institute of Trading Standards Administration; Vice-President, English section of European Food Law Association, and member and former Chairman, Consumers in the European Community Group (U.K.). He is Chairman of the Salamander Oasis Trust and lives in London EC1.

Recently John Cromer's writing has been in collaboration with composer Leonard Salzedo, writing words for choral works, songs, madrigals and a mini-opera.

J. E. BROOKES, Private with 2/5 Bn A.I.F. Served 1940 to 1945. Today living at Galhampton, Yeovil, Somerset.

David BURK, international reporter, writer, and broadcaster, was a bookworm at six, a writer at twelve when a favourite aunt gave him an ancient three-bank typewriter, wrote a mystery novel at thirteen, and got his first newspaper by-line while playing truant from school in London.

An understanding headmaster let him stay on at the weekly paper as a reporter—and a career was launched.

At seventeen he was in Fleet Street with the *Daily Mirror* thanks to a barely visible moustache liberally treated with eyebrow pencil which made him look nineteen. He lived, breathed and prospered on the thrills of Fleet Street in the late 1930s.

The Savoy Hotel barber thought the young Mr. Burk, who gave up dinner once a week to use his services, would appreciate meeting a publisher and gave him a ticket to a cocktail party hosted by Lord Southwood, chairman of Odham's Press. His Lordship offered him a junior's job in the papers' Vienna bureau, which led to a fascinating year reporting on events from Munich up to the start of World War Two.

A year in the infantry, a counter intelligence posting in the Middle East, then a split personality job helping to edit the *Tripoli Times*, and serve with Psychological Warfare Executive. He then ran the news department of the Anglo-Greek Information services.

December 1946 *Daily Mail* as foreign correspondent in Greece then Paris. 1948 feature writer *Daily Mail*. 1953 foreign staff, *Daily Express* in mid-East. 1956 N.B.C. New York and won two Emmy's for documentary TV programmes. 1956 A.B.C. in Paris, then Athens to set up own film company, returning to active reporting during dictatorship of Greek Colonels.

Recently resigned as Roving Editor in Europe for top American weekly and is now a writer for a leading German daily newspaper in Hamburg.

Ken BURROWS, Served in the Middle East from January 1943 to 1947, first with the 16/5 Lancers in the 6th Armoured Division.

Writes . . . 'I used to amuse myself by writing poems on scraps of paper, but most of them were lost or thrown away'. Today living at Alvaston, Derby.

Graham CAWTHORNE, Squadron Leader R.A.F., stationed at 216 Group in the Desert Museum on the Suez Road near Heliopolis, Cairo. Journalist.

Louis CHALLONER, born 1911 in Blackpool, for 29 years primary school Headmaster in Newham, now lives in Ilford, Essex.

Educated Preston, and University College, Southampton. Pre-war schoolmaster in East London he served with 2 R.H.A. (25-pounders) in North Africa from Bir Hacheim to Cairo, and Alamein to Cape Bon and Algiers.

B. COLE, a private soldier with the Royal Sussex Regiment at El Alamein now living at Westcliff-on-Sea, Essex.

J. M. COLLARD, historian, living at Gerrards Cross, Bucks.

Molly CORBALLY, S.R.N., working in nursing home on French Riviera at Munich crisis time, returned to U.K. and enrolled in the T.A.N.S. Called up January 1940, spent 'phoney war' pic-

nicking in Sussex woods then shuttled cross-channel just before Dunkirk, spending one night in Cherbourg then back home.

Next posting Egypt, travelling in *Mauretania*, for four years' service at 19th General Field Hospital, Bitter Lakes, nursing battle casualties—ours, allies, and enemy's—and working with the eminent surgeon Professor Ian Aird, then Lt-Col in charge surgical division. 1945 nursing ex-Japanese P.O.W.s in mental unit.

Now retired from career of looking after mothers, babies, handicapped and elderly in small English town and surrounding villages, and lives in Chichester, Sussex, writing for variety of newspapers and magazines.

Michael CROFT, O.B.E., born Oswestry 1922. Educated at Gobowen Council School and then in Manchester at Plymouth Grove Elementary School and Burnage Grammar School. Served in the Royal Air Force 1940–1 and with the Royal Navy 1942–6. Became professional actor for short time after the war, then went to Keble College Oxford. Taught at Alleyn's School 1950–5 and produced school plays. Founded the National Youth Theatre in 1956 and has directed it ever since. Also directs Shaw Theatre Company in London. Wrote best selling novel *Spare the Rod* in 1954 and travel book *Red Carpet to China* in 1956.

John CROMER *see* John Cromer BRAUN.

J. A. R. DAKIN (1903–79), born Warrington, Lancashire. Clerk, factory manager in Belgium, then joined Burroughs in Paris 1930, became manager in Spain in 1931 until forced out by Civil War.

Assignments in Holland, Belgium, Italy, Switzerland, back to Spain, Portugal and France. Royal Navy 1940, Greenwich, Bletchley, Admiralty and Eastern Mediterranean as S.O.Y. afloat as Lieutenant. At sea all operations from 1941. Torpedoed in *Naiad*, transferred with Admiral Vian to *Cleopatra* and mentioned in despatches at battle of the Gulf of Sirte. Relief of Malta in *Cleopatra*. 1943 joined Force 'S' and ended service as Lt-Cdr, S.O.I. Northern Ireland.

Main hobby for thirty years, restoring pictures in oils, watercolours or prints, picture-framing and advising.

Married Paris 1931. Four children.

D. M. DAVIN, Platoon Commander with 23rd N.Z. Battalion in Greece, wounded in Crete in 1941, transferred to Military Intelligence, Cairo. Served in Italy. N.Z. Intelligence Representative in the Joint Control Commission until end of the war. During the war had verse published in John Lehmann's *New Writing and Daylight*.

Erik de MAUNY, born 1920 in London, French and English parents. Married with two children. Journalist, foreign correspondent, broadcaster, writer, linguist. Educated Wellington College, New Zealand; Victoria University College, Wellington; School of Slavonic and East European Studies, University of London; B.A. Hons.

1938–40 journalist on *The Dominion* and *The New Zealand Listener*, Wellington, N.Z. Began writing plays, short stories and poetry. 1940–5 service with N.Z. Expeditionary Force in Pacific, Middle East and Italy.

1946 studying for degree in Russian language and literature, London, writing for *The Times Literary Supplement* and working as translator. 1949 joined B.B.C.

External Services Foreign News Department. 1955–7 Foreign News Presenter with B.B.C. TV news.

1958 Foreign Correspondent B.B.C. Vienna and S.E. Europe; then Middle East, U.S.A. Washington, Cuba, and Canada 1961–3; first permanent B.B.C. correspondent Moscow 1963–6; Paris 1966–72; Moscow again 1972–4. Covered assassination attempts Mideast; race riots U.S. deep South, fall of Kruschev, death of Shastri, dissident trials U.S.S.R. Publications: Editor (with John Waller) *Middle East Anthology*; *The Huntsman in his Career* (novel); *Russian Prospect, Notes of a Moscow Correspondent*; short stories, poems and literary criticism published in *The Times Literary Supplement*, *Penguin New Writing*; *London Magazine*; *Poetry Quarterly*; *Yale Review*, etc. Numerous translations including *A Time to Keep* by Andre Chamson which won the Denise Clairouin prize for translation 1960. Lives near Caen, Normandy, France.

C. P. S. DENHOLM-YOUNG, Colonel, O.B.E., F.C.I.S. Commanded the Signal Regiment of the 51st Highland Division from 1941 in Scotland until Tripoli in 1943. Went to the 'shop' in 1925 and retired in 1950. Today works as a genealogist. Lives in Oxford.

Keith DOUGLAS (1920–44), Captain, Royal Armoured Corps, professional soldier and professional poet, independent-minded, he disobeyed orders to take a tank into action at El Alamein, had to be with the action, wounded; recorded his experiences in *Alamein to Zem Zem*, also illustrated by him, one of the finest descriptions of war which contains the authentic text of his war poems; made final revision of his poems and arranged for the revenues to go to his mother, before leaving for Normandy, June 1944, where he was killed three days later.

Edward DUDLEY, Chief Librarian, City of London, now Lecturer in Librarianship at North West Polytechnic, London.

David DUNHILL, born 1917 in London, escaped business career in family tobacco firm by taking diploma course in journalism at London University.

1937 junior reporter, *Swinton Evening Advertiser*. 1940, joined R.A.F. as clerk. 1941, Middle East with Western Desert units. Freelance writings led to posting to *Tripoli Times*. 1943 Cairo, Inter-services Publications Directorate producing *Air Force News*, *Parade*, *Gen* and *World Press Review* which he edited in 1944 as Acting Sergeant.

1945, announcer with Middle East Forces Broadcasting ('This is your Forces Station from Cairo . . .'). Later in 1945 a 'Summer holiday relief' job as an announcer with B.B.C. a job which lasted twenty-five years!

Announcer and participant in *Take It From Here*—'brought a measure of ephemeral fame'. 1970 left B.B.C. staff to freelance as broadcaster and writer. Recently involved in vocal training of local radio station staff. 1973 and 1974 wrote scripts for Son-et-Lumiere productions at Bristol Cathedral and Winchester. Married thirty years, four children, four grandchildren. Lives at Plymouth, Devon with a *pied-a-terre* on edge of Dartmoor.

A. DUNN, Poem 'Soldiers' Lament', written when a L/Bdr, Royal Artillery in the Middle East. Served in Tobruk. Shared a tent with another Lance-Bombardier, Sidney Cole from Skipton, Yorks. Today lives in Bradford.

George Sutherland FRASER (1915–80), M.A. St Andrews, 1936 in English Literature and American and Colonial History. Trainee journalist *Aberdeen Press and Journal* at a salary of three pounds a week. This excellent training enabled a physically inept man, who could never hit a target and hardly march in step, to find various niches in Army journalism, on the Cairo magazine, *Parade*, as assistant editor in Asmara of the *Eritrean Daily News* (*Il Quotidiano Eritreo*) and towards end of the war with help of John Waller, into the Ministry of Information, Cairo (as a sergeant-major) churning out information and propaganda.

After the war lectured in Japan and at Leicester University. Many books of poems and of literary criticism, especially on twentieth-century poetry. Helped found The Salamander Oasis Trust and a most useful editor of *Return to Oasis*. New edition of his collected works, edited by Ian Fletcher, to appear next year.

Alan FREEDMAN, for eleven years London editor of the *Manchester Evening News*, and since 1977 chairman of the Newspaper Conference which represents one hundred evening and daily papers and over 1,000 weeklies outside London.

Served in the R.A.F. during the war in the Middle East and Europe; R.A.F. Intelligence at R.A.F. H.Q., Cairo, and later posted to Air Attache's Office, British Embassy, Ankara, and British Embassy, The Hague. Worked as journalist in Bristol, Manchester, and Fleet Street.

Hobbies: Classical guitar and clarinet. Lives in Isleworth, Middx.

Brian GALLIE, Captain, Royal Navy, D.S.C., served in Mediterranean now living in Portugal

John GAWSWORTH, G. S. Fraser called him 'last of the Jacobites'. Gawsworth claimed descent from the Jacobite nobility, his brother, a Brigadier in the Canadian Forces, was the Jacobite Earl of Gawsworth. 'As a poet' Fraser said, 'Gawsworth had great potential. His poetry was always promising something.' Ian Fletcher, who looked after him in his last days in the 1950s, described him as 'Generous, uncompromisingly romantic and anti-intellectual, and with the romantic virtue of spontaneity in his life and in his lyrics . . . Gawsworth could also be passionately exact, a bibliographer. He conducted his life as if it were a tactical exercise against an enemy . . . There were two Gawsworths . . . John fallen into strong water and John sober. John sober was not a frequent figure, and not as likeable as his cellmate.'

He left Merchant Taylors School at age of sixteen before World War Two, worked for a short time with Ernest Benn, the publisher. In the 1930s he ran his own private printing press on which he printed the early work of Lawrence Durrell. In the Middle East in Cairo he instituted his own Bohemia.

After the war he was in Fleet Street until his sad end from alcoholism.

Hamish HENDERSON, born 1919 in Blairgowrie, Perthshire, educated Blairgowrie High School, Dulwich College, and Downing College, Cambridge. Joined Army 1940, commissioned 1941 and posted to Africa.

Intelligence Officer with 1st South African Division at Alamein, and with 51st Highland Division in Libya, Tunisia, and Sicily. Mentioned in despatches. On Anzio beach-head with 1st British Infantry Division. Organized Graziani's surrender order to German and Italian troops of the Armata Liguria after his capture by partisans (April 1945). Returned to Cambridge to read Italian. 1947–9, District Secretary of Workers Educational Association in Belfast.

Elegies for the Dead in Cyrenaica published by John Lehmann in 1949. Somerset Maugham Award 1949. Translated Gramsci's *Lettere dal Carcere* (*Prison Letters*) while in Italy (1949–50).

Since 1951, Research Fellow in the School of Scottish Studies, Edinburgh University, collecting and editing folk-songs and folk-tales. *Freedom Come All-Ye,* an L.P. of poems and songs issued in 1977. Lives in Edinburgh.

W. G. HOLLOWAY, served in Royal Artillery, Regiment hammered in First Battle of Alamein. Returned to base at Cairo (Almaza), where he wrote his war-time verse.

Leslie HOWE, Bombardier, Royal Artillery, with the 7th Armoured Division, the original Desert Rats. Spent Christmas 1940 outside Sidi Barrani. Also served with L.R.D.G. Returned to England in 1941 after being blinded. His sight was later partially restored. Died in 1975.

Barbara HOWROYD, 3rd Officer, W.R.N.S., H.M.S. Nile, Fleet Mail and Censor Officer at Ras-el-Tin (1943–46) now Mrs Barbara Grant, living at Ilminster, Somerset.

Norman HUDIS, born 1922 in Stepney, R.A.F. Middle East 1941–5, first on R.S.U., then briefly, a fighter squadron (Desert), finally on staff of *Air Force News*, Middle East H.Q.

Publicity man for Rank Organization, mostly at Pinewood Film Studios after demob in 1946, then two years under contract as screenwriter at same studios. Went freelance, wrote twenty-plus second-feature thrillers.

Big break was *The Tommy Steele Story* screenplay, followed by *Carry on Sergeant* and the next five *Carry on* films (including record-breaking *Carry on Nurse*). Created and wrote own TV series *Our House* for British A.B.C. Invited to Hollywood 1964, liked it, and went back with family to live and work there in 1966. Written scripts for most major TV series in America, but still feels urge to burst into poetry—and stage drama. Devoted to James Joyce, Bach, and modern jazz. Married a nurse called Marguerite and they have two sons. Needs little persuasion to wear R.A.F.V.R. tie to Hollywood social functions and says: 'It's such a kick to tell 'em, "No, it's not my yacht club".'

Lives in Canoga Park, Ventura County, California.

John JARMAIN, officer with the 51st Highland Division, anti-tank unit; as with Keith Douglas, served in the Desert only to return to England and then be killed in Normandy (26th June, 1944). The night before, he had worked through the records of his unit, assessing each N.C.O. and man, making recommendations for promotion, as if like Keith Douglas he foresaw his end; early next morning, against advice—he had no need to do so but wanted to make sure—he went on a recce into Ste Honorine la Chardonnerette to be hit by a German mortar bomb. In the desert, and before, he had written extensively. A poet of the top rank.

Sidney KEYES (1922–43), born Dartford, Kent, Tonbridge School, at sixteen wrote 'Elegy' and 'Prospero', Queens College, Oxford; published poems in 1941 under title *The Iron Laurel*. Enlisted April 1942 in Northern Ireland; Commissioned Queens Own Royal West Kent Regiment, September 1942; wounded, captured whilst with forward patrol to die on 19th April, 1943.

Uys KRIGE, South Africa's leading poet in World War Two.

L. K. LAWLER, former B.B.C. executive, living at Henley-on Thames, Oxon.

Sorley MACLEAN, Gaelic poet, colleague of Hamish Henderson; to know more of Sorley Maclean's involvement in the Middle East, read his preface to Hamish Henderson's *Elegies for the Dead in Cyrenaica*. In print his *Selected Poems 1932–72* and *Spring Tide and Keep Tide* (Cannongate, Edinburgh). Lives on Skye.

George Ian MALCOLM, Lt-Col Lord of Poltalloch, D.L., J.P., Duntroon Castle, Lochgilphead, Argyll, Scotland. Died March 1976.

Dennis McHARRIE, O.B.E., Wing Commander R.A.F., posted to 38 Bomber Squadron in Middle East in 1942 as a Flight-Lieutenant, moving to Barce near Benghazi. Now living at Blackpool, Lancashire.

J. G. MEDDEMMEN (pen-name of J. G. BARKER also an *Oasis* poet), born 1917, wanted to be University Don, but, through force of circumstances, became a junior railway clerk.

Conscripted 1940 into army 'and marriage', served in twelve foreign countries, highest rank 'honorary Bimbashi in Sudanese Defence Force with a hate relationship with a camel.'

Demobbed, in urgent need of any money—re-joined railway and loathed it ever since, acquiring on the way, sailing dinghy, yacht, daughter, appreciation of Greek hospitality and barren islands, and diploma in Prehistoric Archaelogy. Also taught marine navigation for three years at evening classes. Lives in London SE23.

Began versifying at fifteen. Believes that like a rose or a killer whale a poem is complete in itself, carries its own message and shouldn't be forced to carry any other.

G. C. NORMAN, now a retired bank manager, joined the Territorial Army in 1939 and served in France, Egypt, North Africa and Italy.

On demob, he returned to Barclays Bank as a cashier in the West End of London. He has six children, and now lives with his wife at Pyrford in Surrey.

Since the war he has written articles and humorous pieces for newspapers and magazines in the U.K. and abroad, and a quantity of verse mostly of a lighter nature. He has also published two books, one about banking and the other on married life, entitled *How to Win at Sex*.

J. NUGENT, A trooper with the 7th Armoured Brigade, taken prisoner at Tobruk. Today living at Fleetwood, Lancashire.

Gordon O. PHYSICK, born 1918 in Malaya, artist, designer and sculptor, he comes from family with four generations of sculptors whose works were shown at the Great Exhibition of 1851.

Examples of his work can be seen in Coventry Cathedral, on the European Continent, and in America.

His poems have also appeared in *Poems from the Desert*, *Citadel*, *Orientations* and other publications, and have been broadcast by the B.B.C. and I.T.V.

Educated privately and at Corpus Christi College, Oxford, where he took a degree in English Literature. Lives in London W5.

F. T. PRINCE, became Professor of English at Southampton University. Now Professor in Boston, U.S.A.

John PUDNEY (1909–77), Gresham School, Holt, Norfolk; *News Chronicle* 1937–40, R.A.F. 1940–5 Book Critic, *Daily Express*, 1947–9; wrote over twenty volumes of verse, plus three plays, ten novels and collections of short stories. The Air Force poet of the war.

M. G. QUINN, Enlisted in 1932 in the King's Own Royal Regiment, served in Egypt and India and then in North Africa with the Royal Armoured Corps. Today lives at Bolton, Lancashire.

John RIMINGTON (1918–77), born Gibraltar, from a naval family; Canford Public School, Dorset, an exceptional scholar; family wanted him to enter the Navy but determined to become a writer: left school at age of seventeen to join a Southampton newspaper; having a strong naval background was drafted into the Army in World War Two; served with R.A.S.C., driving a tank transporter, in the Desert; captured by the Germans, but only briefly, though in process lost many manuscripts; after the war, became copywriter, copychief and finally Director of Brunning Advertising and Marketing Ltd. Whilst pitching for a new account at Plymouth, taken ill and died of a cerebral haemorrhage in a Naval hospital close to the sea, 11th October, 1977.

Had proved invaluable to The Salamander Oasis Trust in helping to set it up. Twice married: two children by the first; leaves widow, Moyna.

Charles ROBINSON, born Australia, attended Melborube Grammar School, Stretcher Bearer in Desert, since the war first represented QUANTAS in London and then set up own travel agency. Lives at Caterham, Surrey.

John ROPES, Brigadier at G.H.Q. Cairo, put on entertainment for the troops.

Peter A. SANDERS, Formerly Captain in Royal Army Ordnance Corps, appointed Inspecting Ordnance Officer, posted to Western Desert in March, 1941. Lives near Godalming, Surrey.

Denis SAUNDERS (Juan ALMENDRO, the poet and inspirer of *Oasis*), born 1920, homeopath, naturopath and osteopath, lives in Ferndale, Johannesburg, South Africa. Four children, five grandchildren.

Greatest interest, astrology. Associate member of American Federation of Astrology. B.A. Hons., Diploma in Homeopathy and Naturopathy.

Plans retirement to North Coast of Natal. If Denis Saunders had not been taking his volume of verse to Schindler that day in Cairo, *Oasis* would not have been born.

C. H. O. SCAIFE, evacuated Tobruk as casualty June 1941, six months hospitalization, then on military establishment Ministry of Information, Middle East.

Spring 1945, Educational Adviser, Government of Iraq. September 1947, British Council's Visiting Professor of English, American University, Beirut. 1957, Permanent staff of University, Chairman Department of English to 1963. October 1968 retired. Professor Emeritus. 1977, elected a Fellow of Royal Society of Literature.

Publications: *In Middle Age*; *Morning Noon and Night*; *In the Levant*; Promoter of, and contributor to *Traffic with Time, an Anthology*; *Tones and Overtones*.

Now living in Arezzo, Italy, amongst the olive groves and vineyards.

Victor SELWYN, born London, graduated in economics, statistics and scientific method and has been learning ever since. Hence book on Navigation and Map Reading in the Army and qualifying in explosives at Combined Ops. In all the years of writing, journalism and research, has investigated and reported on subjects ranging from 'Two Tier Interest Rates' (*Guardian*), 'Psychological Methods of Interview' (*Rationeller Transport*, Frankfurt) to 'Economics of Prostitution'—aside from a range of medical and scientific subjects for various magazines, including dope in sport and horse-racing, also a sports column for the *Sunday Mirror*. Edited and mainly wrote *Investment Guide Western Europe* and *Guide to National Practices Western Europe*, the latter including a seven-country cross frontier depth study among top people in Western Europe on how they saw other nationals (jointly with Professor Stuart Sutherland, Head of Experimental Psychology, Sussex) that made the front page *Sunday Times*. Lectured (as a visitor) at Wormwood Scrubs Prison, London, and universities in America. Manages The Salamander Oasis Trust and lives in Brighton.

Sidney STAINTHORP, Customs and Excise Officer volunteered January 1940. Trained in Royal Armoured Corps. Went to Middle East as sergeant in R.A.C. and commissioned there. In Intelligence Corps, Benghazi.

His widow writes . . . 'It was 1945 when my husband saw my first-born for the first time'.

Theodore STEPHANIDES, born Bombay, India, 1896, of Greek parents. Educated India, Greece and France. Medical doctor, Paris 1929. Diploma in Medical Radio-diagnosis, London 1946.

Served World War One in Greek Artillery (Field-artillery and Howitzers) on Macedonian Front, 1917–18. R.A.M.C. 1940–5 in Western Desert, Greece, Crete and Sicily.

Assistant Radiologist at Lambeth Hospital, 1946–61, and now retired and living in Kilburn, London.

R. N. WALKER, born 1917 in Stoke-on-Trent, teacher and Headmaster of a 900-pupil comprehensive school.

1941, R.A.M.C. Middle East. 1942, Cairo re-training as Cipher Operator, then to Persia, Iraq, India and Burma. Commissioned in India. 1945, H.Q. B.A.O.R. Bad Oeyenhausen and Lubecke. Short spell at Nuremberg for the trial. September 1946, returned to teaching.

Now married with four children and an external degree from London University. Has lifelong passive interest in music, studies languages, likes cooking, but has written no poetry since the war years.

John WALLER, seventh baronet, descendant of Edmund Waller, the courtly seventeenth-century poet, born 1917.

Educated Weymouth College, and Worcester College, Oxford, where he edited *Kingdom Come* 1939–41.

Served in R.A.S.C. 1940–6, chiefly in Middle East. Captain, 1942. Features Editor in Ministry of Information, Middle East 1943–5.

Founder member of the Salamander Society of Poets 1942, awarded Greenwood Prize for Poetry 1947. Keats Prize 1974. 1948, elected a Fellow of the Royal Society of Literature. A Knight Templar and Grand Prior for England 1970–4.

Information Officer, Overseas Press Division, C.O.I., 1954–9. Principle volumes of verse are: *The Confessions of Peter Pan*, 1941; *Fortunate Hamlet*, 1941; *The Merry Ghosts*, 1946; and *The Kiss of Stars*, 1948. Edited *Collected Poems of Keith Douglas*, 1966 and *Alamein to Zem Zem*, 1966. Presently engaged on series of novels proving the existence of God, who takes many forms. Lives in Isleworth, Middx.

Victor WEST, London born, taken prisoner-of-war in Crete and spent years in German prison camps. Poems collected into *The Horses of Falaise*.

Darrell Sheldon WILKINSON, born 1919, now consultant dermatologist in Amersham, Bucks.

Educated Epsom College and St Thomas's Hospital, London. Qualified 1941, he was Surgeon-Lieutenant, R.N.V.R. 1942–6 mostly with S.O.E. (Forces 133 and N.E. 67).

Cyril Bradlaugh WILSON, was inspired to write poetry by the sparseness of the desert, the rigours of life, the comradeship of disaster. He found time to write during the siege of Tobruk as a gunner with the Eighth Army when sent to Gun Operations Room where they needed a man who could communicate clearly with Scottish, Polish, Australian and Cockney gunners. His poems were passed from hand to hand. His *Poems from Italy* written when his battalion moved there, was published by Harrap in 1945.

He sees his poetry as desert flowering, and when war ended, his poetry ended. A quiet man of many parts and talents he is retired from his job at the Wellingborough Co-operative Men's Outfitters and living at Finedon, Northants. He won the Montgomery Poetry Prize in 1943.

"MUSIC FOR ALL"

3 Sharia Maarouf, Cairo (off Sharia Soliman Pasha), between National Hotel and Y.M.C.A., Gresham Court. —Phone 55480.

"Music for All" provides a recreation centre primarily for music and talks. It is for all ranks, men and women, anyone in uniform is admitted. There are 4 entertainments every night in the "Air Conditioned" Music Room. Four nights a week there are concerts, including a military band; one night a week, a gramophone recital (symphonies and operas), one night a talk, and the other night varies from week to week. First-class artists only appear, and all the distinguished visiting artists in Egypt can be heard here. Programmes vary from serious classical to light popular.

In addition to this, the Centre's own Trio plays from 12 to 1 and from 4.30 to 6.30 p.m. every day, and there is also something going on every evening from 6 or 6.30, either talks, bridge, chess, or a gramophone recital or concerts. Teas and light refreshments can be obtained in the Music Room during the day. The Restaurant serves fixed luncheons and dinners as well as meals a la carte, all served at usual city restaurant prices. The catering is by Groppi.

The card room is open all day and there is also a stitting room where Poetry-Reading, etc., are held.

There is a comfortable reading and writing room, (air conditioned), where a large selection of papers and periodicals is to be found.

There is a ladies dressing room with bath and a woman attendant.

The men's bath room has 4 baths as well as showers (hot & cold) and a barber's shop.

There are 2 small gardens where refreshments are served.

Bridge tables and chess available. The entrance fee is P.T. 3 for other ranks and P.T. 5 for officers, and each member of the forces may bring two civilian guests. Civilians with White Passes pay P.T. 10 for concerts and lectures.

The entrance is only 1 P.T. until 2 p.m.

Taken from *Services Guide to Cairo*, 1940.
1 P.T. = 1p in Britain or 2 U.S. cents today.

Explanatory Notes on Poems

Many words recur in the poems, such as *wadi*, a dried valley, or *khamseen*, the hot desert wind that may blow for days. It will be appreciated that there cannot be standard spellings using English characters for Arabic words. As far as possible we have aimed at uniformity. However if this would have meant altering a poem already published we have generally adhered to the original text.

We list certain place-names in this section. However the reader is also referred to the maps in this book.

Part I: Oasis

John Bristow. 'Circles': This poem tells of the blind-folded ox, tethered to a wooden arm, that raised water in buckets from a well, by means of a geared wheel. The ox trod on and on, in the same circle.

Douglas Burnie. 'Seven Pints of Ale': *Mersa* (last stanza), short for Mersa Matruh, a small Egyptian coastal resort.

Louis Challoner. 'Sonnet': *Tobruk* (last stanza), much fought over harbour in Cyrenaica. *Halfaya*, a pass south of Sollum, on the Egypt/Libya border.

Dudley Charles. 'Twilight on Carmel': *Carmel*, the hill overlooking Haifa harbour, from which one saw vivid sunsets.

J. M. Collard. 'Death of a Man of Kent': *Hurricane* (first stanza), R.A.F. fighter plane.

E. P. Dudley. 'Stalingrad': Of great importance to the Middle East. If the Russians had not held it, the Middle East would have been outflanked.

G. S. Fraser. 'Egypt': *Fellah* (last stanza), Egyptian peasant.

Hamish Henderson. 'Hospital Afternoon': *blue pyjamas* (line one), standard issue in military hospitals.

Norman Hudis. '. . . And There Was Light': *Derna* (third stanza), a Libyan town; *Alep*, Aleppo in Syria; *Sarafand*, Army camp in Palestine; *Daba*, Egyptian desert town.

G. C. Norman. 'Halt for Lunch': *dixie* (line 5), pot to boil tea and cook; *M and V* (line 6), canned meat and vegetables, staple diet, see poem of same name in Part III; *bully* (line 14), corned beef; *Stukas* (line 30), German dive bombers; *Bren* (line 33), portable light machine gun, magazine loaded; *shrapnel* (line 48), burst bomb or shell fragments, deadly.

John Rimington. 'Danse Grotesque': *Vulture* (stanza two), ever present in the desert waiting for the dying.

T. Stephanides. 'The Marsh of Death': *Very-lights*, pistol-fired rockets to illuminate battlefields and signal orders.

R. N. Walker. 'Living and Dead': Written in a Casualty Clearing Station.

Part II: Previously Published

Harold Ian Bransom. 'The Twenty-five Pounder': Standard British gun too easily outgunned by German 105 mm. The latter a most accurate gun that was also used as anti-aircraft. 'The Game Old Gentleman': *14 Star* (line 1), First World War medal—many deducted years to enlist again.

C. P. S. Denholm-Young. 'Rommel': *Shepheards*, well appointed Cairo hotel, many officers stayed there until Montgomery threw them out (see Two Types cartoon).

Keith Douglas. 'Elegy for an 88 Gunner' (published elsewhere as 'Vergissmeinicht'): this is poet's own title. The 88 was another highly effective German weapon. 'On a Return from Egypt': see Tambimuttu's contribution to this book; prophetic, as if he knew then he would be killed.

Thomas Eastwood. 'The Draft': A typical occurence of troops sent to the front by those who had to remain at base.

G. S. Fraser. 'Three Characters in a Bar': *Last of the Jacobites*, (stanza 3), John Gawsworth, the poet. 'An Elegy for Keith Bullen': Founder of Salamander Society.

Alan Freedman. 'Overseas Soldier': The poem crystallizes the experience of being posted to the Middle East, beginning with the voyage out, places passed, Durban with its rickshaws and a chance to visit African kraals and the Valley of a Thousand Hills. Then Aden where the heat hits like a sledge-hammer and the Red Sea to Port Tewfiq in Egypt and Cairo. Then leave in Palestine, lush and green after the Desert.

Hamish Henderson. 'Second Elegy': *Nazionale*, Italian cigarette, *laager*, parking place for tanks.

Uys Krige. 'The Taking of the Koppie': also spelt 'Kopjie', a small hill.

N. T. Morris. 'The Jeep': *A. C or B* (Stanza 3), companies in the squadron; R.S.M. (stanza 11), Regimental Sergeant-Major, Warrant Officer Class One (allegedly most important rank in the army —somebody to be wary of!)

Victor Musgave. 'Song of Egypt': *Immobilia* (stanza 8), tall building in Cairo; *Y.M.* (stanza 10), Y.M.C.A.; *Tarbrush* (stanza 11), red brimless hat, green if wearer had been to Mecca.

John Ropes. 'You Musn't Drop Your Aitches at G.H.Q.': *G.H.Q.*, General Headquarters; *D.A.Q.M.G.*, Deputy Army Quarter-Master General; *Gezira*, island in Nile, home of sporting club; *Semira-miss*, pun on Semeris Hotel, H.Q. of B.T.E. (British Troops in Egypt); *Maadi*, fashionable Cairo suburb; *AT*, A.T.S. member of the women's services.

John Warry. 'To a W.A.A.F.': Women's Auxiliary Air Force. As with the A.T.S. the W.A.A.F.s in the Middle East included many nationalities.

Victor West. 'La Belle Indifference': *Quassassin*, base on the Cairo-Ismailia road; *Florina Pass*, Greece.

Part III: Previously Unpublished

Gordon Begg. 'Chanctonbury Ring': Tree topped feature on the Sussex Downs that gave its name to a feature in the desert; *Ack-Ack*, anti-aircraft gun.

Bray. 'The Price': *Oerlikons* and *Vickers*, heavy machine guns.

Ken Burrows. 'It's Churchill's Fault': *Victory V's* (stanza 3), army issue cigarette, powerful aroma to combat smell of latrines. (Note: last stanza of poem written in 1942; somewhat prophetic.)

Graham Cawthorne. 'The Bend': *Galabeah* (stanza 1), loose robe; *backsheesh* (stanza 1), open horse-drawn carriage; *Groppi's* (stanza 2), Cairo patisserie and tea-room . . . made the finest cream cakes and ice-cream; *Gezira* (stanza 2), sporting club on island in the Nile; *suffragi* (stanza 5), servant.

Louis Challoner. 'Ballad of Young Sam Small': Derived from a Stanley Holloway original; *G.P.O.* (line 11), Gunnery Position Officer, barked orders; *char* (line 20), tea, Indian Army word; *midan* (line 21), another Indian

Army word . . . applied to the open space in the desert in front of the guns. 'The Royal Horse Artillery: *Chattanooga Choo Choo,* pre-war popular song with catchy tune.

E. F. Gosling. 'Mechanization': Poem sadly tells of change from cavalry to armoured cars. Yeomany units (Territorial Cavalry) became mechanized in the Middle East; *Tetrarch* (stanza 2), celebrated Derby winner.

W. G. Holloway. 'South of Alamein': *Bofors* (line 12), noisy anti-aircraft gun, mainly used by Navy. 'Night Barrage, Western Desert': *Very-lights* (line 4) (see previous note under **T. Stephanides,** The Marsh of Death).

Peter R. Hopkinson. 'Maleesh Aforethought': *Maleesh,* (everyday Arabic expression) couldn't care less . . . plus a shrug of the shoulders. Why worry? Tomorrow will take care of itself; *P. T.* (stanza 4), physical training.

V. J. Locke. 'Tobruk': This port changed hands a few times and became a status symbol. Hence a number of poems on this subject.

J. G. Meddemmen. 'L.R.D.G': Long Range Desert Group operated independently for long spells behind enemy lines, with no support once they were on their own. High casualty rate. Preceded the S.A.S. founded in the Middle East by David Stirling.

G. C. Norman. 'Night Raid': *Remington* (line 18), a rifle; *Havildar* (line 45), Indian Army N.C.O.; *Mark IV* (line 81), tank; *Mauser* (line 91), German pistol, captured and used. 'Morning in Abbassia': Barracks in centre of Cairo; *D.I.D.,* Detail Issue Department, had a corrugated roof.

J. Nugent. 'The Path of Memory': *Ammo* (stanza 1), ammunition; *M. & V.* (stanza 2), canned meat and vegetables (see poem *M. & V.* under **Anonymous**).

Frank Pike. 'Storks at Khanaquin': Technically this poem comes just outside the M.E.F. but we include it for historical interest, as the Polish troops played their part in the Middle East and later in Italy. The storks flying over Khanaquin reminded Polish troops of home.

John Rimington. 'The Flap': The 'Flap' that made Middle East history was the near panic caused by Rommel's approach to Alexandria and threat to Cairo. The skies became black from the burning documents. This poem is just a one-man flap!; *R.A.M.C.* (last stanza), Royal Army Medical Corps.

T. Stephanides. 'Trochee to Anapaest': Two poetic metres, that correspond with the rhythm of the different warnings on board ship.

E. Storey. 'The Northumberland Fusiliers': *Vickers* (stanza 3), heavy machine gun.

Edward Thoms. 'Desert Funeral': *Gharry* (stanza 2), open horse-drawn carriage.

Anonymous. 'Cairo Love Song': Poem neatly employs the Arabic vocabulary of the soldier; *Gippo bint,* Egyptian girl; *Saheeda,* a greeting when we would say 'How do you do?'; *muskeen,* broke, skint!; *mafeesh falloos,* no money; *stanna swire,* wait-a-minute, usually said to a driver; *talla heena,* come here!; *quois kateer,* quite nice. 'Ali Baba Moorshead': Tells of Australian General, Moorshead, and an early campaign in the desert.

A Brief Chronology of the War in the Middle East

(Note: This chronology does not pretend to be more than a summary of the main events. In a war which lasted almost three years, in which the fighting ebbed and flowed over a territory of some four thousand miles, it has not been possible to list every skirmish or even every minor battle. The intention has been to recall the significant developments of each successive campaign.)

1940

June

10—Italy declares war on Britain.

11—British troops (11th Hussars) ambush column of Italian lorries, and press on to take Fort Maddalena and Fort Capuzzo inside Libya.

End of June—General Sir Archibald Wavell, in command of all British land forces in the Middle East and Eastern Mediterranean, establishes Long Range Desert Group. (At that time, Wavell had about 36,000 men in Egypt: 7th Armoured Division, with four regiments of tanks; 4th Indian Division; New Zealand Division, consisting of one brigade group. All were short of artillery and equipment).

July/August—Period of relative quiet. British forces in North Africa vastly outnumbered. Marshal Graziani has about one million men in Cyrenaica and Tripolitania. The Duke of Aosta has nearly 300,000 in East Africa. Churchill wants swift action, but Wavell insists that critical shortages of equipment must first be made up.

September

8—Large British reinforcements arrive in Egypt. Also, Australian reinforcements.

13—Italians occupy Sollum.

18—Italians occupy Sidi Barrani.

December

9—*First British offensive* in Western Desert —but delayed in order to send help to Greece.

11—British capture Sidi Barrani.

17—British occupy Sollum, Fort Capuzzo, and three enemy frontier forts.

23—Italians taken prisoner up to this date: 23,949.

1941

January

3—Australians pierce defences of Bardia.

5—Bardia surrenders. Over 30,000 prisoners taken.

21—Allies pierce Tobruk defences.

22—Australians enter Tobruk. Over 25,000 prisoners.

30—Allies take Derna.

February

3—British occupy Cyrene.

6—Australians enter Benghazi. Later, El Agheila, on frontier of Cyrenaica, is taken.

14—No Italians left in Egypt.

27—First allied brush with German patrols in Libya.

March

1—Free French occupy Kufra.

24—Enemy re-occupy El Agheila.

30—*First enemy counter-offensive*: German

248

armour and Italian infantry advance east from El Agheila.

April
2—British withdraw from Agedabia.

3—British evacuate Benghazi.

7—Germans take Derna.

10—Australians withdraw to Tobruk. Germans cut Tobruk-El Adem road.

13—German encirclement of Tobruk and capture of Bardia.

17—British naval bombardment of Fort Capuzzo.

21—British naval bombardment of Tripoli.

27—Enemy cross Egyptian frontier and occupy Halfaya Pass.

28—Germans capture Sollum.

May
1—Enemy attack on Tobruk.

15—British retake Sollum.

June
5/6—Enemy air raids on Alexandria.

15—British offensive at Sollum.

July
1—General Auchinleck appointed G.O.C., Middle East.

August
19—Start of relief of Australian and Indian troops at Tobruk (up to 26th October) by British and Polish troops.

November
17/18—British commando raid on German Headquarters in Libya.

18—*Second Allied offensive* in Western Desert. 8th Army under General Cunningham advances into Cyrenaica.

19—British capture Sidi Rezegh.

20—Rommel, commanding Afrika Korps, encircled by British forces, gives battle with tanks over a vast area of more than 40 square miles around Sidi Rezegh.

21—British drive wedge between Rommel's armoured forces in Cyrenaica. Tobruk garrison make sortie (supported by tanks landed by Royal Navy) to effect junction with troops at Sidi Rezegh. New Zealanders capture Fort Capuzzo.

23—New Zealanders occupy Bardia.

24—Tank battle with heavy losses on both sides, followed by hand-to-hand fighting. New Zealand forces take Gambut. British mechanized column captures Aujila.

25—Rommel sends strong raiding column over Egyptian frontier.

26—Tobruk force captures El Duda and joins up with advance main force north-west of Sidi Rezegh.

30—Fierce German attacks from west pierce Tobruk–Sidi Rezegh corridor.

December
8—Allied forces retake Sidi Rezegh and restore corridor to Tobruk.

13—Rommel makes a stand. Five-day tank battle.

17—Rommel's front breaks; enemy retreat from Gazala.

19—British retake Derna and Mechili.

21—British patrols enter Cyrene and Apollonia, and make raid 150 miles into Tripolitania.

23—British retake Barce and Benina.

24—British retake Benghazi.

1942

January
2—Allies retake Bardia, after combined bombardment by land, sea and air.

5—British start attack on Halfaya, last enemy stronghold in eastern Cyrenaica.

6—Rommel, with reinforcements, takes offensive at Agedabia.

8—Under cover of sandstorms, Rommel escapes from Agedabia along coast road.

12—British recapture Sollum.

17—British take Halfaya, with unconditional surrender of about 5,500 Axis troops.

21—*Second enemy counter-offensive.* Rommel's forces turn and advance east from El Agheila.

23—Rommel retakes Agedabia.

29—Rommel retakes Benghazi and advances on Barce.

February
4—British evacuate Derna.

14—Rommel, after fortnight's pause, renews offensive.

May
26—*Third enemy counter-offensive.* Rommel

moves to outflank British forces at Bir Hacheim, south of Gazala, in thrust for Tobruk.

28—R.A.F. pounds enemy armoured transport for three days. Battle takes place 25 miles from Tobruk, in area known as 'The Cauldron', around cross-roads on Trigh-Capuzzo running east–west between 'Knightsbridge' and Rotunda Segnali and north–south between Gazala and Bir Hacheim.

June

1—British capture Rotunda Segnali in Rommel's rear; General Crüwell, Commander of Afrika Korps, taken prisoner.

3—Enemy overruns British 150th Brigade near 'Knightsbridge'.

4—General Ritchie stages counter-attack, but fails after three-day battle.

7—Germans launch heavy attack on Bir Hacheim, held by Free French.

10/11—On General Ritchie's orders, Free French garrison withdrawn from Bir Hacheim under cover of darkness. Next day, Germans occupy the position.

12—All-day tank battle south-east of 'Knightsbridge'. Germans attack Acroma and reach a point 15 miles from Tobruk.

13—British tanks suffer heavy losses near 'Knightsbridge'.

14—Germans strike north to Libyan coast to cut off Allied forces in Gazala sector, but General Ritchie effects their withdrawal. South Africans retreat along Tobruk road. British covering division, left in Gazala, strikes west through Italian infantry and reaches Tobruk road.

15—British withdraw from 'Knightsbridge'.

16—Germans make strong thrust at Sidi Rezegh.

17—General Ritchie withdraws to Egyptian frontier, abandoning Sidi Rezegh, El Duda and El Adem, but leaving strong garrison in Tobruk.

20—Germans attack Tobruk in force, penetrate defences, and occupy a large sector.

21—Fall of Tobruk. Germans continue advance towards Egyptian frontier and take Bardia.

24—Germans advance 50 miles across Egyptian frontier. British forces withdraw from Sollum and Sidi Omar to Mersa Matruh.

25—General Auchinleck takes personal command in Egypt.

27—Battle joined at Mersa Matruh.

29—Germans take Mersa Matruh and advance eastwards to Fuka. Alexandria bombed.

July

1—Germans reach El Alamein. Heavy fighting on 40-mile front from there down to Qattara Depression. General Auchinleck issues Order of Day to 8th Army calling for 'supreme effort'.

2—After all-day battle at El Alamein, Germans withdraw west. British position intact.

14—Germans resume attack at Tel El Eisa. British troops secure objectives on Ruweisat Ridge, south of El Alamein.

August

18—General Sir Harold Alexander appointed C-in-C, Middle East. Lieut-General Sir Bernard Montgomery appointed to command 8th Army.

31/1 September—Battle of Alam Halfa. Germans open offensive around El Hemeimat and advance north towards Alam Halfa Ridge, but with considerable losses.

September

3/4—New Zealand Division attacks, accelerating Rommel's withdrawal from Alam Halfa.

13—From Egypt, British mobile patrols (L.R.D.G.) penetrate to Benghazi and Barce, inflicting heavy losses on enemy bases and airfields. British combined forces raid Tobruk.

October

1—British forces open limited offensive, and capture enemy positions at Deir el Munassib.

23/24—*Battle of El Alamein begins*. 8th Army penetrates Rommel's main positions. Steady allied progress until 3rd November.

November

3—Axis forces begin retreat westwards.

4—Cairo communiqué: 'Axis forces now in full retreat'.

7/8—Allied landing in North Africa.

8—8th Army engages enemy rearguards at Sollum and Sidi Barrani.

10—Axis rearguards driven from Sidi Barrani and engaged at Buq Buq.

11—8th Army captures Sollum and Bardia.

12—8th Army captures Tobruk. General Montgomery issues Order of Day: 'We have completely smashed the German and Italian Armies.'

13—8th Army captures Gazala, and clears retreating Axis troops from Cyrenaica.

15—Church bells are rung throughout the United Kingdom to celebrate victory in the Battle of Egypt.

17—In Libya, 8th Army occupies Derna, Mechili and Msus.

18/23—8th Army reaches Cyrene, occupies Benghazi, enters Agedabia and Jalo.

December

13—8th Army attacks and occupies enemy positions at Mersa Brega. Rommel begins retreat from El Agheila position.

16—New Zealand Division intercepts part of Rommel's retreating forces, having made outflanking move to south of main position.

25—8th Army occupies Sirte.

1943

January

15—8th Army makes successful attack on enemy positions at Buerat.

19—8th Army occupies Homs and Tarhuna.

23—8th Army enters Tripoli.

26—8th Army captures Zauia.

29—Advance guard of 8th Army crosses into Tunisia.

31—8th Army occupies Zuara.

February

16/18—8th Army occupies, in succession, Ben Gadane, Medenine and Foum Tatahouine.

March

6—Rommel attacks, but is held.

20/22—Heavy fighting on Mareth Line. New Zealand Corps makes flanking attack against El Hamma.

26—8th Army attacks El Hamma.

28—8th Army occupies Mareth, Toujane and Matmata.

29—8th Army occupies Gabes and El Hamma, then passes through Gabes Gap and occupies Oudref and Metouia.

April

6—8th Army attacks and breaks through Rommel's defences at Wadi Akarit.

7—In northern Tunisia, 8th Army makes contact with American 11 Corps.

10—8th Army occupies Sfax.

12—8th Army occupies Sousse.

14—8th Army reaches Enfidaville defence line.

20—8th Army successfully assaults Enfidaville line.

23—8th Army captures Jebel Terhouna.

May

7—Allied forces capture Tunis and Bizerta.

12—All organized Axis resistance in Tunisia ends.

ERIK de MAUNY

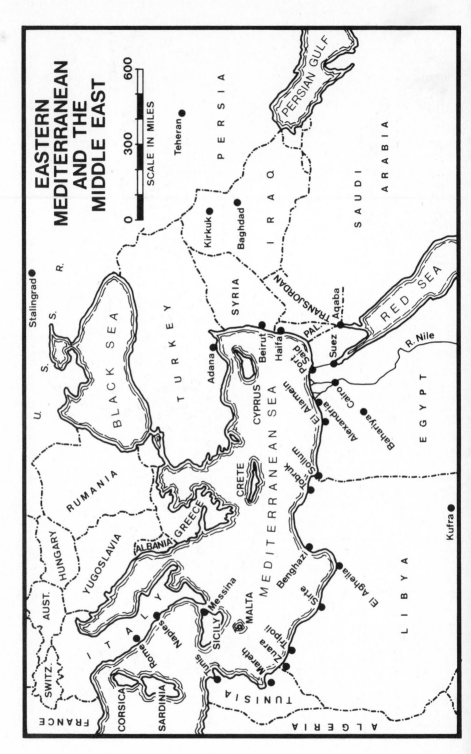

EASTERN
MEDITERRANEAN
AND THE
MIDDLE EAST

SCALE IN MILES
0   300   600

PERSIAN GULF

Teheran●

P E R S I A

Kirkuk●   Baghdad●

I R A Q

Stalingrad●

S.   S.   R.

U.   S.

BLACK SEA

T U R K E Y

SYRIA

TRANSJORDAN

RED SEA

R. Nile

Aqaba●

PAL.

Suez●

Port Said●

Beirut●   Haifa●

Adana●

CYPRUS

El Alamein

Alexandria●   Cairo●

Bahariya●

E G Y P T

SAUDI   ARABIA

Tobruk●

Sollum

RUMANIA

CRETE

GREECE

ALBANIA

YUGOSLAVIA

HUNGARY

AUST.

MEDITERRANEAN SEA

Benghazi●

El Aghelia●

Sirte

L I B Y A

Kufra●

SWITZ.

I T A L Y

Rome●   Naples●

Messina●

SICILY

MALTA

Tripoli●

Zuara●

Mareth●

CORSICA

SARDINIA

Tunis●

T U N I S I A

FRANCE

A L G E R I A

252

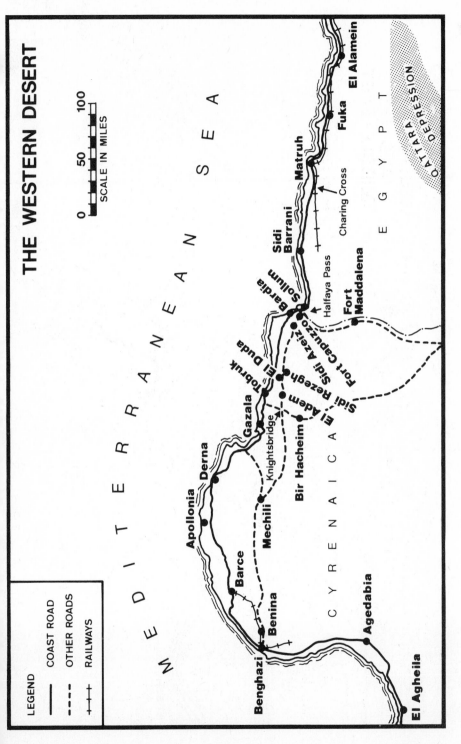

THE WESTERN DESERT

LEGEND

COAST ROAD
OTHER ROADS
RAILWAYS

SCALE IN MILES

0   50   100

MEDITERRANEAN SEA

El Alamein
Fuka
Matruh
Charing Cross
Sidi Barrani
Halfaya Pass
Fort Maddalena
Bardia
Sollum
Fort Capuzzo
Sidi Azeiz
El Duda
Sidi Rezegh
Tobruk
El Adem
Gazala
Knightsbridge
Bir Hacheim
Derna
Apollonia
Mechili
Barce
Benina
Benghazi
Agedabia
El Agheila

CYRENAICA

EGYPT

QATTARA DEPRESSION

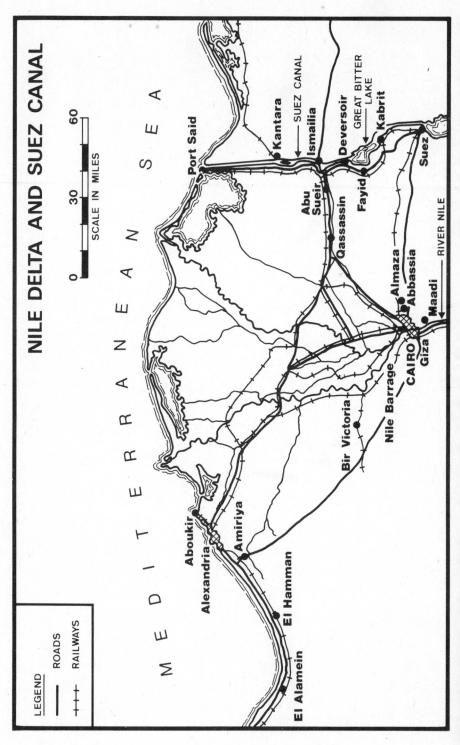

NILE DELTA AND SUEZ CANAL

LEGEND

ROADS

RAILWAYS

SCALE IN MILES

0   30   60

M E D I T E R R A N E A N   S E A

Port Said

Kantara

SUEZ CANAL

Ismailia

Deversoir

GREAT BITTER
LAKE

Kabrit

Abu
Sueir

Qassassin

Fayid

Suez

Almaza

Abbassia

Maadi

RIVER NILE

CAIRO

Giza

Bir Victoria

Nile Barrage

Aboukir

Alexandria

Amiriya

El Hamman

El Alamein